Foundational
Issues in
Christian Education

Foundational Issues in Christian Education

An Introduction in Evangelical Perspective

Third Edition

Robert W. Pazmiño

Baker Academic

a division of Baker Publishing Group
Grand Rapids, Michigan

Published by Baker Academic
a division of Baker Publishing Group
P.O. Box 6287, Grand Rapids, MI 49516-6287
www.bakeracademic.com

Printed in the United States of America

Library of Congress Cataloging-in-Publication Data
Pazmiño, Robert W., 1948–
    Foundational issues in Christian education : an introduction in evangelical perspective / Robert W. Pazmiño.—3rd ed.
        p.   cm.
    Includes bibliographical references and indexes.
    ISBN 978-0-8010-3593-7 (pbk.)
    1. Christian education. I. Title.
BV1471.2.P39 2008
268—dc22
                                                                                                2008003935

To
Albert A. Pazmiño
1909–1986
My father and a modern-day Andrew
and
Laura R. Pazmiño
1920–2007
My mother and a postmodern Dorcas

Contents

Introduction

In commenting on the future of Christianity in 1995, the theologian Alister McGrath saw the potential for evangelical Christians to make a contribution. This continuing contribution relates to the viability of orthodoxy and the need to teach a living faith for the postmodern world.[1] For this to be possible, Christians are called to be faithful in the theory and practice of Christian education to assure the transmission of a living faith to the rising generations. In support of this task, Christian educators are called upon to reappraise their thought and practice in relation to the foundational issues of Christian education. These foundational issues represent perennial or recurrent questions for those involved in the teaching ministries of the church. They deserve careful consideration by those who reflect upon their ministries of the past, present, and future.

This book in its third edition explores the disciplines used to form a holistic and integrated conception of Christian education from which guiding principles and guidelines for practice can be drawn. Christian educators who are evangelical in theological orientation need to make a concerted effort to affirm the biblical insights that provide the essential authority for theory and practice.[2] Christians also need to incorporate insights from other disciplines.

---

1. Alister McGrath, *Evangelicalism and the Future of Christianity* (Downers Grove, IL: InterVarsity, 1995); for a discussion of the postmodern setting, see the two appendixes of this work.

2. Evangelical educators have made major contributions in this area. See the following works as examples: Michael J. Anthony, ed., *Foundations of Ministry: An Introduction to Christian Education for a New Generation* (Wheaton: Victor Books, 1992); Perry G. Downs, *Teaching for Spiritual Growth: An Introduction to Christian Education* (Grand Rapids: Zondervan, 1994); Ronald Habermas and Klaus Issler, *Teaching for Reconciliation: Foundations and Practice of*

Such incorporation, however, is subject to the continuing authority of God's Word as found in Scripture. By critically exploring the various foundations that have been and are predominant in Christian thought, educators can better deal with current needs and future challenges.

✓   Christian educators have been conscious of the need to balance concerns for both continuity and change. Continuity is affirmed in emphasizing essential biblical truths that have guided the Christian faith and educational ministries throughout the centuries. Change is affirmed in emphasizing the need for applying theological truths in relation to specific historical, cultural, social, and personal variables. This effort requires careful reappraisal of biblical and theological sources, as well as evaluation of the various trends that are confronting the wider society and world.

In exploring these areas, it is appropriate to pose questions that have continuing significance in Christian education. A European educator once confronted an educator from the United States with the observation that "American educators are always raising questions and never answering them." In response to this remark, the educator from the United States asked yet another question, "Is that so?" To avoid this real danger, we must propose possible answers to the questions that are raised for consideration.

It is crucial that foundational questions be raised by Christian educators before they form a set theory and practice of Christian education. Raising these questions enables Christian educators to explore new possibilities and to consider "new wineskins" for Christian education. Through such exploration, persons concerned with education in various settings can identify principles and implications for practice.[3] The process by which various educational questions are raised in relation to foundations, principles, and practice is suggested by Denis Lawton, who outlines these areas in relation to a systems diagram (see fig. 1).[4]

At each point in the process, thought and practice are subject to the continuing authority of God's written Word. The Bible is a critical instrument that discerns and judges the educator, the educatee, and the educational process.[5] By exploring biblical and theological foundations first, Christian educators can affirm transcultural universals that may then guide all

---

Christian Education Ministry (Grand Rapids: Baker, 1992); and Jim Wilhoit, *Christian Education and the Search for Meaning*, 2nd ed. (Grand Rapids: Baker, 1991).

  3. For insights into the division of foundations, principles, and practices, see Émile Durkheim, *Education and Sociology* (New York: Free Press, 1956).

  4. Denis Lawton, *Class, Culture, and Curriculum* (London: Routledge & Kegan Paul, 1975), 85–87.

  5. Hebrews 4:12 and 2 Timothy 3:16 affirm this critical and evaluative function of God's written Word.

Figure 1
Foundations, Principles, and Practices

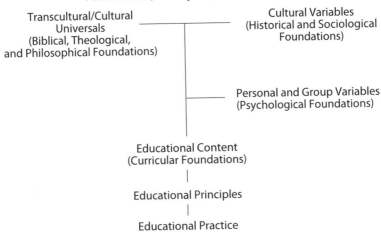

educational conceptions and efforts. The consideration of biblical and theological foundations can also serve to identify distinctive assumptions that Christians bring to their thought and practice of education. The consideration of philosophical foundations also assists the educator in specifying cultural universals in the purposes of education and the nature of knowledge. Transcultural and cultural universals are elements of continuity, less subject to change and various contingencies, though not exempt from interpretation in each educational setting.

The second step in the educational process involves the investigation of cultural variables through the disciplines of history and sociology, or anthropology. This step provides the Christian educator with a sense of his or her location in time and space. Cultural variables give the educator a sense of context, though cultural variables are more subject to the variations of time and space. Yet these cultural and subcultural variables are no less the concern of the Christian educator who seeks to contextualize her or his educational efforts. Thus the Christian educator endeavors to make the universal and transcultural truths of God's revelation real to those participating in the educational event. The educator seeks to so know, understand, and love students that her or his teaching speaks directly to the students' needs and concerns. This, of course, does not exclude the educator's role as one who raises critical questions and provides perspectives unknown to the students. But some sense of one's location in time, space, and society is crucial for faithful educational practice.

Beyond the questions of cultural universals and variables, the educator is confronted with individuals to whom she or he is responsible. The Christian educator needs to consider psychological foundations in order to discern the personal and group variables that influence education. In particular, the students or those being educated who are present and involved, voluntarily or involuntarily, must be considered. Also, educators are responsible to parents, administrators, boards, peers, pastors, and a host of other persons and groups, depending on the context of service. Psychological foundations provide insights to understand how persons develop, learn, and interact with others. Insights are also derived from sociological foundations for understanding how the teacher herself or himself relates and interacts with a variety of other persons, groups, and structures endemic to educational settings, whether in the home, the school, the church, or the community. The impact of sociological factors on psychological foundations indicates the interactions of the various dimensions of the educational process, as well as the potential limitations of a strictly systemic or analytical view of education. The diagramming of the system and process in figure 1 should include several connecting lines between each of the steps to reflect the complexity of the relationships. Additional lines could also be drawn to note the feedback from actual educational practices to the various foundations and their issues.

An additional step in the proposed model involves questions of educational content, the organized knowledge shared in Christian education. This step identifies the Christian heritage that will be shared with the persons and groups assembled. This living heritage draws on sources from the various foundations already identified in the model to form a curriculum. Curricular concerns at this point are organization of knowledge and identification of values and skills to be passed on from one generation or group to the next. In our current situation, questions of curriculum include the exposure of students to new knowledge and skills required for participation in a rapidly changing society. The inclusion of computer competency units in elementary and secondary schools is one example of curricular concern, given the impact of technology. Another curricular concern is the need for biblical and theological literacy in the Christian community.

Finally, the Christian educator needs to state educational principles that have been culled from the various foundations and then apply those principles to actual educational practices. A careful exploration of foundations is essential before one can specify principles and guidelines for practice. Too often, foundational questions have been ignored or the answers to such questions have been assumed in addressing the tyranny of urgent pressures in churches, homes, schools, and other ministry settings. While these fifth and sixth steps are not the focus of this text, suggestions are made in these areas for the reader's consideration.[6]

The entire educational process, though discussed in terms of a system, is subject to numerous contingencies that suggest Christian education combines aspects of an art, as well as of a science. The Christian educator is called upon to creatively combine and integrate insights from various disciplines in the thought and practice of education. This artful integration includes disciplines beyond those identified in this book as foundations for Christian education. Educational thought and practice have incorporated insights from such diverse studies as fine and applied arts, economics, political science, life sciences, physical sciences, systems theory, management theory, engineering, and mathematics. This reality supports the proposition that all truth is God's truth. The Christian educator can incorporate God's truth wherever it may be revealed in the created world in ways that reflect on humanity's God-given creativity.

In discussing Christian education, one readily becomes conscious of its "pre-paradigmatic" character.[7] Thomas Kuhn has suggested this term to describe an area of study or academic discipline that has not developed a paradigm—a dominant and widely accepted understanding, framework, or concept that serves to guide all thought and practice. In the physical and biological sciences, it is possible to identify dominant paradigms.[8] In the case of the social sciences and education, it is more difficult to identify a dominant paradigm that guides *all* thought and practice, in part because the subjects for study in the social sciences and education are human beings. Human beings are infinitely more complex than physical, chemical, and biological processes. From a Christian theistic perspective, one can also affirm this complexity because persons are created in the very image of God. Each person is unique, and exceptions can be cited for any given paradigm or model.

This preparadigmatic stage of Christian education, which by virtue of persons' created nature may be a perennial one, implies that any educational

6. For a focus on steps 5 and 6, see Robert W. Pazmiño, *Principles and Practices of Christian Education: An Evangelical Perspective* (1992; Eugene, OR: Wipf & Stock, 2002), which is a companion volume to this work.

7. Robert A. Drovdahl has raised appropriate questions about characterizing Christian education as preparadigmatic. See "Toward a Paradigmatic Christian Education," *Christian Education Journal* 11 (Spring 1991): 7–16. From my perspective, his pursuit of settledness and a paradigm may limit the place of freedom and creativity, but his pursuit of a framework for Christian education is to be affirmed. The pursuit of a framework and form results in an educational approach rather than a paradigm.

8. See Thomas Kuhn, *The Structure of Scientific Revolutions*, 2nd ed. (Chicago: University of Chicago Press, 1970), 10–51.

conception or practice remains incomplete and subject to renewal and change. This is due in part to the nature of persons with their unlimited potential for good as well as evil. The realization of this potential depends on the Christian educator's relationship with God and the extent to which he or she follows God in educational thought and practice. Thus a major challenge facing Christian educators is to be faithful, obedient, and creative in their thought and practice. By drawing on various resources, Christian educators are further challenged to develop an integrated understanding of Christian education that will guide practice. To ignore this challenge is to potentially be victimized by a mindless effort that fails to give glory to God. An affirmation of the preparadigmatic character of Christian education also acknowledges the creation of space for the surprising and gracious work of the Holy Spirit in any educational approach or design.

The preparadigmatic stage of Christian education requires that each new generation of Christian educators reconsider the foundational questions. Without raising these questions, Christian educators are likely to perpetuate antiquated conceptions and practices that are not faithful to the gospel; to be captive to a culture devoid of significant impact; and to be unresponsive to what the Holy Spirit is saying. Whereas this task is the particular responsibility of those professionally called to Christian education at various levels, the people of God as a whole must recognize their accountability for the direction and quality of Christian education in churches, homes, schools, communities, and societies. A lack of commitment to foundational issues results in limited possibilities for present and future generations.

The chapters in this book are organized to suggest a relationship in the order of the educational foundations as they appear in pairs. In an evangelical tradition, priority is given to the biblical and theological foundations as they provide normative categories for the theory and practice of education. These foundations are discussed in chapters 1 and 2. The philosophical and historical foundations, explored in chapters 3 and 4, are also often paired because their mutuality and complementarity support the task of integration in forming an understanding and appreciation of educational practice within distinct contexts. This is the case because philosophies and histories vary over time and place, and conjoint study fosters the discovery of connections. Also, both sociological and psychological foundations, the topics of chapters 5 and 6, are linked as social sciences that have been readily drawn upon in the field of education. Their interrelationship is noted in the discussion of a systems analysis of the various foundations. Finally, curricular foundations in chapter 7 serve as a bridge from wrestling with foundational issues to applying the actual principles for and practices of education. Additional relationships can be suggested to weave together the various foundational issues explored here, but these vary with the educational approach and rationale embraced by Christian educators.

The rationale for the first and subsequent editions of this book is captured in the wisdom shared by the Jewish educator Abraham J. Heschel, who said, "Thinking without roots will bear flowers but no fruits."[9] Christians must think about Christian education if they are to faithfully bear fruit in their practice. The consideration of the roots of Christian education calls for careful attention to the foundations that we draw upon. A good theory that emerges from grappling with foundational issues will well serve those engaged in the practice of Christian education in a wide variety of settings. A good theory enables those who teach to see, analyze, and respond to educational tasks in creative and faithful ways.

This work is written from a bicultural North American Hispanic perspective. The author is also an ecumenical evangelical Christian in theological persuasion. For many this may pose an irreconcilable tension. First, Hispanics have generally been associated with Central and South America and the Caribbean rather than with North America.[10] Second, ecumenical Christians are generally viewed as not being those who identify themselves as evangelical. Nevertheless, it is from the ecumenical vantage point that I address the current and enduring challenges of Christian education. My distinctive identity and perspective have enabled me to draw from diverse sources in my thought and practice.

This work is intended to be an introductory textbook for upper-level college and seminary courses. Its approach draws heavily on secondary sources to provide a wide exposure for students. My hope is that students will be encouraged to explore the references provided for further study. Although the primary audiences for this work are persons of evangelical persuasion, it is also intended to engage the wider ecumenical community of religious educators.

I wish to thank those communities and individuals who have made this book possible through their nurture and those who have used the first and second editions. I am grateful to Gordon-Conwell Theological Seminary, which I have known both as a student and as a faculty member for five years. The students in the courses I have taught have challenged me to consider various

9. Samuel H. Dresner, ed., *I Asked for Wonder: A Spiritual Anthology, Abraham Joshua Heschel* (New York: Crossword, 1995), 83.

10. For a discussion of the Hispanic heritage and developments in Latin America as related to Christian education, see Robert W. Pazmiño, *Latin American Journey: Insights for Christian Education in North America* (Eugene, OR: Wipf & Stock, 2002).

aspects of Christian education and to develop my thoughts. I am also grateful to Andover Newton Theological School, which has supported my calling to serve a multicultural and theologically diverse church and world over these past twenty years. I also appreciate the fellowships and congregations that have supported and guided me throughout my ministry.

I am indebted to the friends who patiently typed and edited the original manuscript and those colleagues who fostered the process of writing through their feedback and reviews. In particular, I thank Virginia Steadman and Deborah Perkins for their service on earlier editions.

My greatest appreciation goes to my family, immediate and extended, who have loved and encouraged me in the midst of my work. My parents, Laura and Albert Pazmiño, always believed in me and modeled the Christian life. My children, David and Rebekah by birth and Larisa by marriage, along with my grandson, Oliver, have always challenged me to be a better teacher and model in our home. Finally, I thank my wife, Wanda, for being a close companion and friend throughout the joys and struggles of my pilgrimage.

A Note on the Third Edition

Foundational issues in Christian education are raised in the changing contours of societal landscapes. Since the writing of the second edition of this work, postmodernism has emerged as a movement influencing educational thought and practices. The appendix to the second edition subtitled "Proclaiming Truth in a Postmodern Setting" noted one part of a Christian response to postmodern trends in emphasizing the search for truth that undergirds all educational efforts. The appendix to a subsequent work, *God Our Teacher: Theological Basics in Christian Education*,[11] noted the other part of a Christian response in emphasizing the stance of love. This second appendix was titled "Crossing Over to Postmodernity: Educational Invitations." (Both appendixes are included in this third edition.) The holistic Christian response calls for living and speaking the truth in love. This third edition of *Foundational Issues* reexamines the roots of Christian thinking on education, honoring a second nugget of wisdom penned by Abraham Heschel: "Religion begins with a question and theology with a problem."[12] This third edition explores

11. Robert W. Pazmiño, *God Our Teacher: Theological Basics in Christian Education* (Grand Rapids: Baker Academic, 2001).

12. Reuven Kimelman, "Abraham Joshua Heschel: Our Generation's Teacher in Honor of the Tenth Yahrzeit," *Religion and Intellectual Life* 2 (Winter 1985): 17.

educational questions and problems from the perspective of the Christian faith. Postmodernism emerges as an additional educational philosophy or impulse noted in chapter 3. Despite the questions that postmodernism raises about the possibility of enduring foundations, the examination of the roots of educational thoughts and practices is essential. Such reexamination in this third edition honors the distinctive elements of Christian revelation and faith while actively engaging the task of loving God with all of our minds. This is the responsibility and privilege of all Christians who teach today and in the years to come. Each chapter of this third edition was updated, clarified, and reviewed in the process of reexamining foundational issues while maintaining the basic structure of earlier editions. Each chapter includes questions for personal reflection or classroom use under "Points to Ponder."

1

Biblical Foundations

To think responsibly about and practice education from a distinctly evangelical theological position, Christians, and in particular Christian educators, must carefully examine the biblical foundations for Christian education. Scripture is the essential source for understanding distinctively Christian elements in education. Therefore, it is crucial that the Christian educator's thoughts and practices be guided by God's revealed truths as he or she seeks to be obedient to Christ in the task of education. Christians are subject to a confusing plurality of educational theories in contemporary society. In such a situation, the exploration of biblical foundations provides an essential standard for judging education. The examination of these foundations does not result in a sterile or rigid theory and practice, devoid of diversity and creativity. Rather, Christian education patterned on biblical foundations provides for a dynamic and diverse educational experience.

Several foundations can be identified in both the Old and the New Testaments. These biblical sources provide models or approaches even at the basic level of a commonsense reading of the text. All educators have models or approaches that guide their thought and practice. In most cases, these models remain unexamined. The challenge for Christians is to examine their models for education, to make them explicit, and to undergird them with biblical foundations. The models suggested by various biblical foundations provide guides with which to consider past, present, and future educational efforts. What follows is a sampling of foundations that must be elaborated by educators in various settings, making use of more extensive critical, canonical, and contextual studies.[1]

1. Gabriel Fackre in *The Christian Story: A Pastoral Systematics* (Grand Rapids: Eerdmans, 1987), 157–210, identifies four senses of Scripture: common, critical, canonical, and

The Old Testament

The Old Testament provides a wide variety of historical and communal settings in which to explore the nature of teaching and learning within the faith community. The work of the Latin American educator Matías Preiswerk is particularly insightful in identifying the various agents who were engaged in education. They included prophets, priests and Levites, wise persons or sages, scribes and rabbis, along with the people themselves as a nation. Each educational agent had a distinct purpose, content, method, and institutional expression as summarized in table 1 below.[2]

TABLE 1
Education in the Old Testament
Focus on the Educational Agents

	People Nation	Prophet	Priest Levites	"The Wise" Wise Persons Sage	Scribe-Teacher Rabbi "Doctor of the Law"
Purpose	Popular Liberation	Realize Liberation	Transmit the Tradition	A Better Life	Interpret the Sacred Scriptures (Ezra 7:6, 10)
Content	Historical Events	Anticipatory Historical Perspectives	Religious Practices Laws	Advice for Daily Living	Theological Commentaries
Method	Memory Popular Culture	Word Symbolic Actions	The Torah: Its Celebration, Transmission, Explanation, and Application	Popular Wisdom	Instruction
Institution	Nation Itself Community	Schools of Prophets	The Temple	Occasionally the Court of King, Queen	Synagogue

Beyond this summary, it is instructive to consider the particular emphases in major portions of the Hebrew Scripture, or Old Testament. The book of Deuteronomy stresses passing on the basic content and norms essential for the

contextual. This discussion is largely limited to the common sense, recognizing that evangelical constituencies make varied use of critical, canonical, and contextual insights. For further inquiry in this area, see Mary C. Boys, *Biblical Interpretation in Religious Education* (Birmingham, AL: Religious Education Press, 1980); for a good example of the fruits of canonical work, see Walter Brueggemann, *The Creative Word: Canon as a Model for Biblical Education* (Philadelphia: Fortress, 1982).

2. See Matías Preiswerk, *Educating in the Living Word: A Theoretical Framework for Christian Education* (Maryknoll, NY: Orbis, 1987), 50–66.

life of the faith community. Walter Brueggemann identifies this component of the Old Testament canon as the ethos of the Torah, the disclosure of that which is binding upon the faith community.[3] In the Christian faith community, the evangelical heritage has stressed the transmission of these basics. Instruction in traditional and accepted ways or heritage provides continuity across the generations, especially in times of transition and change.[4] The transformation made possible by the recovery of this heritage is described in Psalm 78 and the book of Nehemiah. New life and joy are experienced by the entire nation in returning to the source of their faith. The Wisdom literature embodies how the norms of faith relate to particular questions and issues of the day. Wisdom is required to relate faith demands to particular contexts. The counsel of wise persons guides the connection of faith to life. Brueggemann identifies this component of the Old Testament canon as logos, the discernment of practical wisdom for life that provides meaning and order.[5] Finally, the words of the prophets explore the social dimension of faith and decry breaches in faithfulness both within and beyond the faith community. The prophets are the social educators of their times, and they disclose the passion of God with their timely words that confront and hopefully heal the nation and its leaders. Brueggemann calls this portion of the canon pathos, which brings disruption to the life of the faith community or nation in the service of justice and righteousness.[6] One additional element identified and not emphasized by Brueggemann, but of significance for the formation of faith, is the place of doxology, the place of praise and joy that denotes the embrace of believers by God and their embrace of God.[7] Each of these portions of Scripture is instructive for educational thought and practice in contemporary contexts.

The Book of Deuteronomy

Within the Torah, the book of Deuteronomy stands out as one that outlines the norms for the faith community to follow and teach to the rising generations. In Deuteronomy 6:1–2, 4–9, Moses is described as exhorting the people of Israel to remember God's activities in their history, to teach God's commands, and, above all, to love, fear, and serve God:

---

3. Brueggemann, *Creative Word*, 13, 108. He uses Jeremiah 18:18 as the key text for his analysis of the Old Testament canon.
4. The stress on the norms of orthodoxy is one distinctive of evangelical Christians. Other distinctives are explored in chap. 2.
5. Brueggemann, *Creative Word*, 13, 108–9.
6. Ibid.
7. Ibid., 117.

These are the commands, decrees and laws the LORD your God directed me to teach you to observe in the land that you are crossing the Jordan to possess, so that you, your children and their children after them may fear the LORD your God as long as you live by keeping all his decrees and commands that I give you, and so that you may enjoy long life.

Hear, O Israel: The LORD our God, the LORD is one. Love the LORD your God with all your heart and with all your soul and with all your strength. These commandments that I give you today are to be upon your hearts. Impress them on your children. Talk about them when you sit at home and when you walk along the road, when you lie down and when you get up. Tie them as symbols on your hands and bind them on your foreheads. Write them on the doorframes of your houses and on your gates.

Moses's teaching called the believing community to relate their faith in God to all of life. This passage from Deuteronomy provides insights about the goals, the teacher, the student, the content, and the setting of biblical education.[8]

The educational mandate of Deuteronomy 6:4–9 requires passing on the commandments of God to the next generation. Its ultimate goal is to foster the love of God expressed in loyalty and obedience. To love God is to answer to a unique claim (6:4), to be obedient (11:1–22; 30:20), to keep God's commandments (10:12; 11:1, 22; 19:9), to heed them and to hear God's voice (11:13; 30:16), and to serve (10:12; 11:1, 13). In each of these passages, the word *love* refers to obedience from the heart involving all of one's being.[9] Jesus echoes this relationship between love and obedience in John 14:15: "If you love me, you will obey what I command."

The love of God is expressed in obedience to God's commandments and in giving oneself wholly (heart, soul, mind, and strength). Teaching is to be incisive in challenging hearers to such a total life response to God characterized by heartfelt devotion. This teaching was the particular responsibility of parents, yet this goal has significance for all forms of education.

In the ultimate sense, God is the teacher in biblical education. God is the author and discloser of all truth, and both teachers and students alike stand under this truth. God calls teachers and students to understand, grow in, and obey God's revealed Word. In this passage and throughout the biblical record, teachers are responsible as stewards and proclaimers of God's truth. This truth can be communicated in a variety of ways, always involving a relational dimension. A relationship of love, trust, openness, honesty, acceptance, caring, support,

8. For these insights, I am indebted to the work of Timothy C. Tennent, "Personal Philosophy of Christian Education" (unpublished student paper, Gordon-Conwell Theological Seminary, 1984).

9. Ibid.

forgiveness, correction, and affirmation is to characterize interactions between teachers and students.[10] Teachers, like parents, are called upon to model the love of God, which they hope to encourage students to follow.

Through the teaching and example of the teacher, the student is called to understanding, growth, and obedience in relation to God's revealed Word. While the teacher is encouraged to diligently and incisively teach, it is assumed that the student will be open and willing to receive this instruction. Other passages of Scripture, in particular the book of Proverbs, provide clear injunctions for children to be attentive to the instruction of their parents. The teachers in the context of Jewish life were primarily the parents, and Deuteronomy 6 therefore focuses on this primary role. But this perspective has implications for other educational relationships beyond the home, as was the case in postexilic synagogue schools.

The essential content of biblical education in Deuteronomy 6 is the commandments, decrees, and laws of God that Moses was directed to teach. But this content is vitally related to the whole of life. The content of God's revelation is to be taught or impressed upon students, to be talked about at various times, to be tied and bound upon one's body, and to be written in public and readily observed locations. Truth is to be integrated into all of life and is to affect the moment-to-moment and day-to-day existence of the people of God. This content is both foundational and radical. It is foundational in providing the basic truth and structure on which all else must be built. It is radical in providing the roots from which all life is nourished or affected. Thus both stability and growth are assured to the extent that the content of education is based on God's revelation.

The setting for teaching described in this passage includes all those situations in which parents can impress upon their children the commandments of God. There are various occasions when this is to be done: when sitting at home, when walking along the road, when lying down, and when getting up. God's commandments are to be present even as symbols on people's hands and foreheads and the doorframes of houses and gates. The whole of life provides situations in which persons can be discipled and nurtured in the ways of God, recognizing that God is the ultimate teacher for humanity.

The primary focus in Deuteronomy 6 is parents and their essential role in education. Despite the multiplicity of educational influences today, parents are still the primary educators who actively or passively determine what influences their children. The challenge is for the Christian church to equip parents for

10. Lawrence O. Richards, *A Theology of Christian Education* (Grand Rapids: Zondervan, 1975), 314.

their roles as ministers and educators in their homes and to assist them in the choice of other educational influences in the lives of their children. Parents need the support and guidance of leaders in their faith communities.

In Deuteronomy 6, Moses exhorts the people of Israel to remember and to teach. The context for this teaching is the home, in which persons learn to relate their faith in God to all of life. Because of the contemporary tendency to compartmentalize life, faith is often relegated to those limited occasions when one is involved in church-related activities, typically confined to a few hours on Sunday mornings. The book of Deuteronomy demonstrates that faith in God is related to all of life. Wherever faithful persons interact, there is an occasion for Christian education—provided this interaction is deliberate, systematic, and sustained.[11]

Education entails conscious planning, implementing, and evaluating of educational experiences. Intentionality in Christian education involves the effort to share biblical content, to grapple with its implications for life, and to suggest avenues for appropriate response. A similar point is emphasized in James 2:14–17. This approach has been advocated by Lawrence O. Richards, whose conceptions have clarified the place of nonformal and informal aspects of education.[12] Richards largely depends on a socialization or enculturation model for education that focuses on education for life.[13]

Richards assumes that the values of formal education will be implicitly addressed in the Christian community; however, it is clear that these values must be planned in educational ministries that enable persons to move beyond a community norm, in a prophetic sense, as well as nurturing them in the ways of a particular community. Prophetic education calls persons and communities to be accountable to biblical norms and demands at points where sin, injustice, and oppression are evident, where the life of the home or nurturing community is critiqued rather than affirmed. These two foci—affirmation and critique—are patterned after the blessings and warnings of God's covenant (see Deuteronomy 27–28) with all humanity. These foci are implied in Deuteronomy 6, which emphasizes attentiveness to God's commands and parental instruction.

Affirmation and critique are as essential in today's contexts as they were in biblical times. Thus, while a family or community may faithfully pass on to

---

11. These terms for describing education are explored in chap. 3 when the definition of education is considered. See also Lawrence A. Cremin, *Traditions of American Education* (New York: Basic Books, 1977), 134–45.

12. For a complete discussion of the content-implications-response sequence, see Lawrence O. Richards, *Creative Bible Teaching* (Chicago: Moody, 1970).

13. Richards's conceptions are elaborated in his *Theology of Christian Education*.

the next generation the truth of God through its socialization and enculturation processes, this transmission may also at key points need correction and
reorientation. Formal education can often serve as a vehicle for correction and
reorientation of the efforts of a particular home or community. Likewise, a
particular home or community may minister to an agency of formal education, such as when parents take an active role in the policies and goals of a
Sunday, private, or public school.

Deuteronomy 30–32 also provides essential insights for understanding the
nature of Christian education. Jesus himself is reported to have made repeated
reference to the book of Deuteronomy during his wilderness temptations.[14] In
the current educational wilderness of a plurality of educational philosophies,
Christian educators can likewise gain strength and clarity by considering the
insights offered from the following three passages in Deuteronomy: 30:11–20;
31:9–13; and 31:30–32:4. The education described in these passages comes to
its full fruition in the life and ministry of Jesus Christ.

Deuteronomy 30:11–20: Finding Life. Deuteronomy 30:11–20 clarifies some
of the issues at stake in current Christian education efforts. This passage records a covenant renewal challenge given to the people of Israel and describes
the curses or warnings that result from disobedience of God:

> Now what I am commanding you today is not too difficult for you or beyond
> your reach. It is not up in heaven, so that you have to ask, "Who will ascend
> into heaven to get it and proclaim it to us so we may obey it?" Nor is it beyond
> the sea, so that you have to ask, "Who will cross the sea to get it and proclaim
> it to us so we may obey it?" No, the word is very near you; it is in your mouth
> and in your heart so you may obey it.
>
> See, I set before you today life and prosperity, death and destruction. For I
> command you today to love the LORD your God, to walk in his ways, and to
> keep his commands, decrees and laws; then you will live and increase, and the
> LORD your God will bless you in the land you are entering to possess.
>
> But if your heart turns away and you are not obedient, and if you are drawn
> away to bow down to other gods and worship them, I declare to you this day
> that you will certainly be destroyed. You will not live long in the land you are
> crossing the Jordan to enter and possess.
>
> This day I call heaven and earth as witnesses against you that I have set
> before you life and death, blessings and curses. Now choose life, so that you
> and your children may live and that you may love the LORD your God, listen
> to his voice, and hold fast to him. For the LORD is your life, and he will give
> you many years in the land he swore to give to your fathers, Abraham, Isaac
> and Jacob.

14. See Matthew 4:1–11 and Luke 4:1–13.

Christian educators are to make clear God's offer of life or death. Christian education is one of the church's ministries that seek to encourage persons of all ages to choose life—the spiritual life found in Jesus Christ for the Christian church. Choosing life requires loving, listening to, and holding fast to God. This choice is imperative because God is the source of life, a truth echoed in 1 John 5:12: "He who has the Son has life; he who does not have the Son of God does not have life." Christian education entails sharing knowledge of and encouraging a response to God that results in life.

Deuteronomy 31:9–13: The Word of God and Human Response. Deuteronomy 31:9–13 emphasizes the importance of reading and hearing God's Law. This passage records the sabbatical legal renewal of God's covenant with God's people:

> So Moses wrote down this law and gave it to the priests, the sons of Levi, who carried the ark of the covenant of the LORD, and to all the elders of Israel. Then Moses commanded them: "At the end of every seven years, in the year for canceling debts, during the Feast of Tabernacles, when all Israel comes to appear before the LORD your God at the place he will choose, you shall read the law before them in their hearing. Assemble the people—men, women and children, and the aliens living in your towns—so they can listen and learn to fear the LORD your God and follow carefully all the words of this law. Their children, who do not know this law, must hear it and learn to fear the LORD your God as long as you live in the land you are crossing the Jordan to possess."

Those addressed are to listen, learn to reverence God, and follow carefully in God's ways. God's Law is a trust, a heritage that is to be shared not only with adults but also with children and youth in the community of faith. These formal and legal arrangements are finally fulfilled and transcended in the new covenant. From the perspective of the New Testament, the importance of God's Law is extended to all of Scripture (2 Tim. 3:14–17). God's Word provides the essential content for teaching. Christian education can be further distinguished by the focus on God's revelation as expressed in the Old and New Testaments. God's Word is to be passed on from generation to generation with the intent of fostering a response of faithfulness on the part of the hearers. The authority of God's Word is understood within the community of faith, the church of the living God, which is described as the "pillar and foundation of the truth" (1 Tim. 3:15). With this understanding, educators must submit any private interpretations of Scripture to the shared wisdom of the church in both its historical and present expressions.

Deuteronomy 31:30–32:4a: Fostering Liberation and Facilitating Worship. Deuteronomy 31:30–32:4a provides a description of education in Old

Testament times. This passage is an unusual introduction to a long poetic curse upon the nation that is followed by the promise of restoration:

> And Moses recited the words of this song from beginning to end in the hearing
> of the whole assembly of Israel:
>> Listen, O heavens and I will speak;
>> hear, O earth, the words of my mouth.
>> Let my teaching fall like rain
>>> and my words descend like dew,
>> like showers on new grass,
>>> like abundant rain on tender plants.
>> I will proclaim the name of the LORD.
>>> Oh, praise the greatness of our God!
>> He is the Rock, his words are perfect,
>>> and all his ways are just.

This passage describes an education that liberates persons to grow and be refreshed in God. It is also an education that encourages them to celebrate, to attribute worth to God. It liberates in the sense of enabling persons to be and become all that God has intended them to be as God's creatures and as members of the covenant community. The threat of curse along with the anticipation of blessing were opportunities for learning. Such a liberating education requires the effectual working of God to restore persons and groups so that they can reflect God's image in their lives, just as rain and dew restore and renew plant life in a desert. Liberation is the empowerment to be and become all that God intended persons to be by the Creator's continual care and transformation of individuals, communities, and societies.[15] This liberation includes the denouncement of sin, along with the announcement of forgiveness and reconciliation. Christian education is characterized by teaching and learning that result in the liberation of persons. Jesus affirms this emphasis in John 8:31b–32: "If you hold to my teaching, you are really my disciples. Then you will know the truth, and the truth will set you free."

The education described in Deuteronomy 31:30–32:4a also entails celebration. It is celebration in the sense of encouraging participants to praise, adore, and glorify God. God is praised for God's gracious activity, care, providence, judgment, justice, and righteousness. Participants in this educational event are called by Moses to recognize their utter dependence on God and to respond with obedience to divine demands in all spheres of human activity.

15. See Exodus 6:6–8 for a description of liberation as God worked in the life experience of the nation of Israel.

Therefore, in addition to liberation, celebration is an outcome of education that is biblical in character.

The life and ministry of Jesus is the fullest expression of the nature of education described in these passages from Deuteronomy. Christ is the life, the Word Incarnate, and the ultimate source for liberation and celebration. Jesus Christ is the life (John 14:6), the bread of life (John 6:35), and the resurrection and the life (John 11:25). He comes to offer everlasting life to all who believe in him (John 3:16, 36; 1 John 5:12). Jesus Christ as the Word Incarnate (John 1:1–18) fulfills God's Law (Matt. 5:17–20). In Christ there is the fullest realization of liberation (John 8:31–36) and the occasion for celebration (John 15:9–11). His discipling ministry with the twelve disciples provides a model for the kind of education that affects the total life of participants.[16] More than just imparting content as revealed truth, Jesus shared his very life with his disciples as the Word Incarnate. This sharing of life then issues in life for those who respond in faith to God's disclosure.

What possible educational implications can be drawn from consideration of these biblical foundations from the book of Deuteronomy?[17] Several can be suggested in relation to the need for reform in local church education using the categories suggested above. Other implications might be suggested in relation to education in various settings, but our focus is on the implications as they relate to the local church. Such implications emerge from a common-sense reading of the Scripture that must be evaluated in relation to the other foundational considerations explored in subsequent chapters of this work.

From Deuteronomy 30:11–20—"Finding Life"—the following implications can be suggested:

1. Reemphasize the evangelistic functions of Sunday school and other educational programs of the local church.

16. For an insightful description of Jesus's teaching ministry, see these classic works: A. B. Bruce, *The Training of the Twelve* (Grand Rapids: Kregel, 1971); and Herman H. Horne, *The Teaching Techniques of Jesus* (Grand Rapids: Kregel, 1920). A more recent work is Joseph A. Grassi, *Teaching the Way: Jesus, the Early Church, and Today* (Washington, DC: University Press of America, 1982).

17. One can raise the question of how one moves from biblical texts to educational or ministerial implications. This assumes that educators are dealing with the authority for teaching, which is the subject of Robert W. Pazmiño, *By What Authority Do We Teach? Sources for Empowering Christian Educators* (Eugene, OR: Wipf & Stock, 2002). But, basically, in moving from biblical texts to implications, one moves through one's experiences and reflections as prayerfully enlightened by the work of the Holy Spirit in illuminating the texts. In this process, one interacts with the experiences and reflections of other Christians, but no easy formula exists for such a journey to acquire wisdom, which is a lifelong task. Teaching becomes incarnated as truth through the person of the teacher.

2. Train Sunday school teachers and adult participants in areas of evangelization and follow-up.
3. Explore the possibilities of classes and Bible study groups geared to those inquiring about the Christian faith.
4. Pray for and anticipate decisions for a life commitment to Jesus Christ as Sovereign and Savior.

From Deuteronomy 31:9–13—"The Word of God and Human Response"— the following implications emerge:

1. Develop and work toward goals of biblical literacy for all age groups.
2. Evaluate and select curriculum that is Bible centered and comprehensive in dealing with the whole counsel of God.
3. Relate biblical themes to contemporary life and help students in all educational programs to grapple with the implications of biblical truth for their response in the world.

Deuteronomy 31:30–32:4—"Fostering Liberation and Facilitating Worship"—suggests the following implications:

1. Maximize the active participation of everyone in educational programs. Complement action with time for serious thought and reflection in dialogue with others.
2. Raise questions concerning distinctive Christian lifestyles in a pluralistic society. Ask, What does it mean to affirm Christ's lordship in various areas of life?
3. Consciously rely on the renewing work of the Holy Spirit in the lives of individuals, groups, and structures.
4. Work toward the coordination of education programs with the themes and emphases of weekly corporate worship.
5. Prepare children and youth for and expose them to corporate worship. Provide assistance for parents in this area of preparation.
6. Allow for spontaneous and planned occasions of worship during educational events.
7. Inquire about the spiritual growth of persons in your programs.

Psalm 78

Psalm 78:1–8 is another key Old Testament passage providing insights for understanding the setting for covenant education. This passage speaks about the attention given to God's activities in history on behalf of God's creation and the redeemed community:

O my people, hear my teaching;
   listen to the words of my mouth.
I will open my mouth in parables,
   I will utter hidden things, things from of old—
what we have heard and known,
   what our fathers have told us.
We will not hide them from their children;
   we will tell the next generation
the praiseworthy deeds of the LORD,
   his power, and the wonders he has done.
He decreed statutes for Jacob
   and established the law in Israel,
which he commanded our forefathers
   to teach their children,
so the next generation would know them,
   even the children yet to be born,
   and they in turn would tell their children.
Then they would put their trust in God
   and would not forget his deeds
   but would keep his commands.
They would not be like their forefathers—
   a stubborn and rebellious generation,
whose hearts were not loyal to God,
   whose spirits were not faithful to him.

Wherever God's words and deeds are passed on to succeeding generations, a context for Christian education is formed. By necessity, intergenerational relationships must be present for this to occur. Both the Old and the New Testament communities have a shared memory or history. In rehearsing the accounts of God's activities in both distant and recent history, the meaning and purpose of life in God are shared. Followers of the living God are not to forget but rather should learn from the victories and failures of persons in the past. God's community is called to reflect on God's covenant and the responses of persons, groups, and communities that have resulted in both blessing and curse. Where this reflection and dialogue are facilitated is the place where the covenant can be renewed. Reflection depends on a faithful recounting of history, which emphasizes the need to explore historical foundations.

In Old Testament times, the family was the primary setting for education. The efforts of the family were supplemented and complemented by the instruction in the covenant community as it gathered. In exilic and postexilic times, the agencies of education expanded to include both synagogues and schools.[18] Even with these developments, the extended family continued to be important in education.

In the New Testament, the church functions as the extended and adopted family of God. It is the responsibility of those so gifted and experienced to pass on to the next generation accounts of the acts, the power, and the wonders of God in the past and present. Those who are gifted and experienced have responsibilities as stewards to transmit this life-giving message to new members of the faith community. This transmission is crucial if persons are to gain a sense of rootedness and identity in relation to a faith community. Constant diligence is necessary to sustain this faithful transmission that also calls for interpretation.

Nehemiah 8:1–18

Following the return of the exiles from captivity, Ezra reads the Law to the people (Neh. 8:1–18). Ezra's ministry is an instrument for renewal in the life of the community; those able to understand are assembled to hear God's Word.[19] The hearing and heeding of God's Word issues in the restoration of life and worship. The uniquely educational aspect of this event is the Levites' instruction of the people. They clarify the words of God so that the people can understand. When the people clearly see the implications of biblical teachings, they can then respond in ways that are pleasing to God. The tasks of education include enabling others to come to an understanding of God, divine revelation, and expectations for personal and corporate human life.

The responsibilities of the educators or teachers include: (1) *proclamation*, that is, the reading, speaking, or sharing of God's Word; (2) *exposition*, that is, the translation and explanation or opening up of the meaning of God's Word; and (3) *exhortation*, that is, the suggestion of direct application and response for those who hear.

The responsibilities of the hearers or students include the following: (1) *knowing* God's Word by listening attentively to its proclamation; (2) *understanding* God's Word by responding to its exposition; (3) *obeying* God's Word by responding wholeheartedly to its exhortation; and (4) *worshiping* God, who is encountered through the proclaimed Word, and celebrating the restoration realized in personal and corporate life.

18. For a full description of education in Old Testament times, see William Barclay, *Train Up a Child: Educational Ideals in the Ancient World* (Philadelphia: Westminster, 1959), 11–48.

19. Cf. Romans 10:14–18; see also the discussion of Ezra and Nehemiah in Robert W. Pazmiño, *Latin American Journey: Insights for Christian Education in North America* (Eugene, OR: Wipf & Stock, 2002), 123–44.

In general, hearers or students are expected to have reverence for God's Word (the people stand while Ezra reads the book of the Law) and to respond at several levels, including one's thoughts, decisions, and affections. A response includes the intellect in terms of understanding, the will in terms of obedience, and the emotions in terms of repentance and worship. A call is made to set one's mind, will, heart, and affections upon God. Here is an example of education that goes beyond the immediate family situation to include the whole community and nation.

Wisdom Literature

Crucial to understanding education from the perspective of the Old Testament is the concept of wisdom and, in particular, its embodiment in Wisdom literature. In the Hebrew worldview, wisdom was intensely practical, resulted in successful living, and applied to the heart. A special group of persons was endowed with the gift of wisdom and had the responsibility of sharing their advice with others. Their task was to develop workable plans and to prescribe advice for successful living (Jer. 18:18). But wisdom in its fullest sense was only to be understood in relation to its source, namely, God.[20] David H. Hubbard provides helpful insights in his description of wisdom:

> Wisdom in the fullest sense belongs to God alone (Job 12:13ff.; Isa. 31:2; Dan. 2:20–23). His wisdom is not only completeness of knowledge pervading every realm of life (Job 10:4; 26:6; Prov. 5:21; 15:3) but also consists in his irresistible fulfillment of what he has in mind (J. Pedersen, *Israel: Its Life and Culture*, I–II, page 198). The universe (Prov. 3:19f.; 8:22–31; Jer. 10:12) and man (Job 10:8ff.; Ps. 104:24; Prov. 14:31; 22:2) are products of his creative wisdom. Natural (Isa. 28:23–29) and historical (Isa. 31:2) processes are governed by his wisdom, which includes an infallible discrimination between good and evil and is the basis for the just rewards and punishments which are the lot of the righteous and the wicked (Pss. 1, 37, 73; Prov. 10:3; 11:4; 12:2). Such wisdom is inscrutable (Job 28:12–21). God in his grace must reveal it if man is going to grasp it at all (Job 28:23, 28). Even wisdom derived from natural abilities or distilled from experience is a gracious gift, because God's creative activity makes such wisdom possible.
>
> Biblical wisdom is both religious and practical. Stemming from the fear of the Lord (Job 28:28; Ps. 111:10; Prov. 1:7; 9:10), it branches out to touch all of life. . . . Wisdom takes insights gleaned from the knowledge of God's ways and applies them in the daily walk. This combination of insight and obedience (and all insight must issue in obedience) relates wisdom to the prophetic emphasis

20. David H. Hubbard, "Wisdom," in *The New Bible Dictionary*, ed. J. D. Douglas (Grand Rapids: Eerdmans, 1962), 1333.

on the knowledge (i.e., the cordial love and obedience) of God (e.g., Hos. 2:20; 4:1, 6; 6:6; Jer. 4:22; 9:3, 6; and especially Prov. 9:10).[21]

What implications emerge from this Old Testament understanding of education? First, God imparts wisdom, and people are dependent on this grace for any claim to wisdom. Therefore, wisdom that is apart from or inconsistent with the truths of God's revelation must be suspect and questioned. Education at its best must be God-centered, seeing God as the source. Educators are called to integrate all areas of knowledge with God's revelation.

A second implication is that education should have an impact on people's lives and should enable them to grapple with the practical consequences of the truths studied or discerned. Therefore, the appeal to a strictly theoretical or academic agenda that addresses the mind divorced from affections and actions cannot claim to be faithful to the biblical tradition. Questions of character, ethics, and lifestyle are appropriate, along with how truth and commitment relate to all areas of life. Herein is the need for a holistic and integrated perspective on education that affects the head, heart, and hands of both teachers and students.

A third implication for education is that those who are identified as teachers must be evaluated in terms of the extent to which they give evidence of having received the gift of wisdom from God. Teachers are ultimately responsible to God for the use of their gifts and responsible to students in sharing the fruit of their insights. Approaches to education that exclusively emphasize student-directed learning may not provide adequate opportunities for a teacher's wisdom to be shared. The Wisdom literature affirms the need to contextualize norms that can speak to people where they live.[22]

Prophetic Literature

The prophets are the social educators of their times who call the people, the leaders, and the nations to account for their ways. They express the passion of God for righteousness and justice in the land. Those within and outside the faith community are scrutinized for the values they espouse and live out in their lives. In response to the lack of faithful living, the prophets in their teaching bring a message of hope, anger, and courage that the great North African teacher Augustine described: "Hope has two lovely daughters, anger

21. Ibid.
22. For a discussion of wisdom in relation to education, see Peter C. Hodgson, *God's Wisdom: Toward a Theology of Education* (Louisville: Westminster John Knox, 1999); and Charles F. Melchert, *Wise Teaching: Biblical Wisdom and Educational Ministry* (Harrisburg, PA: Trinity, 1998).

and courage. Anger at the way things are, and courage to see that they need not remain as they are."[23] The prophets' teachings provide hope for those who are oppressed as they express God's anger at human sin, as suggested by Isaiah's words: "The Sovereign LORD has given me an instructed tongue, to know the word that sustains the weary. He wakens me morning by morning, wakens my ear to listen like one being taught" (50:4). After listening to God, the prophets teach with courageous words, declaring the alternatives to the current situation.

As outlined by Ezekiel, the Levites have a distinctive role in teaching the people the ways of the Lord: "They are to teach my people the difference between the holy and the common and show them how to distinguish between the unclean and the clean" (44:23). Whereas the Levites' teaching may be primarily applicable to personal, familial, and religious or cultic ethics, the prophets' role is to set an agenda for the nation in the public sphere as well as the area of social ethics. This is modeled in the message of Micah: "He has showed you, O man, what is good. And what does the LORD require of you? To act justly and to love mercy and to walk humbly with your God" (6:8). The works of justice, righteousness, and mercy encompass all of life and include the social, economic, and political spheres. The prophets speak of God's values for all of life that bring human efforts under judgment and disrupt everyday patterns. God's demands are made explicit in the teachings of the prophets, who pose choices for all their hearers, their students in the public arena.

The prophetic tradition suggests the need for Christian educators to grapple with the social, political, and economic implications of faith commitments. The prophets were commentators in their time who took risks in clearly outlining God's demands. Prophetic teaching was not always welcomed, and a silencing of the prophets was one response to their teaching. One important consideration of the prophetic teacher in the present day is the manifestation of love in confronting hearers, realizing that care is required to confront others in their sinful and destructive ways.

The New Testament

The New Testament, as was the case with the Hebrew Scripture, or Old Testament, provides a variety of insights regarding the tasks of teaching the

23. This quote, which may well be part of an oral tradition attributed to Augustine, is noted by Wilbert J. McKeachie, *Teaching Tips: Strategies, Research, and Theory for College and University Teachers,* 9th ed. (Lexington, MA: D. C. Heath & Co., 1994), 384. This work is one that I wish I had read before teaching in higher education. It has many helpful suggestions.

faith. The Gospels and the Epistles set an agenda for the propagation of the Christian faith in what often was an alien or hostile setting. Jesus as a teacher had to contend with an unwelcome reception by many to what he was proclaiming. The facts of his incarnation, the threat to his life in Bethlehem, his rejection at Nazareth, and his crucifixion in Jerusalem all point to the risks and costs of teaching the truth in his time. These experiences of Jesus are explored in appendix A.[24] Christians in the first two centuries had similar challenges to their sharing the gospel. Much can be learned regarding education from a careful study of several New Testament teaching patterns, some of which are considered below. Kevin Giles points out in relation to the New Testament that every leader of the faith community was a teacher. Those leaders included apostles, prophets, bishops, deacons, elders, women, church members, and even children who were brought within Jesus's circle of teaching. The vision was for everyone to be teachers.[25] This was particularly the case for Matthew's Gospel, which served in many ways as both a teaching manual and curriculum.

Matthew: Sharing Vision, Mission, and Memory

In the New Testament, the Old Testament patterns of education persist, but the followers of Jesus are provided with a new agenda for their educational efforts. This agenda is most explicit in Matthew 28:16–20. The purpose of the disciples' ministry is to enable other persons to become obedient disciples of Jesus Christ. This teaching of responsibility is for all who are disciples of Jesus. It is a difficult task to teach obedience. Those who have taught others can appreciate this difficulty. Yet there is the promise that Christ's very presence, as well as his authority, will empower his disciples to disciple others, be it in the home, the church, the classroom, or the wider community. The purpose of making disciples is totally dependent on sharing the content of Jesus's own teachings, those truths revealed by God with direct implications for life. The challenge posed for current efforts in Christian education is this question: Are obedient disciples of Jesus Christ being nurtured and taught all that Jesus taught? If so, there is a basis for affirmation and continued reliance on God's gracious undertaking. If not, there is a challenge for careful evaluation and renewed efforts.

24. See also the forthcoming work: Robert W. Pazmiño, *So What Makes Our Teaching Christian? Teaching in the Name, Spirit, and Power of Jesus* (2008). This book explores insights from Jesus's teaching in the Gospel of John particularly with Nicodemus and the Samaritan woman known as Photini and the apostles' teaching in the book of Acts.

25. Kevin Giles, *Patterns of Ministry among the First Christians* (Melbourne, Australia: Collins Dove, 1989), 114–18.

In addition to this educational commission, the pattern of instruction in Matthew's Gospel shows how teaching was conducted in the early church. Matthew's Gospel is a teaching manual for discipling Christians. Jesus's teaching is organized into blocks of instruction that provide a curricular guide for the emerging Christian church. The five major teaching sections of instruction include the following: 5:1–7:27; 10:1–42; 13:1–52; 18:1–35; 23:1–25:46. These sections address major areas of Christian life.[26] They can be categorized in terms of three elements that a Christian community shares with its members, namely, a vision, a mission, and a memory.

The first teaching section is the Sermon on the Mount (Matt. 5:1–7:27). This passage contains Jesus's teaching on the personal and social ethics of the kingdom. It provides a vision for participation in God's kingdom.

Matthew 10:1–42 records Jesus's charge to the twelve disciples, outlining his teaching on mission. Jesus sends out his disciples as an extension of his own ministry with specific directives to guide their ministries.

The third teaching section (Matt. 13:1–52) includes the parables of the kingdom, in which Jesus teaches about redemptive history and provides insights for discerning the nature of the kingdom itself. The kingdom has small beginnings but grows in the midst of an evil world. This history of the kingdom provides a framework for understanding past, current, and future developments in the mission of the kingdom.

Matthew 18:1–35 contains Jesus's discourse on church discipline, in which he describes the nature of his disciples' commitments to one another in love and truth. This passage addresses the area of mission as related to a local body of disciples who are called to model a community of love, healing, reconciliation, and justice.

The final teaching section (Matt. 23:1–25:46) contains Jesus's teaching on eschatology. The happenings at the end of the present age with the inbreaking of the coming age of God's kingdom fulfilled on earth are described. Thus the focus is again on vision.

The New Testament model for Christian teaching, then, centers on the shared Christian vision, mission, and memory, as the followers of Jesus Christ seek to be faithful to God's calling in the world.

In relation to current educational efforts, Christians are called to evaluate the extent to which the Christian vision, the Christian mission, and the Christian memory are effectively shared. Such criteria provide standards for evaluating Christian education today. As was illustrated with Deuteronomy

26. Glenn W. Barker, William L. Lane, and J. Ramsey Michaels, *The New Testament Speaks* (New York: Harper & Row, 1969), 264–66.

30–32, possible educational implications can be suggested for local church educational efforts based on the consideration of Matthew's teaching model.

From the first element of education—sharing vision—the following implications for Christian educators can be identified:

1. Explicitly state, preferably in written form, their vision for God's work in their specific locality.
2. Provide an extended period of time, perhaps in a retreat format, when persons involved in educational ministries can study biblical insights for education and can share their vision for ministry.
3. Periodically devote time to evaluate the implementation of a vision for a specific ministry and to reorient efforts.

From the second element of education—sharing mission—the following implications for Christian educators can be suggested:

1. Develop a statement of mission to guide educational work that identifies specific purposes and goals for long- and short-term periods.
2. Consider needs both within and outside of the immediate Christian community and biblical demands in considering mission. (Challenges in home and foreign missions cannot be neglected in focusing on local concerns.)
3. Delegate specific responsibilities and establish avenues of accountability for various components of mission implementation.
4. Evaluate existing programs and efforts in terms of an agreed-upon mission statement.
5. Periodically reconsider the mission statement in light of new challenges and changing situations.

The third element of education—sharing memory—suggests the following implications for Christian educators:

1. Plan times when the history of God's work in a particular local church community and/or denomination can be recounted and celebrated.
2. Relate local history to the advance of God's kingdom over the centuries.
3. Identify specific points of continuity and discontinuity with the past in relation to the present and future of the local church.
4. Include children, youth, and adults in exploring historical roots.

These implications are suggestive and serve to illustrate the value of exploring foundations for the actual practice of education in the setting of the local church. Various other factors must be considered, but biblical models can be reappropriated and reinterpreted to provide helpful frameworks in which to conceptualize and practice Christian education. This approach is an alternative to the uncritical appropriation of dominant models current in society, which nevertheless can be considered for secondary insights.

Luke: Methods from the Master Teacher

Another passage of particular significance for a discussion of education, and of methods in particular, is Luke 24:13–35, in which Jesus talks with two disciples on the road to Emmaus.

> Now that same day two of them were going to a village called Emmaus, about seven miles from Jerusalem. They were talking with each other about every-thing that had happened. As they talked and discussed these things with each other, Jesus himself came up and walked along with them; but they were kept from recognizing him.
>
> He asked them, "What are you discussing together as you walk along?"
>
> They stood still, their faces downcast. One of them, named Cleopas, asked him, "Are you only a visitor to Jerusalem and do not know the things that have happened there in these days?"
>
> "What things?" he asked.
>
> "About Jesus of Nazareth," they replied. "He was a prophet, powerful in word and deed before God and all the people. The chief priests and our rulers handed him over to be sentenced to death, and they crucified him; but we had hoped that he was the one who was going to redeem Israel. And what is more, it is the third day since all this took place. In addition, some of our women amazed us. They went to the tomb early this morning but didn't find his body. They came and told us that they had seen a vision of angels, who said he was alive. Then some of our companions went to the tomb and found it just as the women had said, but him they did not see."
>
> He said to them, "How foolish you are, and how slow of heart to believe all that the prophets have spoken! Did not the Christ have to suffer these things and then enter his glory?" And beginning with Moses and all the Prophets, he explained to them what was said in all the Scriptures concerning himself.
>
> As they approached the village to which they were going, Jesus acted as if he were going farther. But they urged him strongly, "Stay with us, for it is nearly evening; the day is almost over." So he went in to stay with them.
>
> When he was at the table with them, he took bread, gave thanks, broke it and began to give it to them. Then their eyes were opened and they recognized him, and he disappeared from their sight. They asked each other, "Were not our hearts burning within us while he talked with us on the road and opened the Scriptures to us?"

They got up and returned at once to Jerusalem. There they found the Eleven and those with them, assembled together and saying, "It is true! The Lord has risen and has appeared to Simon." Then the two told what had happened on the way, and how Jesus was recognized by them when he broke the bread.

Key components of this teaching episode for consideration are discussion (v. 14), open inquiry (v. 17), correction and clarification (vv. 25–27), role modeling (vv. 30–31), and the need for response (vv. 33–35). Whereas this educational encounter includes the dimension of declaration as evidenced in Jesus's exposition of the Scriptures, it also includes the dimension of dialogue, which enables the disciples to be engaged not only at the level of their minds but also includes their affections, wills, and actions. Here is an educational encounter that calls for a head, heart, and hand response to the good news declared by Jesus.

Jesus's approach in interacting with these disciples includes three noteworthy elements. First, Jesus asks them questions (vv. 17–19). The Master Teacher knows the answers, yet he wants his students to think for themselves. Second, Jesus listens. He hears their response to the questions he asks. Teachers often fail to listen to students and to allow adequate time for thought. Third, it is only after questioning and listening that Jesus both exhorts these disciples and opens the Scriptures, explaining their meaning. Jesus explains the truths discussed by Moses and the Prophets through his interpretation of the texts. In response to Jesus's teaching, these disciples describe their encounter as one in which both their eyes and the Scriptures were opened. The word for "open" here is the same word used to describe how a womb is opened at the birth of a child. There is a sense of joy and the burning of the heart that parallels a birth experience in terms of its personal impact. The joy associated with such a disclosure is a desperately needed dimension in each and every Christian education endeavor.

In addition to this account of Jesus's teaching, the Gospels provide examples of the wide variety of methods that Jesus used in his teaching ministry.[27] James Stewart identifies some general principles and particular features of Jesus's methodology. The general principles are: Jesus's teaching was authoritative; Jesus trusted in the power of truth to convince his hearers; Jesus sought to have persons think for themselves; Jesus lived what he taught; and Jesus loved those he taught. The particular features are: Jesus's teaching was oral instruction; it

---

27. Robert H. Stein, *The Method and Message of Jesus' Teachings* (Philadelphia: Westminster, 1978), provides a helpful categorization of the forms of Jesus's teaching. He points out that three important considerations in teaching include what is taught, who the teacher is, and how the teacher teaches.

was occasional in nature; it was elicited by quite casual events; it was adapted to his audience; and it included figurative elements such as illustrations, epigrams, paradoxes, and parables.[28] Christian educators are not limited to the oral instruction that Jesus employed but have access to a wide variety of media and methodologies. Nevertheless, the example of Jesus as the Master Teacher must be studied if one is to effectively and faithfully minister. In this study one must recognize the unique role and mission of Jesus's teaching.

1 Corinthians 2:6–16: Wisdom from the Holy Spirit

Christian educators must consider the extensive teaching ministry of Paul in the first century. Paul's focus is wisdom from God, a wisdom whose source is the Holy Spirit. Paul teaches in words taught by the Spirit, expressing spiritual truths in spiritual words. The reception of these words also requires the work of the Holy Spirit in the lives of the hearers. A person without the Spirit does not accept the things that come from the Spirit. Paul reflects the words of Jesus to his disciples: "But the Counselor, the Holy Spirit, whom the Father will send in my name, will teach you all things and will remind you of everything I have said to you" (John 14:26); "But when he, the Spirit of truth, comes, he will guide you into all truth. He will not speak on his own; he will speak only what he hears, and he will tell you what is yet to come" (John 16:13). The Holy Spirit, whose responsibility is to teach the disciples of Christ all things and remind them of Jesus's teachings, equips the Christian teacher to effectively minister and releases the creativity necessary to appropriately share and understand Christian truths.

Effective teaching and learning require the continuing presence and work of the Holy Spirit. Teaching itself is described as one of the gifts bestowed on the church by Christ through the Holy Spirit (Rom. 12:3–8; 1 Cor. 12:27–31; Eph. 4:7–13; 1 Pet. 4:10–11). Teaching is not only a Spirit-endowed and motivated gift but also requires that the teacher be continually filled and guided by the Holy Spirit in the process of teaching (Eph. 4:29–32; 5:15–20). The spiritual dimensions of education are foundational in a New Testament perspective.

The wisdom from the Holy Spirit contrasts with the knowledge or wisdom from the world. This distinction is also explicit in James 3:13–18. In 1 Corinthians, Paul describes "a wisdom of this age" (2:6) and a knowledge that puffs up (8:1–3). In comparison, spiritual knowledge and wisdom are characterized

---

28. James D. Stewart, *The Life and Teaching of Jesus Christ* (Nashville: Abingdon, n.d.), 64–71. For a detailed exploration of these dimensions of Jesus's teaching, see Pazmiño, *Principles and Practices of Christian Education: An Evangelical Perspective* (1992; Eugene, OR: Wipf & Stock, 2002), 124–32.

by a love that builds up or edifies. Knowledge easily breeds conceit, provides glib answers, and at best is incomplete. What matters more is spiritual wisdom expressed in a love that promotes the good of others and glorifies God. Paul prays that the Ephesians might know the love of Christ that surpasses knowledge (3:19). Paul does not denounce knowledge but sees it being transcended through the work of the Holy Spirit, making the love of Christ a reality.

From the experience of teaching a group of twelve to fifteen active fifth- and sixth-grade boys in East Harlem, New York City, the author can testify to the essential dimension of love shared both within and outside the classroom. Beyond any knowledge shared in the lessons, students have commented over the years on the glimpses of God's love seen during Saturday outings and service projects that extended scriptural lessons into everyday life.

Ephesians: Pattern and Purposes

A general pattern of Paul's ministry as reflected in the book of Ephesians, but also in his other writings, is one that incorporates instruction, intercession, and exhortation.[29] Instruction consists of a focus on the content of Christian faith, on what God has done. Intercession is prayer for those instructed, with a conscious dependence on God and the work of the Holy Spirit. The third element of the pattern is exhortation. Paul specifies what believers are to be and do in light of God's activities and revelation in Christ.

In addition to this general pattern, Ephesians 4:7–16 provides specific insights for discerning the purposes of the teaching or educational ministries of the church. Teaching is a spiritual gift. The immediate purpose of teaching is the preparation of God's people for works of service within the church and the world. A truth of particular significance for the Christian church in the twenty-first century is the ministry of all believers. The sixteenth-century church affirmed the priesthood, and in some cases the prophethood, of all believers, which is now being understood in terms of a ministry that each believer possesses. All of God's people must be equipped, taught, and trained for their varied ministries, making use of the gifts God has bestowed on a covenant people.

Beyond this immediate purpose of preparation for works of service, there is an ultimate purpose for teaching, for educating. This ultimate purpose is

---

29. John Stott, God's New Society: The Message of Ephesians (Downers Grove, IL: InterVarsity, 1979), 146. See also Roy B. Zuck, Teaching as Paul Teaches (Grand Rapids: Baker, 1998); Richard R. Osmer, The Teaching Ministry of Congregations (Louisville: Westminster John Knox, 2005), 3–56; for my discussion of Paul as teacher, see "Teachings of Paul," in Evangelical Dictionary of Christian Education, ed. Michael J. Anthony (Grand Rapids: Baker Academic, 2001), 686–88.

the edification of the church. The gift of teaching is given so that the body of Christ, the church, might be built up. Whereas sanctification generally centers on the personal spiritual growth of an individual, edification centers on corporate spiritual growth that is by necessity mutual, collaborative, and cooperative. The church is Christ's body, and his headship and lordship are essential if edification is to occur. This edification occurs in the areas of unity and maturity. Unity is a unity in the faith and knowledge of the Son of God, and it is a unity in the truth. Maturity takes place in terms of the whole measure of the fullness of Christ. The church grows into this maturity by truth and love. Speaking the truth in love involves maintaining, living, and doing the truth within relationships of love.

Edification requires the corresponding work of sanctification; both processes are mutually supportive. Thus the purposes of education must include both corporate and personal dimensions of growth in the Christian faith. Also, the immediate purpose of preparation for service must be seen in relation to the ultimate purpose of edification. It is through the actual opportunities for service that the body of Christ is built up. Therefore, education in the Christian faith that does not issue in service can be questioned as being inadequate in the same way that the book of James questions a faith devoid of deeds (James 2:14–26).

Colossians and Philippians: Wisdom in Christ

In Colossians 1:9–14 Paul prays that God will fill the Colossian Christians with knowledge of God's will through all spiritual wisdom and understanding. He prays this so that these Christians might live their lives worthy of the Lord, pleasing God in every way. Paul specifies ways in which this worthiness might be expressed: bearing fruit in every good work, growing in the knowledge of God, being strengthened with all power according to God's glorious might, and joyfully giving thanks to God. In other words, service, spiritual growth and empowerment, and worship are evidences of the application of Christian knowledge and wisdom to life.

In this epistle Paul goes on to emphasize the supremacy of Christ in creation and his centrality in the experience of Christians. It is in Christ that Christians have redemption, the forgiveness of sins (1:14). It is in Christ that Christians must center their education. Paul describes his purpose in ministering that fellow believers "may have the full riches of complete understanding, in order that they may know the mystery of God, namely, Christ, in whom are hidden all the treasures of wisdom and knowledge" (2:2–3). It is in Christ that integration and wholeness in education can be found because in him are all the treasures of wisdom and knowledge. Reality itself is found in him (2:17). Paul warns of hollow and deceptive philosophy, which depends on human tradition and the basic principles of this world, rather than on Christ (2:8). It is essential that the christocentric character of Christian education be recognized and affirmed at its roots. Christ himself is at the center of all life from a Christian world and life view.

In relation to the centrality of Christ and the treasures of wisdom and knowledge in him, Christians are called to a rigorous task in the area of education. This task is suggested in Paul's exhortations to the Christians at Philippi. In Philippians 4:8–9, Paul shares a vast agenda for Christian educators at all levels of society:

> Finally, brothers, whatever is true, whatever is noble, whatever is right, whatever is pure, whatever is lovely, whatever is admirable—if anything is excellent or praiseworthy—think about such things. Whatever you have learned or received or heard from me, or seen in me—put it into practice. And the God of peace will be with you.

This is an agenda encompassing all the areas of human intellectual endeavor and study. In relation to these areas, Christians are to think about such things and take such things into account. They are to allow such valuable knowledge to shape their attitudes and lives. But the obligation does not end with mere thought or reflection. Whatever these Philippian Christians had learned, received, or heard from Paul, or had seen in him, was to be put into practice. Thought without practice is incomplete. It is also helpful to note that Paul's influence was not only direct and intentional through what was learned, received, and heard; it was also unintentional and indirect. Paul himself served as a model so that what was seen in his life was also taught. This is the dimension of teaching that is more caught than taught through relationships with students.

John: Supremacy of Relationships

While emphasizing wisdom and knowledge, Christian educators must also be aware of the dimension of interpersonal relationships addressed in the New Testament. Christian education centers on relationships with the Triune God, with other persons, and with all of creation. Various Scriptures could be cited that deal with the relationships among persons as they are to be patterned after the foundational relationship with God. One passage of particular significance is John 15:12–17, which presents Jesus's new commandment to love others as he himself has loved his disciples. Jesus modeled this love in how he taught both Nicodemus and the Samaritan woman in his encounters with them as recorded in the Gospel of John. This commandment to love is overwhelming and yet foundational for all interpersonal interactions in Christian education.

Also of significance is the nature of Jesus's relationship, as the Master Teacher, with his disciples, his students. Jesus shared his very life by laying it down for his disciples. They were viewed not just as servants but more significantly as friends. Wherever possible, teachers are called upon to foster friendships with students and to give of themselves sacrificially following the model of Jesus. Sacrificial giving can include such efforts as being available both before and after scheduled teaching times for interaction and active listening with students.

Paul describes his relationship to his Thessalonian disciples as one that includes both maternal and paternal dimensions (1 Thess. 2:7–12). In verse 8, Paul says that the ministers and teachers were delighted to share not only the gospel of God but their lives as well.[30] The maternal dimension included caring and nurturing, while the paternal dimension included encouraging, comforting, and urging others to live lives worthy of God. The challenge is for Christian teachers to be open to this level of servanthood, which places the teacher in a position of risk and vulnerability in loving and interacting with students. This interaction requires the sharing of one's very life and the willingness to serve as an example in guiding others. Being an example means not that the teacher is a complete and sinless person, but rather that he or she, like other persons, is in need of forgiveness and yet still seeks to be faithful.

Complementing the focus on love in relationships is the dimension of truth. Ephesians 4:15, 1 Peter 1:22, and 2 John 1 link the virtues of love and truth in encouraging Christians to speak or maintain the truth in love or to love in truth. There must be a standard of truth. For the Christian educator, this is provided in the Scriptures and consummately in the person of Jesus Christ. There is the assurance that all truth, wherever discerned, is God's truth, for God alone is its source. Truth without love results in harshness, and love without truth results in compromise. The Christian gospel maintains both of these virtues together in a creative complementarity.[31] It is a constant challenge in every educational setting to balance both love and truth through one's teaching. These themes are explored in the appendices of this third edition in relation to postmodernism.

An additional responsibility for teachers is suggested by the admonition issued in 2 Timothy 2:2. Teachers are called to duplicate their efforts through the teaching ministries of their students (Luke 6:40). Persons who are taught are to be prepared and equipped to teach others. Thus the Christian teacher

30. See also 1 Timothy 4:16.
31. See Thom Hopler, *A World of Difference: Following Christ beyond Our Cultural Walls* (Downers Grove, IL: InterVarsity, 1981), 185–95, for a helpful general discussion of these themes.

is to be sensitive to opportunities to disciple others. To fulfill this obligation, the Christian teacher depends on the work and presence of God the Creator, Redeemer, and Sustainer.

Hebrews: A Question of Readiness

Hebrews 5:11–6:3 provides insights for the important question of readiness prior to and during teaching interactions:

> We have much to say about this, but it is hard to explain because you are slow to learn. In fact, though by this time you ought to be teachers, you need someone to teach you the elementary truths of God's word all over again. You need milk, not solid food! Anyone who lives on milk, being still an infant, is not acquainted with the teaching about righteousness. But solid food is for the mature, who by constant use have trained themselves to distinguish good from evil.
>
> Therefore let us leave the elementary teachings about Christ and go on to maturity, not laying again the foundation of repentance from acts that lead to death, and of faith in God, instruction about baptisms, the laying on of hands, the resurrection of the dead, and eternal judgment. And God permitting, we will do so.

The writer to the Hebrews warns against those who may fall away from the faith and explains that some need to be retaught the elementary truths of God's Word. This is the case because they had not understood, accepted, or exemplified these truths in their lives. These persons are slow to learn. Using the metaphor of food, the writer notes that some persons need the milk of elementary teaching because they cannot handle the solid food of teachings for the mature. Other passages also describe various levels of maturity (1 Cor. 2:6–3:4; 9:19–23; Titus 2:1–15; 1 Pet. 5:1–7) that must be assessed and considered in any teaching endeavor. Christian educators are called to exercise discernment in adjusting their teaching to the spiritual, social, cultural, economic, and political characteristics of their hearers in the effort to address participants at appropriate levels of understanding and readiness.

The issue of adequately assessing the readiness of participants in Christian education efforts is complex and can be overwhelming, given the many variables that influence persons individually, corporately, and contextually. Yet there is a resource person available to Christian educators for this task. That person is the Holy Spirit. But in discussing the ministry of the Holy Spirit, who assists Christian teachers in assessing the readiness of participants and planning appropriately for it, teachers must realize that their readiness also is an issue. Educators are reminded of the warning in James 3:1: "Not many of you should presume to be teachers, my brothers, because you know that we who teach will be judged more strictly." Part of that judgment involves the discernment that one in fact has the gift of teaching.[32] Confirmation of that gift involves active service and a genuine openness to the feedback of others and to the improvement of one's skills.

An Integrated Model

Based on the biblical foundations for Christian education, it is possible to suggest a model to guide current thought and practice. Dr. E. V. Hill uses the image of a softball or baseball diamond to suggest the tasks of the Christian church.[33] But moving beyond the confines of a baseball diamond, a network or web of education can be proposed for the church's tasks. These tasks have direct implications for the purposes of Christian education (see fig. 2).

Figure 2
The Educational Tasks of the Church

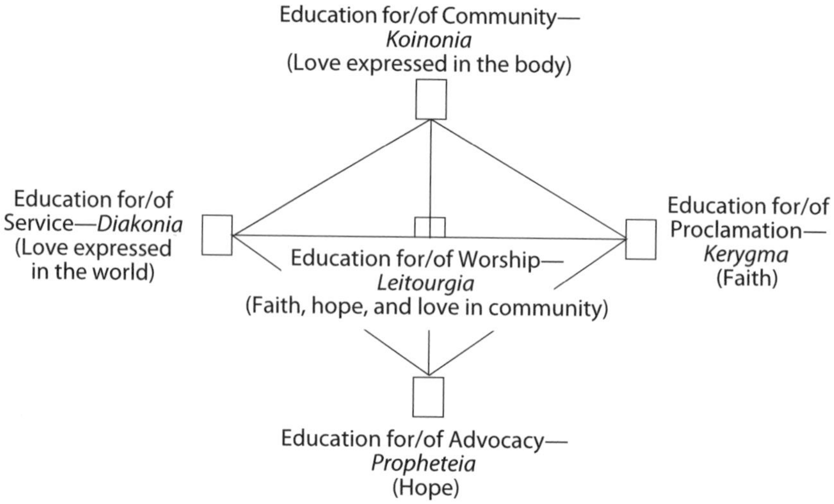

Education for/of Community—
Koinonia
(Love expressed in the body)

Education for/of
Service—*Diakonia*
(Love expressed
in the world)

Education for/of Worship—
Leitourgia
(Faith, hope, and love in community)

Education for/of
Proclamation—
Kerygma
(Faith)

Education for/of Advocacy—
Propheteia
(Hope)

In this model, one base represents education *for* proclamation (*kerygma*), which seeks to enable persons to consider their personal commitment to Jesus Christ. The task of proclamation involves teaching and preaching the gospel along

32. For a discussion of the gift of teaching, see Pazmiño, *By What Authority Do We Teach?* 59–76.
33. Edward V. Hill, "A Congregation's Response" (lecture presented at Gordon-Conwell Theological Seminary, South Hamilton, MA, January 21, 1976).

with the ministry of evangelism. By necessity this purpose includes sharing the basic content of the Christian faith. It also includes teaching about the need for personal response, about the need to make a decision regarding the new life offered in Jesus Christ. Persons are not educated into God's kingdom, but educational ministries are opportunities for them to explore the dimensions of faith in response to the gospel. The Christian virtue most closely, but not exclusively, associated with this emphasis in Christian education is faith.[34]

Faith can be viewed as including the dimensions of *notitia* (intellectual affirmation), *assensus* (affective affirmation), and *fiducia* (intentional affirmation) as persons respond to God's activities and revelation in Jesus Christ. Education for proclamation or evangelism focuses on enabling persons to explore and grapple with these dimensions of faith and encouraging their response. This response includes one's initial personal response and then efforts to share the Christian faith with others. The proclamation of the *kerygma* is crucial in this process (Rom. 10:17), with educational encounters providing for dialogue on the issues of faith in addition to the proclamation of the gospel. This base centers on faith, which is most often related to the temporal dimension of the past with an assurance based upon Christ's completed work in history.

In addition to education *for* proclamation with its explicit and active emphasis on the *kerygma*, this base also represents the education *of* proclamation. The education *of* proclamation denotes a more receptive and implicit teaching and learning that occurs through the witness of the Christian faith in word and deed. Education *for* proclamation includes encouraging the response of non-Christians to the claims of Christ and training Christians for their witness in various settings. Education *of* proclamation includes the nonformal and informal learning that occurs when Christians personally and corporately acknowledge their commitments to Christ and the implications of such commitments before the world in various ways. For example, a local church's advocacy and/or outreach to single parents and their participation in church life, or a church's commitment to honesty and integrity in its economic and political life can be a proclamation of the gospel.

A second base represents education *for* community (*koinonia*)—fellowship with God and with other Christians. It includes the processes of training, instruction, and nurture, which enable persons to grow and mature in their faith.[35] Maturation and growth, given the nature of Christian community and

---

34. Christian virtues or values become important in Christian education because who and what persons are and are becoming in Christ are central concerns. See, for example, 1 Timothy 4:12–16.

35. *Training* can be defined as education that deals with predictable, replicable situations. Training is a conserving element of education that emphasizes continuities with the past and the

fellowship, include not only personal sanctification but also corporate or mutual edification. For the purpose of analysis, it is possible to distinguish training, instruction, and nurture, and to include both personal and corporate dimensions. In actuality, however, these various elements should complement one another and foster an integration of biblical content and personal experience, of faith and life. Education *for* community involves the quest for sameness or what persons hold in common with others. One responsibility of both pastoral and lay leadership is to explore areas of sameness that help to form a sense of corporate identity or community. The sameness sought does not deny the realities of difference and the place of distinct individuals in the community. The Christian virtue most closely but, again, not exclusively associated with education for community is that of love as it is expressed within the body for others. Love as a virtue relates most closely to the temporal dimension of the present, with a focus on maximizing the potential of each current situation and interaction.

Paralleling the active and receptive models of the first base described, this second base can also be seen as encompassing two facets. The education *of* community includes the knowledge and implied insights and values that are communicated through the shared life of the faith community itself as it reflects its fellowship with God. For example, church dinners that seek to include everybody and perhaps share dishes of various ethnic, cultural, and racial groups communicate and teach values and attitudes beyond formal training and instruction. Lessons more caught than taught comprise the elements of education *of* community, and each faith community, group, family, or school must ask itself what in fact is being nurtured during time spent together.

A third base represents education *for* service (*diakonia*)—service to God, to other persons, and to the world. Christian educators are called to equip Christians for the task of service within the local church and the task of incarnating their faith in life through efforts and actions. In terms of the wider society, Christians are called in an incarnated ministry to be vehicles for Christ's transforming power, which can be effective at several different levels. Christians are called to be salt and light in various organizations and institutions, to work for justice and righteousness in various economic, political, social, educational, and ecclesiastical structures. The church order outlined in

---

passing on of an unchanging heritage. *Instruction* can be defined as education that deals with unpredictable situations. Instruction is a transforming element of education that emphasizes renewal and change in response to changing situations in society and a consideration of the discontinuities with the past. It envisions new possibilities and calls for the personal and corporate responses of Christians. *Nurture* involves love, nourishment, and spiritual direction. Nurture, by its very nature, requires a vital and intimate relationship and interaction with others.

Ephesians 4:7–13 points up the need to work for the ministry of all believers, with all serving and ministering in the contexts of their homes, workplaces, communities, societies, and world.

Christ's transforming power is also operative in the intentional and ideational realms, where knowledge and meanings are produced and distributed. A Christian world and life view is crucial for realizing meaning, purpose, and integration in life, and the call is to bring every thought captive in obedience to Christ (2 Cor. 10:5), recognizing that it is the Lord who gives wisdom and that from his mouth come knowledge and understanding (Prov. 2:6).

This renewing power of Christ is also needed in the realm of culture, with its various values, beliefs, and attitudes. Christ seeks to preserve, redeem, and transform cultures. Christians need spiritual discernment in exploring how the Christian faith interacts with surrounding cultures. The Christian virtue most closely associated with this third base, as with the second base, is love. But in this instance, love is primarily focused on the world and expressed in deed and word through service. As with second base, the temporal focus is on the present.

This third base includes a receptive mode to complement the active stance of education *for* service. Actual deeds *of* service for various persons, groups, and causes provide occasions when others can learn from the perspective of both Christians and non-Christians. Christians, for example, can learn the real human costs of certain political, social, and economic policies through ministries with the poor and in the process be spiritually enriched through contacts with disadvantaged Christians. On the other hand, non-Christians can gain insights about the Christian faith from the sacrificial service of Christians in the world as they serve as living epistles to the transforming power of Jesus Christ.

The fourth base signifies education *for* advocacy (*propheteia*). Christians are called to realize that their hope is in God and God's reign in history. With this perspective they are able to advocate those concerns that fulfill God's purposes in the world. Advocacy works for the restoration of hope in the wider community and society. As noted in the discussion of the Old Testament's prophetic legacy, the great church teacher Augustine suggested that "hope has two lovely daughters, anger and courage. Anger at the way things are, and courage to see that they need not remain as they are."[36] Human efforts in various areas of life and ministry must be evaluated in terms of kingdom values. Outcomes must be evaluated in terms of God's creative and redemptive purposes for all humankind, which include concerns for justice,

36. This quote attributed to Augustine is cited in McKeachie, *Teaching Tips*, 384.

peace, and righteousness throughout creation. God's purpose is "to bring all things in heaven and on earth together under one head, even Christ" (Eph. 1:10). All creation awaits the future glory that God will bring to fruition in the completed adoption of God's children and the redemption of their bodies (Rom. 8:18–27). There will be a new heaven and a new earth that will be the home of righteousness as God has promised (2 Pet. 3:13). John speaks of God's future in Revelation 21:1–5:

> Then I saw a new heaven and a new earth, for the first heaven and the first earth had passed away, and there was no longer any sea. I saw the Holy City, the new Jerusalem, coming down out of heaven from God, prepared as a bride beautifully dressed for her husband. And I heard a loud voice from the throne saying, "Now the dwelling of God is with men, and he will live with them. They will be his people, and God himself will be with them and be their God. He will wipe every tear from their eyes. There will be no more death or mourning or crying or pain, for the old order of things has passed away."
>
> He who was seated on the throne said, "I am making everything new!" Then he said, "Write this down, for these words are trustworthy and true."

This perspective of God's future kingdom negates neither an appreciation of the past nor an active working in the present to cooperate with God's purposes within the church and within the world. Education *for* advocacy encourages Christians to gain this perspective on the future and God's purposes in addressing current realities. Moses serves as a model advocate for his people in the Old Testament. Moses worked for the political, economic, social, and spiritual liberation of the people in Egypt. He sought their empowerment as a fulfillment of God's plan. In the New Testament, Jesus as the Second or New Moses fulfills this role of advocacy and upon his departure from earth sends another advocate, the Holy Spirit, to intercede on behalf of the people. In response to such advocacy, Christians are to advocate for the persons and concerns that are close to the heart of God. The Christian virtue logically associated with this fourth base is hope, which envisions God's future and human participation in that future along with calling persons, communities, and societies to account just as the prophets of old did. In commenting on the place of advocacy with older adults, Arthur Becker identifies three aspects of advocacy: the correction of injustice, the positive pursuit of justice, and the prevention of injustice.[37]

---

37. Arthur Becker, *Ministry with Older Persons* (Minneapolis: Augsburg, 1986), 196, as cited by Harriet Kerr Swenson, *Visible and Vital: A Handbook for the Aging Congregation* (New York: Paulist Press, 1994), 108, 129.

These three aspects of advocacy are components of the prophetic calling of God's people.

The challenge inherent in the prophetic task of the church calls for risk and vulnerability as modeled by the prophets of the Old Testament. To avoid this risk is to neglect the ministry of reconciliation that is given to the church (2 Cor. 5:16–21). The prophets of old assumed this task of calling peoples and nations to account before God. Christians in each age are not to shrink from such a demand. This requires that prophetic words be honored in corporate life and that believers demonstrate a willingness to respond to the demands of the gospel of Christ.

Education for/of advocacy includes both acculturation and disenculturation. Acculturation is a process that affirms the place of a particular Christian culture and involves becoming a responsible member of a community in which that culture is affirmed. In contrast to acculturation, disenculturation is a process that places the values of God's kingdom above any given cultural expression and community of the Christian faith. Both processes are interdependent and necessary, for as Lesslie Newbigin has aptly observed, "the gospel provides the stance from which all culture is to be evaluated; but the gospel . . . is always embodied in some cultural form."[38]

Education for advocacy can be seen as acculturation into the vision of God's future as embodied and expressed in a particular community with its proximate purposes for God's reign. Education of advocacy involves a receptive stance that enables a critical consciousness of proximate purposes in light of the ultimate purposes of God's reign. A particular Christian community, for example, may emphasize the need for its participants to use the most updated media and technological resources to equip children and youth for the challenges of influencing modern Western culture. This can be viewed as an appropriate proximate purpose. But from the perspective of the kingdom values of shalom for all and stewardship of global resources, the tremendous outlay of capital to secure such media and technology may be questioned in terms of ultimate purposes.

The emphasis that centers and integrates educational efforts at each of the four bases is education for worship (leitourgia), located at the center of the diamond network. In educational ministries, persons are to be encouraged to see the sovereign God as Lord of all and therefore worthy of worship, honor, glory, and praise. Education for worship encourages persons to celebrate the presence of God in all areas of life and to respond with the sacrifice of their

---

38. Lesslie Newbigin, Foolishness to the Greeks: The Gospel and Western Culture (Grand Rapids: Eerdmans, 1986), 21.

very lives (Rom. 12:1–2). Abraham Heschel is a religious educator who has spoken directly to this need. Heschel observes that the Greeks learned in order to comprehend, the modern person learns in order to use, but the Hebrews learned in order to revere. Heschel reminds Christian educators of the need to encourage students to revere, to sense wonder and awe in response to God and to our multifaceted creation.[39]

A legitimate question can be raised as to why worship should be identified as the hub in my proposed model.[40] It is the worship, praise, and adoration of God that unites persons with all creation.[41] The potential for connection and integration in Christian education is enhanced if we center on the worship and adoration of God in a world that is struggling with increased fragmentation and a corresponding loss of meaning in life. But Christian educators have not adequately addressed education for worship. Instead, models of education emphasizing production and efficiency have been perpetuated. Alternative models based on biblical sources can provide the opportunities for persons to reflect on the majesty and wonder of God and God's workings. They can tap the creative potential of persons that finds expression in praise of God. The chief end and purpose of education, as of life, can thus be seen in terms of the glorification and enjoyment of God. Archbishop William Temple has said: "To worship is to quicken the conscience by the holiness of God, to feed the mind with the truth of God, to purge the imagination by the beauty of God, to open the heart to the love of God, to devote the will to the purpose of God."[42] Christian education at its best enables persons to worship the one true God in all of God's fullness and grandeur.

In addition to education *for* worship, the education *of* worship must be noted. Worship is active participation in the liturgy of the faith community, which attributes honor, glory, praise, and worth to God. The word "liturgy" is derived from the term *leitourgia* and emphasizes the need to connect education to the liturgical life of faith communities. Active liturgical participation can result in receptivity to new insights regarding God, self, others, or the world. Such receptivity can include cognitive, aesthetic, emotional, intuitive, volitional, and spiritual insights and bring a greater sense of wholeness and integration to life. A fulfilling liturgical life can have an impact on all of life in liberating ways.

39. Abraham J. Heschel, *Between God and Man: An Interpretation of Judaism from the Writings of Abraham Heschel*, ed. Fritz A. Rothschild (New York: Free Press, 1959), 35–54.

40. Debra Dean Murphy explores this question in *Teaching That Transforms: Worship as the Heart of Christian Education* (Grand Rapids: Brazos, 2004).

41. "Escape into Africa," in *Whole People of God Adult Curriculum,* December 31, 1995 (Inver Grove Heights, MN: Logos Productions, 1995), A 111–21.

42. William Temple, *The Hope of a New World* (London: Student Christian Movement Press, 1941), 30.

Beyond the particulars of each base, educators must be aware of the interconnections among the bases in order to form a network. The first base of *kerygma* primarily emphasizes knowing, and its complement at the third base of *diakonia* emphasizes doing. For effective educational ministry, both knowing and doing of the faith must be addressed along this first axis. The second basis of *koinonia* emphasizes feeling at one or being reconciled with God, others, and all creation while being in the world. The complement of this second base is the fourth base of *propheteia*, which stresses not so much feeling at one as feeling distinct or being not of the world in relation to the values of God's kingdom. As with the first axis, understanding educational ministry along this second axis requires balancing the Christian vocation of being in but not of the world, balancing the reconciliation of the already present blessings of God with the anticipation of the "not yet." The fifth and central base of *leitourgia* serves as the nexus of the two axes, where the challenges of knowing, feeling, and doing are brought into perspective in relation to discerning the eternal purposes of God and orienting all of life to God's glory and praise. It is on these bases that the educational ministry of the Christian church is to be founded.

Conclusion

The biblical foundations for Christian education are multiple but can be woven together to provide an impressive tapestry of ministry in the service of Jesus Christ. The warp and woof of that tapestry are the efforts of the sovereign Triune God and those of God's adopted family who have been gifted and equipped for educational ministry.

The perspective of Scripture provides the essential basis for educational ministries. In their various efforts, Christian educators may well take to heart Peter's exhortation:

> Each one should use whatever spiritual gift he has received to serve others, faithfully administering God's grace in its various forms. If anyone speaks, he should do it as one speaking the very words of God. If anyone serves, he should do it with the strength God provides, so that in all things God may be praised through Jesus Christ. To him be the glory and the power for ever and ever. Amen. (1 Pet. 4:10–11)

Table 2 summarizes some of the foundational passages and major insights suggested in this chapter. Other portions of Scripture could be cited that provide additional insights and potential models. These specific passages are noted only to provide an initial basis for discussion and dialogue in grappling with biblical foundations. In considering these foundations, Christian educators must evaluate their theological commitments; doing so raises issues taken up in the second chapter, which explores theological foundations.

TABLE 2
Biblical Foundations for Christian Education

Passage	Audience/ Focus	Insight	Implication/ Question
Deut. 6:1–9	Family/parents	God's commands foster loving obedience.	Formal and nonformal instruction must be deliberate.
Deut. 30:11–20	Nation	A decision for life as offered by God is crucial.	The priority of education emphasizing personal response must be seen.
Deut. 31:9–13	Faith community	God's Word must be shared.	Focus on the Word of God must include opportunities for response.
Deut. 31:30–32:4	Nation	Liberation and celebration are purposes for teaching.	Does our teaching empower and issue in worship and joy?
Ps. 78	Intergenerations	The stories/accounts of God must be passed on.	Intergenerational sharing is indispensable.
Neh. 8:1–18	Nation	Teachers must foster understanding and obedience.	A holistic response to God's Word can bring personal and communal renewal.
Wisdom literature	Teaching relationships	Wisdom must be shared.	Biblical wisdom is practical.
Prophetic literature	Nation	We are accountable to God.	Lordship applies to all of life.
Matthew	Jesus's disciples	Jesus suggests a new educational agenda.	Obedient disciples are nurtured by sharing vision, memory, and mission.
Luke 24:13–35	Disciples	A teacher must be attentive to students.	Dialogue and listening are valuable for disclosure.
1 Cor. 2:6–16	Faith community	Spiritual wisdom is distinct.	How can one foster the message and work of the Holy Spirit in teaching?
Ephesians	Church	Equipping and training for ministry is the purpose of education.	Mutual edification requires active commitment and service.
Colossians/ Philippians	Christian wisdom	We must use our minds for Christ.	The pursuit of truth requires diligence in thought and practice.
John 15:12–17	Christian relationships	Love and truth are both needed.	Interpersonal relationships require attention.

Passage	Audience/ Focus	Insight	Implication/ Question
1 Thess. 2:7–12	Discipling relationships	Teachers share their life and message in teaching.	Female and male dimensions of nurture must be affirmed.
Heb. 5:11–6:3	Teaching relationships	A varied diet may be necessary.	Consider readiness in teaching.

Points to Ponder

- What additional biblical texts or passages might be added in exploring biblical foundations for Christian education from your educational experiences?
- How do Old and New Testament perspectives relate to and compare with those identified in the appendices of this work as characterizing postmodernism, and why?
- Walter Brueggemann notes components of the Old Testament canon to guide education. What components of a New Testament canon could be proposed to guide Christian education?
- Suggest additional models beyond the five-task model presented here and discuss the strengths and weaknesses of any models to guide Christian education using biblical foundations.
- Identify gaps and additional implications and questions for the biblical foundations noted in table 2.

2

Theological Foundations

In emphasizing the essential authority of Scripture as divine revelation, evangelical Christians have been predisposed to grapple seriously with biblical sources in all areas of their faith and practice. Therefore, in dealing with education, both as a theoretical and a practical endeavor, evangelicals have turned to Scripture and to biblical theology in considering various principles. In general, evangelicals have been inclined to emphasize a theological approach in education over against one that exclusively highlights the social sciences. Specifically, evangelicals have tended to emphasize propositional theology[1] over against process, liberation, existential, neoorthodox, natural, or other theologies in their educational efforts. Thus evangelicals have preferred the term *Christian education,* rather than *religious education,* to denote an emphasis on distinctly Christian aspects of theology that guide thought and practice. This preference has occasionally resulted in limited dialogue with those who identify the academic community of religious educators with a more pluralistic and diverse effort.

Four Distinctive Theological Elements

An evangelical approach to religious education emphasizes four distinctive elements that are primarily theological in nature: biblical authority, the

1. In my work *God Our Teacher: Theological Basics in Christian Education* (Grand Rapids: Baker Academic, 2001), I as an evangelical educator opted for "prepositional theology" using the prepositions of *for, despite, with, in, through,* and *beyond* in addition to *above* to explore theological loci and to emphasize relationships.

necessity of conversion, the redemptive work of Jesus Christ, and personal piety. Each of these elements can be viewed as a grace of the evangelical tradition, as a gift that God has graciously bestowed on the church for the advance of God's work in the world.[2] But in relation to each of these distinctive elements or graces, a potential danger exists: each distinctive element must be related to the greater revelation of God's truth, which holds each grace in proper balance with other graces. This is the case in individual experience as well as in the corporate experience of evangelicalism.

An individual's strength can potentially become a weakness if it limits his or her awareness of other dimensions of life, truth, or relationships. For example, a person can so emphasize his or her physical development that mental, social, psychological, or spiritual development is inappropriately ignored. Likewise, one may be so consumed with a particular aspect of personal spiritual growth that responsibilities to others are largely unfulfilled. Given the need for balance in the whole of Christian life, evangelical educators can appreciate their distinctive gifts and be aware of potential dangers that result from overemphasis, imbalance, and lack of sensitivity.

Biblical Authority

Evangelical educators consciously grapple with biblical revelation and claim to be "under the Word of God." The written Word of God is Scripture in its entirety and variety, and evangelicals seek to teach the whole counsel of God. In this way believers are connected to their primary source or authority for discerning the Christian faith. This stance implies not a mindless literalism but an appropriation of the plain or commonsense meaning of Scripture as normative for thought and practice. The Scriptures are viewed as divinely inspired, and believers are called to discern a biblical agenda in Christian education, as in all areas of thought and practice. The Scriptures function as the final authority and serve as the filter through which all other truths are examined for their consistency with a Christian world and life view.[3]

As compared with a relatively greater emphasis in other traditions on persons reading the Bible to discern truths that relate to their experience,

2. For a discussion of the contributions of evangelicalism, see Alister McGrath, *Evangelicalism and the Future of Christianity* (Downers Grove, IL: InterVarsity, 1995); as related to religious education, see Ronnie Prevost, *Evangelical Protestant Gifts to Religious Education* (Macon, GA: Smyth & Helwys, 2000).

3. For a discussion of authority in teaching ministries, see Robert W. Pazmiño, *By What Authority Do We Teach? Sources for Empowering Christian Educators* (Eugene, OR: Wipf & Stock, 2002).

evangelicals emphasize that the Bible itself "reads" or confronts persons and proposes a world and life view that persons are to appropriate and to live. Certainly, evangelical educators do not exclude the practice of reading the Bible, but emphasize that final authority resides in biblical revelation over against residing in reason, tradition, or experience, which are conjoint and secondary sources for understanding and important for educational practice. Scripture functions as the written Word of God that discloses the living Word Jesus Christ and provides perspective on the creative Word described in Genesis 1 and John 1.[4] Thus evangelical Christians carefully attend to the biblical foundations such as those cited in chapter 1 to guide their educational programs.

The danger of such a distinctive element is that it can lead to a dead orthodoxy, a literalism or biblicism emphasizing biblical propositions divorced from life and relationships. It can also result in an educational practice that imposes truths on persons without enabling them to think seriously about and grapple with the implications of affirming such truths. Such an imposition is manipulative indoctrination, and it does not result in personal appropriation, internalization, and the transfer of learning to other situations. Such an authoritarian stance in education demands mindless compliance and obedience at the loss of personal integrity and rationality. It reduces the response of loving obedience to God to a superficial conformity that is contrary to a biblical understanding of persons. A mindless and spiritless focus on the written Word may not result in vital contact with the living Word, Jesus Christ. The spirit of the Word can be lost in haggling over the letter of the Word with a subsequent loss of vitality and joy.

The Necessity of Conversion

Evangelism and conversion are issues in evangelical education that can complement a focus on catechesis and nurture. Catechesis is instruction that fosters the integration of Christian truth with life. Nurture is the interpersonal sharing among Christians characterized by love and spiritual nourishment resulting in the edification of the Christian church. Both catechesis and nurture presume that the teacher, parent, model, or discipler is a committed Christian and that the student is either a Christian or one who is and will be seriously considering a lifelong commitment to follow Christ as Lord and Savior.

Through educational efforts the basic truths of biblical faith are shared, and, in particular, the great saving acts of God in the birth, life, death, and

4. Ibid., 22–29.

resurrection of Jesus Christ. But in sharing these basic truths, one constantly emphasizes personal response and the need for commitment. In his letter to the Thessalonians, Paul thanks God for the faith response of these Christians to his ministry among them. Their response evidences the new life they have found in their conversion to the living and true God:

> For we know, brothers loved by God, that he has chosen you, because our gospel came to you not simply with words, but also with power, with the Holy Spirit and with deep conviction. You know how we lived among you for your sake. You became imitators of us and of the Lord; in spite of severe suffering, you welcomed the message with the joy given by the Holy Spirit. And so you became a model to all the believers in Macedonia and Achaia. The Lord's message rang out from you not only in Macedonia and Achaia—your faith in God has become known everywhere. Therefore we do not need to say anything about it, for they themselves report what kind of reception you gave us. They tell how you turned to God from idols to serve the living and true God, and to wait for his Son from heaven, whom he raised from the dead—Jesus, who rescues us from the coming wrath. (1 Thess. 1:4–10)

Paul provides a similar description of the experience of salvation, of being made alive in Christ, in Ephesians 2:1–10:

> As for you, you were dead in your transgressions and sins, in which you used to live when you followed the ways of this world and of the ruler of the kingdom of the air, the spirit who is now at work in those who are disobedient. All of us also lived among them at one time, gratifying the cravings of our sinful nature and following its desires and thoughts. Like the rest, we were by nature objects of wrath. But because of his great love for us, God, who is rich in mercy, made us alive with Christ even when we were dead in transgressions—it is by grace you have been saved. And God raised us up with Christ and seated us with him in the heavenly realms in Christ Jesus, in order that in the coming ages he might show the incomparable riches of his grace, expressed in his kindness to us in Christ Jesus. For it is by grace you have been saved, through faith—and this not from yourselves, it is the gift of God—not by works, so that no one can boast. For we are God's workmanship, created in Christ Jesus to do good works, which God prepared in advance for us to do.

This matter of conversion is also made explicit by John in 1 John 5:9–12, in which faith in the Son of God is essential for a walk with God:

> We accept man's testimony, but God's testimony is greater because it is the testimony of God, which he has given about his Son. Anyone who believes in the Son of God has this testimony in his heart. Anyone who does not believe God has made him out to be a liar, because he has not believed the testimony God

has given about his Son. And this is the testimony: God has given us eternal life, and this life is in his Son. He who has the Son has life; he who does not have the Son of God does not have life.

It is essential that evangelism or invitation be a key purpose of the educational ministry of the church. Evangelism can be defined as the presentation of Jesus Christ in the power of the Holy Spirit, which enables persons to place their faith in God through Christ and to serve Christ, to accept Christ as their Savior, and to serve their Lord in the fellowship of his church and world.[5] Evangelism is not simply "soul winning," because the Christian faith, as Harold Carlton Mason has pointed out, is concerned with Christian intelligence, Christian nurture, Christian culture, and personal choice and commitment.[6] Educational evangelism, then, can be defined as reaching and guiding persons toward a personal encounter with Christ as Lord and Savior. This effort does not replace either personal or mass evangelism, which has a greater appeal to the will of persons, whereas education tends to emphasize their thought processes in responding to the gospel presented through teaching.[7]

In relation to the three dimensions of saving faith mentioned in chapter 1 (*notitia, assensus*, and *fiducia*), educational evangelism focuses primarily on *notitia*, the intellectual dimension of faith. Education generally appeals to reason and deals with intellectual content. Although it does not exclude the dimensions of *assensus* and *fiducia*, which emphasize the emotional and volitional dimensions of faith, by its essential nature education shares those *indicia* or facts about the faith that support an intellectual grappling with the person and work of Jesus Christ.

What impact does this distinctive element have on practice? Mason suggests some helpful corollaries for this emphasis on educational evangelism:

1. The student must know the moral law and the implications of the Christian ethic for morally responsible persons.
2. The teacher/evangelist must have personally experienced that which she or he teaches to others, that is, must be a Christian.
3. The teacher must devote time and special concern to students who must be nurtured in the faith and grow in grace.
4. Educational evangelism involves a knowledge of basic principles of Christian theology.

5. This definition is adopted from that of William Temple, cited in Michael Green, *Evangelism Now and Then* (Leicester, England: InterVarsity, 1979), 13–14.
6. Harold Mason, *The Teaching Task of the Local Church* (Winona Lake, IN: Light & Life Press, 1960), 173.
7. Ibid.

5. One of the functions of the church's educational ministry is enlistment or recruitment of new participants.

6. One of the evangelistic functions of any Christian education program, such as Sunday school, is to encourage students to hear the preaching of God's Word.

7. United prayer for those considering Christian commitment should be a regular component of preparation for teaching.

8. Parents in Christian homes must be supported in their efforts to make the Christian faith significant in their personal lives and in the lives of their children and youth.[8]

The danger of such a distinctive element is that it may lead to easy believism, shallow discipleship, and "soul winning" devoid of substance in the effort to encourage a personal faith response to Jesus Christ. Dietrich Bonhoeffer poignantly warns of a cheap grace that ignores the costs of discipleship and the implications of affirming Christ as Lord as well as Savior.[9] Educational evangelism therefore must be explicit about the costs and responsibilities of faith in Christ. Such evangelism must also evidence a concern for the whole person and not merely the person's soul or spirit. Educational programs that teach a spiritual gospel that ignores physical and social needs and neglects discipleship are shallow and abortive.

There is a real danger inherent in an educational evangelism that fails to represent the whole gospel. This danger is captured in the following poem, which suggests a broader faith challenge:

Your Holiness and My Loneliness

I was hungry and you held meetings to discuss my hunger.
I was imprisoned and you crept off quietly to pray for my release.
I was persecuted and you explained to me how Christ was persecuted.
I was sick and you knelt down and thanked God for your health.
I was homeless and you preached to me of the spiritual shelter of the
    love of God.
I was lonely and you left me alone to pray for me.
You seem so holy and I'm still very lonely.[10]

8. Ibid., 173–83.

9. See Dietrich Bonhoeffer, *The Cost of Discipleship*, rev. ed. (New York: Macmillan, 1959).

10. This poem was discovered by Michael Green on the door of a chaplain's office in a hospital in Africa. It was recounted in his lecture series *Foundations for Evangelism from the New Testament Churches* (Miami, FL: Mobile Media, 1978).

Evangelicals must likewise beware of a social involvement or ministry that
ignores the proclamation of the gospel and the vital place of evangelism. But
educational evangelism includes a concern with presenting the full implications of following Jesus Christ and the costs of discipleship.

The Redemptive Work of Jesus Christ

Carl F. H. Henry observes that evangelical Christians "affirm the fundamental doctrines of the gospel, including the incarnation and virgin birth of
Christ, his sinless life, substitutionary atonement, and bodily resurrection as
the ground of God's forgiveness of sinners, justification by faith alone, and
the spiritual regeneration of all who trust in the redemptive work of Jesus
Christ."[11] Such doctrines provide the theological foundation on which Christian educators can function.[12]

Evangelical educators affirm these fundamental doctrines because they provide
the essential framework in which the Christian faith has been historically defined.
Frank Gaebelein clarifies how these doctrines function for the evangelical:

> It is these that make up the framework of our Christian world view. What are
> they? They are the facts upon which Christianity rests. Included in them are
> the existence of the living God, the Maker of heaven and earth; man's creation
> in the image of God, an image ruined through the fall beyond human power to
> repair, but not beyond God's power to regenerate; the incarnation of God the
> Son and His redemption of lost humanity; the activity of God the Holy Spirit
> in calling out of this present world a community of believers which is Christ's
> Body, the Church; and, finally, the end of earthly history through the "glorious
> appearing of the great God and our Savior Jesus Christ."
>
> Let us understand once and for all that there is nothing sectarian about these
> truths; they are common to all branches of the Christian church. Granted that
> in many quarters they have been and are today being watered down through
> concessions and reservations, or obscured through man-made tradition and
> dogma, the fact remains that such truths as these stand as both the foundation
> and frame of reference for a Christian world view. It is upon them that Christian
> education must build; it is within them that it must work.[13]

In dealing with the actual impact of these beliefs on the thought and practice of education, it is appropriate for the educator to consider some possible

---

11. Carl F. H. Henry, "Evangelical," in *The New International Dictionary of the Christian
Church,* ed. J. D. Douglas, rev. ed. (Grand Rapids: Zondervan, 1978), 358–59.

12. Also see my reformulation in *God Our Teacher.*

13. Frank E. Gaebelein, *The Pattern of God's Truth: Problems of Integration in Christian
Education* (New York: Oxford University Press, 1954), 34–35.

implications. For example, if one affirms God as Creator, what is the proper attitude to the use of the land and resources as an outworking of ecological responsibilities?

Whereas this distinctive element enables clarity of belief and continuity with biblical revelation, it may lead to a static and uncritical stance that fails to address the need for contextualization. Contextualization is the continual process by which truth is applied to and emerges from concrete historical situations. This process grapples with the implications of the gospel's values for the actual transformation of realities and with commitments to that transformation.[14] This process also raises questions about cultural impositions that distort the radical demands of the New Testament.

Faithfulness to Christ requires scrutiny in relation to various personal, cultural, political, economic, and social realities. These realities may be affirmed, rejected, or transformed in relation to the demands of affirming Christ as Lord and working for the advance of his kingdom in the world. God's sovereign rule in the person of Jesus Christ and allegiance to Christ requires Christians to live out the good news as well as believe it. Evangelicals may be reluctant to address such realities and opt for a "ghettoized" existence that fails to struggle with how Christ relates to various cultures and societal issues. They do so at the peril of denying the Christian faith and its power. A theological certainty that eliminates the need for contextualization denies God's creative and providential works in history and in the present world. It also fails to embrace an incarnational stance embodied in Jesus the Christ.

A crucial issue is the relationship of theology to Christian education. Sara Little suggests the following possibilities:

1. Theology is the content to be taught in Christian education.
2. Theology is the point of reference for what is to be taught and for methodology, and functions as the norm for the critical work of analysis and evaluation of all Christian education.
3. Theology is irrelevant to the task of Christian education; therefore, Christian education is autonomous.
4. "Doing theology" or theologizing is Christian education in the sense of enabling persons to reflect on their current experiences and perspectives in light of the Christian faith and revelation.

14. For a discussion of the place of transformation in Christian education, see Robert W. Pazmiño, *Latin American Journey: Insights for Christian Education in North America* (Eugene, OR: Wipf & Stock, 2002), 55–75.

5. Theology and Christian education are separate disciplines that are engaged mutually and collegially in the advance of God's kingdom.

Little also points out that no one alternative is the only way to relate Christian education and theology.[15]

While being aware of the danger of positing one definitive relationship, evangelical educators can explore the implications of their theology in the resolution of this issue. The basic perspectives of evangelical theology would affirm the first two alternatives, neither of which is mutually exclusive. Theology can be viewed as both content and norm. Yet transmission does not have to be imposed or communicated in an authoritarian manner, but can be done with a sensitivity to persons and their needs. Nevertheless, truths essential for faith and practice must be taught. Without the communication of certain essential truths, teaching that claims to be Christian is suspect.

The third possibility Little mentions—theology as irrelevant to Christian education—may not be an option for the evangelical educator who seeks to be consistent with his or her faith.[16] An affirmation of Christ as Lord assumes the significance of theology, defined most simply as the study of God, for all of life. Theology grapples with the implications of faith as mediated through the experience of God's revelation. Such implications must deal with the thought and practice of education. Thus theology is indispensable for the task of Christian education.

The fourth possibility in Little's scheme poses unique challenges for the evangelical educator. Some religious educators have emphasized the need for education to focus on and encourage the process in which persons become more skilled at using their faith to reflect on contemporary experience and using their contemporary experience to reflect on faith. This reflection seeks to discern the action of God in history as it is being written, and to examine inherited religious conceptions for adequacy in confronting global realities and problems. "Theologizing" or "doing theology" is the term applied to this process of reflection.[17] Evangelicals generally affirm the need for critical reflection and for addressing global realities. But evangelicals are extremely cautious in using contemporary experience to reflect on faith. Their emphasis

15. Sara Little, "Theology and Religious Education," in *Foundations for Christian Education in an Era of Change,* ed. Marvin J. Taylor (Nashville: Abingdon, 1983), 31–33.

16. For a discussion of this issue, see Edward J. Newell, *"Education Has Nothing to Do with Theology": James Michael Lee's Social Science Religious Instruction* (Eugene, OR: Wipf & Stock, 2006).

17. See Norma Thompson's discussion of theology in "Current Issues in Religious Education," *Religious Education* 73 (November–December 1978): 617.

on biblical authority resists the tendency to place experience as a higher authority than Scripture. Evangelicals are not reluctant to discuss or use personal experience. But for evangelicals, experience functions as an evidence of faith, not as a judgment of faith.

Little's fifth possibility—theology in dialogue with Christian education—poses additional challenges. Christian educators can shape the reflection that characterizes the study of God in theology by raising essential questions. These questions recently have been posed by Thomas H. Groome in *Christian Religious Education*. Prior to Groome's formulation, D. Campbell Wyckoff raised these questions with an additional concern for an organizing principle that holds all the educational factors together.[18] Groome poses six questions that can be identified with the interrogative pronouns *what, why, where, how, when,* and *who*:

1. *What* is the nature of Christian education? (nature and content)
2. *Why* is Christian education essential? (purposes)
3. *Where* is Christian education undertaken? (context)
4. *How* is Christian education conducted? (methods)
5. *When* is it appropriate to share particular Christian truths and experiences? (readiness)
6. *Who* is interacting in Christian education? (relationships)[19]

By addressing these six essential questions, Christian educators are dealing with theological issues in the areas of ecclesiology, soteriology, eschatology, anthropology, Christology, and the doctrine of God and Scripture as they affect education. Christian education at its best is an area of practical theology. It also explores the place of theology in the formation of persons who can mature in the Christian faith.

As Christian education can contribute to the tasks of theology, so theology can contribute to Christian education. Theology can be a tool for reflecting on the thought and practice of Christian education. Theology can also inform the faithful practice of education by raising questions regarding consistency in relation to biblical values. A dialectical interaction between theology and Christian education as separate disciplines can be established that enables the actualization of faithful Christian living within the church and the world. Thus cooperative dialogue can enhance the effectual and creative work of each discipline.

18. See D. Campbell Wyckoff, *Theory and Design of Christian Education Curriculum* (Philadelphia: Westminster, 1961).

19. Thomas H. Groome, *Christian Religious Education: Sharing Our Story and Vision* (San Francisco: Harper & Row, 1980), xiv.

Personal Piety

As was the case with the second distinctive element, evangelicals stress the need to personally appropriate the Christian faith and to grow in one's devotion and walk with Christ. John Calvin defined piety as "the union of reverence and love to God which the knowledge of his benefits inspires."[20] One's dedication to Jesus Christ and the Christian faith is demonstrated in a genuine spiritual life. This life initiated at conversion is sustained as a person's connection with God engages the heart and spirit as well as the mind. Because of this distinctive element, evangelicals have historically fostered the development of spiritual affections and disciplines. This has not been done to the necessary exclusion of a reasoned faith, but rather as a complement to one's intellectual devotion to Christ. In some instances this has led to a religion of the heart devoid of a religion of the mind, but a balance of both the emotional and the intellectual dimensions of faith is an ideal of the evangelical educational agenda, which affirms the place of spiritual life and growth. This distinctive element has tended in the past to be more covert or implicit than publicly affirmed and promoted. The recent pervasive interest in "spirituality" represents a departure from this earlier reluctance.[21]

The danger in this distinctive element, given its tendency toward personal and introspective preoccupation, is a piety or spirituality devoid of social consciousness. A blatant disregard of social sins and a corresponding social passivism that condones the status quo can too readily emerge. A conservative theology can also imply a stance with regard to all of life that fails to be sensitive to God's continued activity in the historical process and God's giving the church new wineskins for the advance of God's kingdom in the world. A shallow piety can also result in the proposal of easy solutions to complex social problems and an insensitivity that divorces Christians from cultural concerns.

The matter of culture raises an important question in relation to the place of culture from the standpoint of the Christian faith and Christian education. H. Richard Niebuhr proposes five possible relationships between Christ and culture (see fig. 3):

1. *Christ against culture.* Christ is the sole authority; the claims of culture are to be rejected.

---

20. John Calvin, *Institutes of the Christian Religion*, trans. Henry Beveridge, vol. 1 (Grand Rapids: Eerdmans, 1975), 41.
21. For examples of this shift, see Elizabeth Conde-Frazier, S. Steve Kang, and Gary A. Parrett, *A Many Colored Kingdom: Multicultural Dynamics for Spiritual Formation* (Grand Rapids: Baker Academic, 2004); and Karen Marie Yust and E. Byron Anderson, *Taught By God: Teaching and Spiritual Formation* (St. Louis: Chalice, 2006).

Figure 3
Christ and Culture

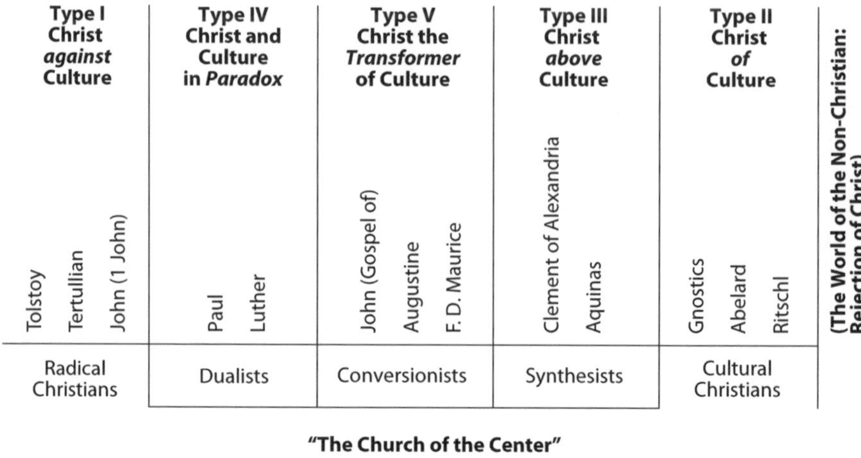

Type I Christ against Culture	Type IV Christ and Culture in *Paradox*	Type V Christ the *Transformer* of Culture	Type III Christ *above* Culture	Type II Christ *of* Culture	(The World of the Non-Christian: Rejection of Christ)
Tolstoy, Tertullian, John (1 John)	Paul, Luther	John (Gospel of), Augustine, F. D. Maurice	Clement of Alexandria, Aquinas	Gnostics, Abelard, Ritschl	
Radical Christians	Dualists	Conversionists	Synthesists	Cultural Christians	

"The Church of the Center"

Taken from *Communicating Christ Cross-Culturally* by David J. Hesselgrave. Copyright ©1978 by David Hesselgrave. Used by permission of Zondervan.

2. *Christ of culture.* The Christian system is different from culture not in kind but only in quality; the best culture should be selected to conform to Christ.

3. *Christ above culture.* The reception of grace perfects and completes culture, although there is no "smooth curve or continuous line" between them.

4. *Christ and culture in paradox.* Both are authorities to be obeyed; the believer therefore lives with this tension.

5. *Christ the transformer of culture.* Culture reflects the fallen state of persons; in Christ, persons are redeemed and culture can be renewed so as to glorify God and promote God's purposes.[22]

David J. Hesselgrave notes that from a biblical perspective, there seems to be some value in emphases that fall under types 1, 4, 5, and, possibly, 3.[23] The danger of emphasis on personal piety is that evangelical Christians may opt exclusively for type 1 or type 2 and thereby be unaware of either the impact of culture on Christians or the potential influence of Christians on culture. Evangelical Christians have generally opted for types 1, 4, and 5 in their

22. David J. Hesselgrave, *Communicating Christ Cross-Culturally* (Grand Rapids: Zondervan, 1978), 79–80.
23. Ibid., 80.

educational thought and practice at various times and in various contexts.[24] A type 1 response results in a countercultural posture with the isolation of the Christian community from the wider culture, which is viewed as hostile. A type 4 response opts for a posture in which the church and the wider society are viewed as complementary and the status quo is maintained. A type 5 response assumes a proactive stance in working for renewal and reform at all levels of society.

An Orthodox Foundation

Beyond these four distinctive theological elements, it is possible to outline the theological foundations of evangelical education by referring to the Apostles' Creed, which provides a helpful framework for exploring questions of theology with affirmations regarding Scripture.[25] Each affirmation has implications for Christian education. In relation to these major theological doctrines of the orthodox or evangelical faith, examples of implications are provided that have direct relationships with the biblical foundations explored in chapter 1.

God the Creator

Because God is the creator of the world and of humankind, God is the source of life and persons are responsible to God. God has, in fact, established a creative covenant with persons. A God-centered educational approach that depends on divine revelation and that encourages persons to find meaning in the life that is in God is essential. Persons must be instructed in their responsibilities as creatures of God. The status of creaturehood undermines an exclusive emphasis on human autonomy. Such an emphasis on autonomy ignores dependency on God and interdependency with other persons and the created world. God has initiated efforts to be in communion with persons, and educational efforts should foster the response of persons to God. Persons are adopted as members of God's family with all the resulting privileges and responsibilities.

Because God is the redeemer-liberator of persons, groups, and societies, God is the source of righteousness, justice, and freedom; the one on whom persons must depend for fulfillment; and the initiator of a redemptive covenant.

24. A further discussion of culture is found in chap. 5.
25. For a further discussion of the place of the Apostles' Creed, see James D. Smart, *The Creed in Christian Teaching* (Philadelphia: Westminster, 1962); and Bernard L. Marthaler, *The Creed* (Mystic, CT: Twenty-Third Publications, 1987).

Human understanding and efforts in the areas of righteousness, justice, and freedom therefore must be subject to the divine agenda for actualization. This does not relieve human responsibility but subjects it to God's sovereignty.

Christian educators are called upon to raise the consciousness of persons in issues that relate to righteousness, justice, and freedom as components of God's continuing activity in the world. Given the realities of sin and its effects in personal and corporate life, persons are dependent on God for redemption to realize fulfillment and freedom. The realities of sin and human fallenness must be addressed in Christian education. The need for structure, discipline, forgiveness, and reconciliation applies to educational interactions in which persons confront one another. The place of evangelism in Christian education is to be recognized; the outworkings of God's redemptive work in all human endeavors must be explored, which is a lifelong task.

Jesus Christ

Jesus Christ is the Son of God, Lord and Savior, Son of Man, and King. Since Jesus Christ is the giver of life, Christian education must strive to be christocentric in the sense of enabling persons to know the living Word and to mature in him. Christian educators are called upon to help persons grapple with the implications of Christ's lordship personally and corporately. The reality of a new creation in Christ provides hope for educators and students alike in their joint efforts. As Son of Man, which was his preferred way of identifying himself, Jesus Christ is sensitive to the needs and dilemmas of human existence and actively intercedes for those who are committed to him. The example or model of Jesus Christ in his earthly life and teaching ministry is instructive for both teachers and students. Those who identify with Christ and his kingdom have obligations in relation to that kingdom. Teaching and learning can be seen as activities that glorify the name of Christ and extend his kingdom in the world.[26]

The Holy Spirit

The Holy Spirit is the activator and sustainer of life, the Spirit of truth, and the transformer of persons. Christian teachers, parents, administrators, and students must be sensitive to the work of the Spirit in motivating persons and pray for the Spirit's effectual working in their lives. The Holy Spirit applies, complements, and corrects human teaching.[27] The human quest for truth in education must be

---

26. See Robert W. Pazmiño, *So What Makes Our Teaching Christian? Teaching in the Name, Spirit and Power of Jesus* (forthcoming, 2008).

27. See Roy B. Zuck, *Spirit-Filled Teaching: The Power of the Holy Spirit in Your Ministry* (Nashville: Word, 1998).

seen in relation to God being the source of all truth. The Holy Spirit enlightens persons' minds so that they can discern truth in special and general revelation. The Spirit also enables persons to live in accordance with the truths disclosed or discovered. The Holy Spirit is the agent working for personal and social transformation among persons in the world. Christian educators must therefore be sensitive to the workings of the Holy Spirit in the areas of renewal and transformation. Ways of cooperating with the Holy Spirit both within and outside of the educational encounter must be explored. Recognition of transformation and renewal becomes a basis for thanksgiving and celebration.

The Written Word of God

The Bible is the basis for authority and is God's revelation and source of truth for all of life. The Bible functions as the final authority or filter through which all truths are evaluated. The authority of teachers and others who educate is derivative. It must be judged in terms of its consistency with God's revealed and discovered truth. The Bible is the essential, though not exclusive, content of Christian education. It provides a sufficient, though not exhaustive, guide for faith and life. Biblical truths must be integrated with all areas of educational thought and practice, with all subject areas and disciplines.

The Holy Catholic Church

The church is the body of Christ. It is holy by virtue of Christ's righteousness, and it is catholic, or universal, in that it includes persons from all cultures, nations, and tribes across the ages. In the church, a variety of ministries parallels the various New Testament descriptions. The educational mission of the church has manifold expressions. A diversity of gifts for teaching and a diversity of insights from learning can be celebrated by the church. The church is both an organization and an organism, and concerns for both structures and relationships are appropriate. Christian educational efforts must relate to the purposes, the tasks, and the mission of the Christian church.[28]

The Communion of Saints

Christians form the Christian extended family or community of faith. Those involved in education are called to maintain positive relationships that balance

---

28. I elaborate on this topic in *Principles and Practices of Christian Education: An Evangelical Perspective* (1992; Eugene, OR: Wipf & Stock, 2002), 45–55.

concerns for truth and love. Relationships are to bring honor to the name of Christ. Being a communion implies the need for Christians to foster positive relationships with one another and with God the Spirit, who sustains the communion.

The Forgiveness of Sins

Christians need reconciliation and healing in their relationships with God and with others. Personal and corporate sins must be addressed as part of the agenda in educational encounters.[29] The ministry of reconciliation must be operative at all levels of personal, interpersonal, and intergroup interactions in Christian education.

The Resurrection of the Body

The biblical view of persons is holistic. Christian educators are challenged to correct an overemphasis on the body/soul dualism and theoretical/practical dichotomies, which confront educational efforts, and work for integration. Christians in the West must learn from Christians in non-Western contexts in this area of their lives. Western cultures, while emphasizing intellectual analysis, have fostered the fragmentation of human personality and the disembodiment of life.

Life Everlasting

The various efforts of persons involved in Christian education must be evaluated in terms of God's ultimate plan for creation and the redeemed community. The efforts of students and teachers are conditioned by God's purposes in history and are to be carefully discerned.

This quick survey of insights comprising an orthodox foundation can be elaborated on by considering additional theological questions that Christians have historically discussed.

A Reforming View of Education

Beyond this orthodox foundation, it is possible to explore theological foundations by considering the particular example of the Reformed wing of the Christian church, which represents just one tradition. The author is most familiar with this tradition, which, nevertheless, has insights for other communities.

29. See Pazmiño, "God Despite Us: Sin and Salvation," in *God Our Teacher*, 37–57.

Reformed educators generally emphasize three distinctive theological tenets that can guide their view of education: the covenant of creation, the fall, and the covenant of redemption.

From the covenant of creation, Reformed educators emphasize that all persons are God's image bearers and therefore are to be instructed to show forth the glory of God. As image bearers, persons are responsible for building the kingdom of God and must be prepared for this end.[30] Educators must be mindful of ecological responsibilities toward nature, religious responsibilities with respect to God, and political, aesthetic, and intellectual responsibilities in relation to other persons and oneself.[31] The task of educators is to encourage persons to fulfill their responsibilities, ultimately with respect to their relation to the Creator God. In serving and worshiping the Creator, Christians are to recognize the unity of culture and the unity of the human race, which implies sensitivity to the world and society.[32] The kingdom of God in this perspective is defined as the rule or reign of God, which extends beyond a spiritual and otherworldly domain to include the created world and human society. Therefore, Reformed education at its best seeks to enable students to grapple with the implications of a Christian view for all of life.

The second tenet of a Reformed view of education considers the fall. Persons freely revolted against God and refused to live in trustful obedience, preferring instead to act as if they were self-normed. As a result they became confused about their responsibilities and in many ways denied them. They mutilated the earth, victimized other persons, squandered their abilities, and set up surrogate gods.[33] This tenet eliminates the possibility of viewing persons as having free will and autonomy in any ultimate sense. Thus any educational strategy that views autonomy as the highest developmental stage or goal must be questioned. Recognizing the reality and extent of sin, Reformed educators have emphasized the demands of divine standards and warnings that issue from rebellion against God.[34]

The third tenet, the covenant of redemption, provides hope for humankind and creation in God's provision for re-creation and renewal in Jesus Christ. Out of God's great love, God acted so that persons can again live in joyful fulfillment with themselves, their neighbors, nature, and God.[35] Persons must accept

---

30. Cornelius Van Til, *Essays on Christian Education* (Nutley, NJ: Presbyterian & Reformed, 1977), 78–80.

31. Nicholas Wolterstorff, *Educating for Responsible Action* (Grand Rapids: Eerdmans, 1980), 9, 33.

32. Van Til, *Essays on Christian Education,* 83–85.

33. Wolterstorff, *Educating for Responsible Action,* 9–10.

34. Van Til, *Essays on Christian Education,* 87–91.

35. Wolterstorff, *Educating for Responsible Action,* 10.

their cultural task and opportunity anew in Christ through the regenerating power of the Holy Spirit. Christians have by grace repented from sin and are called to contribute positively to the coming of God's kingdom through their cultural efforts.[36] The task of Christian education is to equip persons in this vital area of renewal through presenting Christ and encouraging response to him as Savior and Lord of all. In fact, all of life becomes the subject matter of Christian education, given the multifaceted dimensions of the cultural task in relation to God's creation.

Whereas these three tenets are foundational for a thoroughgoing Christian view of education, they may not be of sufficient breadth to address some of the challenges that confront the church of Jesus Christ today. A Reformed view of education has generally emphasized distinctive theological elements that emerged during the Reformation. In choosing this focus, Reformed educators have often failed to be adequately sensitive to historical developments prior and subsequent to the Reformation. Rather than a Reformed view of education, the need is for a reforming view that affirms the distinctive theological elements of a biblical view, but then builds on them in addressing the current historical context.

A reforming view maintains that God is still active in history and that the church is gaining a greater understanding of the implications of God's revelation in Scripture and in Jesus Christ. A reforming view or perspective also recognizes the contextualized nature of theology, which is a continuing and ongoing task, rather than one that has been set definitively at the time of the Reformation. God has chosen Christians to address the needs of their time in categories that necessitate continual renewal. This renewal entails sensitivity to new wineskins with which God is blessing the church for sharing the new wine of the gospel in the postmodern world.

In a reforming view of education, a danger of adulteration in the gospel certainly exists. Nevertheless, while maintaining the orthodox faith, Christian educators can gain insights from other theologies to the extent to which they remain faithful to biblical revelation. One truth regarding the creation is that persons are rational and creative and have the responsibility of glorifying God through their thought. Also, the Holy Spirit is alive and active and provides continued illumination regarding the application of God's truth to the world.

In the development of a reforming view, insights from liberation theology as they relate to the tasks of education are helpful.[37] A reforming view has implications for all traditions in the Christian church beyond Reformed communities.

---

36. Van Til, *Essays on Christian Education*, 87–91.

37. For a detailed discussion of the interface with liberation theologies, see Daniel S. Schipani, *Religious Education Encounters Liberation Theology* (Birmingham, AL: Religious Education Press, 1988); and Pazmiño, *Latin American Journey*.

A Reformed view of education can be identified as a received perspective and a liberation view as a reflexive perspective (see table 3).

TABLE 3
Reformed, Reforming, and Liberation Perspectives

Received Reformed Perspective	Restructuring Reforming Perspective	Reflexive Liberation Perspective
Closed	Both	Open
Traditional-Culture Taking	Both	Futuristic-Culture Making
Determined	Both	Innovative
Conservation	Both	Change
Absolutism	Both	Relativism
Determinism	Both	Voluntarism

A Reformed view emphasizes a somewhat closed system of thought relative to first and essential principles of theology. It is traditional in the sense of affirming or taking a religious culture and thought system as developed during the Reformation and passing it on to the next generations. It assumes a transmissive form of communication. The basic structure of Reformed theology has largely been accepted, and any elaboration occurs within that structure. This view is also characterized by conservation, absolutism, and determinism in doctrine and life. In its extreme form, a Reformed view as a received perspective fails to adequately account for differences or deviations from an existing pattern in the structures of relationships between God and persons, among persons, and between persons and all of creation.

By comparison, a liberation view is a relatively open system of thought and understanding with regard to first and essential principles of theology. It is futuristic in that it emphasizes an open future in which persons must assume responsibility for the development of a religious culture and thought system for the present and the next generation. It assumes a dialogical and interactive form of communication. The basic structure of liberation theology is innovative in the development of new categories to fit changing situations. This view is also characterized by an emphasis on change, relativism, and voluntarism in doctrine and life. Change is taken to the extremes of radical revolution if warranted by the circumstances. In its extreme form as a reflexive perspective, a liberation view fails to account for regularities, similarities, continuities, and absolutes.[38]

38. See John Eggleston, *The Sociology of the School Curriculum* (London: Routledge & Kegan Paul, 1977), 52–92, for a discussion of received and reflexive perspectives.

A reforming view or a restructuring perspective is one in which both received and reflexive perspectives can be brought together as two related modes of understanding both the theological truths in the Scriptures and the possibilities of change in relating those truths to different cultures and historical situations.[39] It mediates between the two extremes of a strict Reformed view and a liberation view. Such a view affirms the need for the conservation of the biblical and theological essentials of the Christian faith while recognizing the need for innovation in relating those essentials to changing needs, forms, and structures. A reforming view stresses both the need for stability, authority, and reliability and the need for critical inquiry and creativity in the areas of theological reflection.

The question that remains to be addressed is how liberation theology affects a reforming view of education. This question can be explored by reconsidering the dangers of each of the distinctive theological elements of an evangelical approach and how a liberation view can help at these very points of potential weakness.

Liberation theology emphasizes the place of praxis, the active interaction between reflection and action in life. Such an emphasis in Christian education can address the danger of a mere verbalism that neglects the implications of biblical truth for life. The clarion call of those who espouse a liberation perspective is the need for active engagement with the world. Serious questions can be raised as to the nature of that engagement in relation to the biblical agenda; nevertheless, the avoidance of a passive, spectator stance in relation to Christian commitments can be wholeheartedly affirmed. The concerns for active participation are also distinctive elements of a liberation view that are a necessary corrective for dead orthodoxy. A danger inherent in the liberation view is that of an activism that fails to adequately address the biblical sources of the Christian faith in favor of an exclusive preoccupation with the current historical context.

Liberation theology also attempts to seriously grapple with what it means to follow Christ and carry out God's agenda in concrete historical contexts. Liberationists do not ignore the physical and social needs of persons while sharing the gospel. They take a stand with those who suffer oppression. Liberationists not only stress the costs of discipleship but also model a willingness to sacrifice for their cause. Unfortunately, in some instances this has included an identification of the oppressed with God's people irrespective of any personal response to Christ as Lord and Savior.

One hallmark of the liberation view is its emphasis on the very nature of theology. It calls for an unambiguous commitment to reality in its historical concreteness. This concrete rootedness issues in the call for contextualization,

39. Ibid., 71.

for a theology that does not stop with mere reflection on the world in its particular setting but rather tries to be part of the process through which the world is transformed. Faith becomes incarnated in the historical process in the effort to understand and liberate various cultures in light of gospel demands. Such a perspective demands careful listening as well as an active and incisive critique of those perspectives and practices that embody ideologies contrary to the gospel. The danger in a liberation view arises when the historical context is allowed to set an agenda contrary to biblical faith and the embodiment of a revolutionary agenda as an alternative gospel.

Liberation theology also maintains a stance so committed to social issues and activism that concerns for personal piety and an appropriate affirmation of points of continuity may be ignored. Liberationists seek to raise the consciousness of persons regarding the extent of social sins and the need for corrective action.

A reforming view of education, as has been proposed, enables the evangelical educator to incorporate insights from a liberation view that are faithful to the distinctive biblical and theological elements of the Christian faith. The inherent dangers of an evangelical approach to religious education can be addressed through an active dialogue and interaction with those who grapple with the implications of liberation theology for Christian education. The God of the Bible is a God of liberation who brings full liberation in the person and work of Jesus Christ. Yet the implications of the gospel of Jesus Christ extend to all areas of personal and corporate life. God speaks through Moses to the Israelite people, promising deliverance from their bondage in Egypt:

> Therefore, say to the Israelites: "I am the LORD, and I will bring you out from under the yoke of the Egyptians. I will free you from being slaves to them, and I will redeem you with an outstretched arm and with mighty acts of judgment. I will take you as my own people, and I will be your God. Then you will know that I am the LORD your God, who brought you out from under the yoke of the Egyptians. And I will bring you to the land I swore with uplifted hand to give to Abraham, to Isaac and to Jacob. I will give it to you as a possession. I am the LORD." (Exod. 6:6–8)

Our God still brings deliverance from spiritual bondage. God's reign embodies redemption of whole persons in this life and in the life to come.

Insights from Paulo Freire

The implications of a reforming view of education can be further explored by considering the work of Paulo Freire, a Brazilian educational philosopher and social educator who is an advocate of liberation education.

Paulo Freire was born in 1921 into a middle-class family. Due to financial reverses caused by the American stock market crash in 1929, he experienced poverty. He was dedicated to the education and advancement of the poor and oppressed of Brazil and to the transformation of society. As a result of his revolutionary work, Freire was imprisoned and later exiled by the Brazilian government after the military coup of 1964. After his exile he first moved to Chile, then migrated to the United States, and later worked as an educational consultant at Harvard University. In the 1970s he worked with the Office of Education of the World Council of Churches in Geneva, Switzerland, and subsequently returned to Brazil in 1980, where he served as a professor and educational leader until his death in 1997.

Freire's religious background was Roman Catholic. He was influenced by various philosophies including phenomenology, personalism, existentialism, and Marxism. Freire referred to himself as a Christian humanist and described his educational philosophy as humanistic. For Freire, humanization is the goal of every valued educational and social activity. Dehumanization is destructive of true human nature and dignity.[40]

Freire described his educational theory in *Cultural Action for Freedom*: "Our pedagogy cannot do without a vision of man and his world. It formulates a scientific humanist conception which finds its expression in a dialogical praxis in which teachers and learners, together, in the act of analyzing a dehumanizing reality, denounce it while announcing its transformation in the name of the liberation of man."[41] Freire affirmed persons as reflective and free, created by God to expand continually the potentialities of their being by living out relationships with God and other persons. This was full humanity and the goal of education.

Freire maintained that learners must be liberated from the oppression of the traditional teacher who limits the activity and power of the students. His solution was to develop a style of teaching that is intrinsically liberating in the sense of enabling persons to become more aware of and responsible for themselves and their world. This occurs through a process of reflection followed by action and further reflection (praxis).

Freire's main contribution to education lies in his concept of "conscientization," a word originally coined to describe the arousing of a person's positive self-concept in relation to the environment and society. Because Freire eventually ceased using the term because it was misused by persons in the West who disassociate action from knowledge, the term *transformation* is used here. Transformation

---

40. John Elias provides a detailed description of Freire's work in "Paulo Freire: Religious Educator," *Religious Education* 71 (January–February 1976): 40–56.

41. Paulo Freire, *Cultural Action for Freedom* (Cambridge: Harvard Educational Review and the Center for the Study of Development and Social Change, 1970), 20.

is a liberating education that treats learners as subjects, as active agents, and not as objects or passive recipients of the wisdom shared. Students are thus viewed as active, creative subjects with the capacity to examine critically, interact with, and transform their world. Transformation is also described as problem-posing education, which encourages freedom for students in cooperative dialogue with the teacher and other students.[42] In contrast to transformation education is banking or problem-solving education, which imposes knowledge on passive students. In banking education, the teacher assumes an authoritarian role, prescribing what the students are to learn and how they are to think and behave.[43]

Freire's theology represents a redefinition of traditional theological understandings in line with the insights of various liberation theologies. God is seen as the Creator who seeks a relationship of liberation with humanity. God is the active and dynamic God of the Hebrews and the human person of Jesus who acts to save persons. God is involved in the ongoing process of creating persons and the world with the cooperation of persons. This cooperative, interactive process is one that Freire sought to replicate in education with teachers and students cooperatively working together.

Jesus is viewed as the radical critic of oppressive institutions and experiences who offers the possibility of redemption and salvation. Redemption is redefined in terms of a Christian's willingness to undergo death by struggling for new life and freedom for oppressed peoples and not remaining neutral in political struggles. Thus sin is viewed as oppression as it is exercised against persons and against God. Salvation is viewed not so much in terms of individuals as in terms of the process of bringing persons and societies to true freedom (humanization). The Christian gospel is the proclamation of the radical reordering of a society in which persons are oppressed.[44]

Freire's theology is problematic:

1. His use of a situational hermeneutic can lead to a distorted interpretation of Scripture; political analysis takes priority over biblical theology. Freire does not consider Scripture a primary frame of reference.

42. Lyra Srinivasan, *Perspectives on Nonformal Adult Learning* (New York: World Education, 1977), 2–7. For a discussion of conscientization, see Freire, *Cultural Action for Freedom*, 27–52; and Paulo Freire, *Education for Critical Consciousness* (New York: Seabury, 1973). Freire ceased using the term *conscientization* when he realized that people did not relate this term to action as indispensable to their knowing and learning. Critical consciousness for him implies a total life response to new understandings and perspectives gained through education. This perspective is also encountered in a Hebraic understanding of knowledge as a total life response to that which is known.

43. Paulo Freire, *Pedagogy of the Oppressed*, trans. Myra Bergman Ramos (New York: Seabury, 1970), 58–74.

44. Elias, "Paulo Freire," 42–46.

2. In Freire's Christology, the absence of the doctrine of the Holy Spirit is apparent. We can encounter the antichrist in our neighbor, in the oppressed. Christ is not mediated through persons alone.

3. Freire's anthropological theology does not consider the extent of sin. He views the oppressed as the people of God—not just potentially, but actually. God is thus dependent on persons and loses transcendence. The God of the Bible makes demands on humanity and is revealed through the living, created, and written Word.

4. Freire adheres to a qualitatively defined salvation, which results in a truncated view of salvation. Freire forgets that salvation is appropriated not automatically in joining a struggle for liberation but through an *act of faith* in God and Jesus Christ as Lord and Savior, which results in works of faith.

5. Freire's theology has little appreciation of the church's role as the proclaimer of the gospel of Jesus Christ. The kerygma is to be declared in word and action. There is little appreciation of the church's mission: enabling persons to place their faith in Christ. No evangelism as historically understood exists for Freire.

6. Finally, a vagueness is present in an unqualified open future. Hope emerges only out of the present and is defined in terms of God's ultimate plans for the creation as revealed in Scripture.[45]

In relation to the implementation of Freire's theory, Bennie Goodwin's critique provides additional insights. Goodwin's insights are particularly helpful in that he represents the African American church, a community that has and is experiencing oppression in the United States.

1. Opting for a godless theology is a major problem resulting from dependence on humanism and personalism. The loss of a biblical or theological base for educational efforts is apparent and limits the value of Freire's theory for Christian education.

2. Open implementation of an avowedly revolutionary strategy results in a great deal of resistance and hostility, which may not be necessary to realize renewal in all contexts.

3. Liberation in the social, political, and economic spheres, falling short of violent revolution, requires the assistance and cooperation of at least

45. For a discussion of these criticisms, see Orlando Costas, *The Church and Its Mission: A Shattering Critique from the Third World* (Wheaton: Tyndale, 1974), 219–64; and Clark H. Pinnock, "Liberation Theology: The Gains and Gaps," *Christianity Today* (January 16, 1976): 13–15.

some of those who are in power. There is the need to work for the conscientization of the oppressors as well as the oppressed. Freire chooses the level of ideas and values in making his appeal to the oppressed and ignores the need to address oppressors. Jesus's gospel calls both oppressed and oppressors to reconciliation with God, each other, and creation.

4. Freire's theory, epistemology, and axiology are not fully developed.[46]

In spite of these criticisms, several commendations of Freire's work can be made:

1. It addresses the concrete historical situation of persons. It is concerned with contextualizing education and theology by drawing out the implications of our faith and the need for response.
2. It emphasizes a service-oriented salvation and education.
3. It provides insights for Christian educators on how to educate for advocacy and social action and how to raise the consciousness of Christians to the realities and needs of persons in other cultural contexts.
4. It takes seriously the need to demonstrate an incarnational theology, one that is lived out. It seeks to relate faith to life.
5. It affirms the biblical emphasis on the poor and oppressed in Christ's ministry (Luke 4:18–19), recognizing the challenges of Marxist ideology.
6. It focuses on the humanity of Christ in reaction to an exclusive emphasis on his deity.
7. It encourages a critical awareness that the Western world is part of the global problem of oppression and injustice.
8. It emphasizes that Christian education is prophetic education, challenging oppressive social structures by questioning those programs and techniques of education that neither consider the social and corporate implications of the gospel nor question the status quo and developing Christian consciousness of the global context of oppression while leading Christians to construct new and faithful lifestyles.
9. It stresses the need for structural and social transformation as well as the personal transformation/redemption inherent in the gospel.
10. It confronts the myth of a life of better "things" and forces an examination of the tension between professed or stated intentions and values (ideas and ideals) and revealed preferences (reality).

46. Bennie Goodwin, *Reflections on Education* (Atlanta: Goodpatrick Publishers, 1978), 86–92.

Much can be gained through critical interaction with educators such as Freire because his insights address areas of weakness that have plagued evangelical educators. It is essential that Christian educators critically examine received traditions and conceptions and grapple with what God is saying to the church of Jesus Christ in our time.[47]

The theological foundations explored in this chapter provide an essential ground for relating biblical directives and principles to Christian education in the postmodern world. A reforming view is one possible contemporary formulation that seeks to build on the Reformed tradition in theology and Christian education along with the insights of liberation theologies. Certainly Lutheran, Anglican, Pietist, Arminian, Wesleyan, charismatic, and other formulations also build on a common evangelical heritage and are equally faithful to a biblical faith. It is essential that Christian educators explore and rediscover those theological sources that provide beacon lights in the stormy waters of educational thought and practice in the world and thus glorify Jesus Christ in all aspects of life.

Beyond the insights of theology, Christian educators are also called to consider those philosophies that further clarify the universals undergirding their thought and practice. These universals are the givens, the assumptions, the ideals, and the values with which persons function in their lives. A tendency exists for one's theology to parallel the particular philosophy of education espoused, but philosophical foundations of Christian education are important to explore on their own terms.[48]

Points to Ponder

- Identify other distinctive theological elements beyond the four named that serve to guide your church or denomination and suggest how they might influence the thought and practice of Christian education.
- Of the five possibilities for the relationship between theology and Christian education that Sara Little suggests, which makes the most sense to you and why?
- Where does your faith community stand on Niebuhr's scale of Christ and culture? How does this stance influence educational practices?

47. For a more extensive discussion of liberation theologies from my perspective, see Pazmiño, *Latin American Journey*.

48. For a discussion of this relationship between theology and philosophy, see Garland Knott, "Undergraduate Teaching of Religious Education," *Religious Education* 85 (Winter 1990): 105–18.

- How does an orthodox foundation serve to guide the lives of persons and communities in postmodern times as compared with earlier centuries? What has changed and what has remained unchanged in theological essentials or groundings?
- What are the strengths and weaknesses of a reforming view as compared with Reformed and liberation perspectives of theology for Christian education? Suggest alternatives that honor your theological roots.
- How do the insights of Paulo Freire's work raise questions for those who make educational decisions? Who are those with legitimate authority and power in Christian education ministries, and how do they serve the real needs of everyone God intends to teach?

3

Philosophical Foundations

The third foundation for Christian education is philosophy, which in conjunction with biblical and theological foundations provides transcultural and cultural universals to guide thought and practice. Charlotte Mason (1842–1923), a Christian educator and school reformer in England during the nineteenth and early twentieth centuries, wrote, "As a stream can rise no higher than its source, so it is probable that no educational effort can rise above the whole scheme of thought which gives it birth."[1] A philosophy of education attempts to articulate a systematic and life-giving scheme of thought that can guide practice. This is crucial because, as Mason sensitively implies, education is the fruit of its philosophic roots. The challenge for the Christian educator is to make that philosophy of education explicit and consistent with a Christian worldview while recognizing the place of paradox.

General Definitions

It is essential in exploring philosophical foundations to consider basic definitions to guide one's inquiry. A worldview can be defined as a collection of underlying presuppositions from which one's thoughts and actions stem. A Christian worldview is comprised of those fundamental Christian beliefs

1. Charlotte Mason, *Home School Education*, vol. 8 of the Home Education Series, 6th ed. (Oxford: Scrivener, 1953), ix.

that most adequately describe the relationship between God and creation.[2] Arthur Holmes, a Christian philosopher, suggests that an overall worldview will have the following characteristics: (1) it has a *holistic* goal, trying to see every area of life and thought in an integrated fashion; (2) it is a *perspectival* approach, approaching things from a previously adopted point of view that now provides an integrative framework; (3) it is an *exploratory* process, probing the relationship of one area after another to the unifying perspective; (4) it is *pluralistic* in that the same basic perspective can be articulated in somewhat different ways; and (5) it has *action outcomes*, for what we think, what we value, and what we will do.[3]

Thus a preliminary task for the Christian educator is to explore a Christian worldview that will then have direct implications and action outcomes for education. The means of developing such an overall worldview is the discipline of philosophy.

Philosophy can be literally defined as "the love of wisdom." Christians are reminded in Scripture that it is the Lord who gives wisdom and that from his mouth come knowledge and understanding (Prov. 2:6), and that the fear of the Lord is the beginning of knowledge or wisdom (Prov. 1:7; 9:10). Indeed, a further and amazing claim is that in Christ are hidden all the treasures of wisdom and knowledge (Col. 2:3). As an academic discipline, philosophy seeks a coherent organization of all knowledge and addresses human concerns to discern the true, the good, the right, the real, and the valuable. These very concerns are those which Paul encouraged the Christians at Philippi to think about and practice:

> Finally, beloved, whatever is true, whatever is honorable, whatever is just, whatever is pure, whatever is pleasing, whatever is commendable, if there is any excellence and if there is anything worthy of praise, think about these things. Keep on doing the things that you have learned and received and heard and seen in me, and the God of peace will be with you. (Phil. 4:8–9 NRSV)

Whereas philosophy in general is an intellectual discipline concerned with the nature of reality and the investigation of the general principles of knowledge, existence, and truth, Christian philosophy is also concerned with the reality and truth of God. For Christians, God is the source of all truth and reality. In the final analysis, the subject matter of Christian

2. See Arthur F. Holmes, *Contours of a World View* (Grand Rapids: Eerdmans, 1983) for a discussion of this perspective.

3. Arthur F. Holmes, ed., *The Making of a Christian Mind: A Christian World View and the Academic Enterprise* (Downers Grove, IL: InterVarsity, 1985), 17.

philosophy is the human relationship with the Creator/Redeemer God.[4] Thus the challenge for Christians is to think "Christianly" and rightly in all areas of human endeavor. One such area of endeavor is education and the challenge for Christians is to think about and realize an education that is in fact Christian.

A philosophy of Christian education or a Christian philosophy of education therefore can be defined as "an attempt to arrange systematically some thoughts on education as they are given their meaning by the biblical teachings that constitute the orthodox Christian faith."[5] For the evangelical educator, this poses the challenge of rethinking education biblically given the prior commitment to biblical authority.

Definition of Education

The definition of the essential terms *education* and *Christian education* poses a unique challenge given the plurality of educational philosophies in the modern world and the preparadigmatic nature of education.[6] Various definitions of education have been suggested that can be placed on a continuum whose poles are formal and informal education.[7]

Formal education can be defined as education that is "conventional, given in an orderly, logical, planned, and systematic manner."[8] Formal education is associated most directly with the institution of the school and the actual classroom experience. Generally, a formal understanding confines education to the experiences of persons within the classroom itself with little or no reference to the students' incidental and varied experiences outside the classroom.[9] This is a limited definition of education in comparison to the various teaching ministries described in the Scriptures, which did not envision the primary place of the school in transmitting the faith.

At the other end of the continuum is informal education that defines education in terms of life. Informal education occurs through shared identity and

4. Colin Brown, *Philosophy and the Christian Faith* (1969; London: InterVarsity, 1973), 288.

5. Norman DeJong, *Education in the Truth* (Nutley, NJ: Presbyterian & Reformed, 1974), 16.

6. See the introduction for a discussion of the "preparadigmatic" state of education as a discipline. A Christian worldview certainly provides the outline of a paradigm for Christians that is nevertheless pluralistic and is, in the final analysis, "preparadigmatic" in Kuhn's terms.

7. Fayette Veverka describes these various definitions in an unpublished classroom handout, "Matters of Definition and Perspective" (Boston College, Chestnut Hill, MA, 1983).

8. Carter V. Good, ed., *Dictionary of Education* (New York: McGraw-Hill, 1945), 175. I am indebted to Douglas M. Sloan, professor of history and education at Teachers College, Columbia University, for his analysis.

9. Ibid.

experience. It takes place in settings other than the school and classroom.[10] This definition of education views all of life and experience as education. It regards informal and unintentional interactions as providing occasions in which learning can occur. This definition is perhaps too broad in that all experience is not education but may be, in fact, miseducation if one considers questions of values.

Figure 4
A Range of Definitions

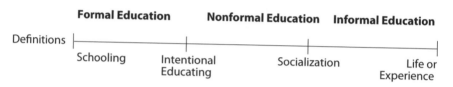

A caution with regard to this definition is warranted given the truths implied by the following proverbs: "Experience is the best teacher, but is the school of a fool"; and "Experience is a dear school, but fools will learn in no other." Experience is not sufficient for education. Having recognized this warning regarding experience without opportunities for serious reflection in schools or other settings, the Christian educator can affirm the reality that God as the teacher can use all of life's experiences to instruct persons. But in terms of a definition, education that includes all of life and experience must be distinct in some ways from other activities in life.

Given these two extreme definitions, one too narrow and the other too broad, alternatives must be explored. In 1960, Bernard Bailyn, an educational historian, proposed a definition to solve this dilemma. In considering developments in colonial America, Bailyn defined education as "the entire process by which a culture transmits itself across the generations."[11] He explored various educational agencies and persons who passed on their understanding to the next generation and proposed that history revealed four great axles or agencies of society involved in education: the family, the church, the community, and the economy.[12] Bailyn's definition shifted focus from

10. For an extensive discussion of formal, nonformal, and informal aspects of education, see Lawrence O. Richards, *A Theology of Christian Education* (Grand Rapids: Zondervan, 1975), 144, 236–39, 317–19.

11. Bernard Bailyn, *Education in the Forming of American Society* (New York: W. W. Norton, 1960), 14.

12. For a discussion of these axles or educational structures, see Pazmiño, *Principles and Practices of Christian Education: An Evangelical Perspective* (1992; Eugene, OR: Wipf & Stock, 2002), 59–90.

formal education to the vast processes of socialization and enculturation, comparable terms for education in the social sciences. Bailyn recognized the important place of nonformal education to complement the place of informal and formal education in persons' lives. The agencies of the family, church, community, and economy have an essential educational role that may not always be recognized.

The Bible reveals the impact of these agencies in the formation of persons in passing on biblical faith and Jewish culture. Many of the educational responsibilities outlined in Scripture are addressed to parents as representatives of the faith community. They are to pass on faith in God to the next generation (Deut. 6:4–9; Ps. 78:1–8; Eph. 6:1–4). Socialization is the process that enables persons to become responsible and contributing members of a community. For Israel and the New Testament church, socialization enabled persons to become responsible members of the faith community. In this perspective, education is equated with socialization or enculturation. But as was the case with the definition of education as life, this focus may still be too broad to identify the distinctive elements of education as compared with ongoing processes of formation.

As persons grow within a community or family, some, or perhaps most, of their learning experiences are not intentionally planned. The dilemma again is the question, what makes education distinct or unique? An additional problem emerges if education is equated with socialization. This entails the limitation of reformation or renewal in the community because not only does a community shape or educate an individual but an individual can also shape or educate a community. History attests to this reality. Also, biblical faith includes the process of disenculturation or prophetic education, in which a community norm or standard is seriously questioned or critiqued in light of God's values. The realization of these values often transcends the processes of socialization and enculturation. The very structure of covenantal faith assumes a place for blessing and warning, for affirmation and critique that would limit the exclusive association of education with socialization. A New Testament perspective affirms the place of socialization to the extent to which the models are consistent with the model of Jesus Christ (1 Cor. 11:1). Scripture provides numerous examples of the disobedience and unfaithfulness of communities, which parents in their efforts to model a righteous life are to avoid rather than emulate.

What becomes apparent is that education includes formal schooling, life experiences, and socialization. But what unique characteristic combines these various aspects? Lawrence Cremin, another educational historian, defines education as "the deliberate, systematic, and sustained effort to transmit, evoke, or acquire knowledge, attitudes, values, skills, or sensibilities, as well as any outcomes of that effort."[13] Cremin's definition includes educational agencies beyond the school while maintaining the deliberate, systematic, and sustained character of education. Education is deliberate in the sense of being intentional and planned. It is systematic in terms of sequential exposure and sensitivity to the readiness of participants. Education is also sustained over time, implying a continuity of exposure and interaction along with a continuing relationship between students and teachers. This definition includes transmission, discovery, and self-education and expands the limited focus on knowledge that has characterized some schooling efforts. While emphasizing the intentional dimension of education that implies responsibility and accountability, Cremin recognizes the unintentional aspects of education in his definition by including "any outcomes of the effort" to educate in it.

While recognizing the strengths of Cremin's definition, Christian educators must also identify potential weaknesses. Cremin's definition is so broad and inclusive that it fails to adequately deal with the normative dimensions of education. There is no way to distinguish miseducation from education that is appropriate and helpful for students. In dealing with education, educators must address fundamental value judgments. For the Christian educator, that which is in accord with a Christian worldview is appropriate education, and that which is not in accord with these foundations is miseducation.[14] To adequately define and determine education, Christian educators must identify the values and desired goals that will guide the entire process. Such values and goals require the clear identification of ultimate foundations. In relation to these ultimate foundations, the words of C. S. Lewis are particularly instructive in a pluralistic society: "An open mind, in questions that are not ultimate, is useful. But an open mind about the ultimate foundations either of Theoretical or of Practical Reason is idiocy."[15] Christian faith identifies specific ultimate foundations to guide life and education in its various forms.

With the discussion of education I have opted to use a descriptive general definition in my work as an educator. I define education as the process of sharing content with persons in the context of their society and community. The content in this case includes the mind, the heart, the body, and life lived personally and in relationship.

13. Lawrence A. Cremin, *Traditions of American Education* (New York: Basic Books, 1977), 134–45.

14. Cornelius Van Til, *Essays on Christian Education* (Nutley, NJ: Presbyterian & Reformed, 1977), 81.

15. C. S. Lewis, *The Abolition of Man* (New York: Macmillan, 1947), 60.

Definition of Christian Education

Given the importance of normative dimensions for defining education, Christians are called upon to propose a definition of Christian education that can guide their efforts. Several possibilities follow:

1. Christian education is a Bible-based, Holy Spirit-empowered (Christ-centered) teaching-learning process. It seeks to guide individuals at all levels of growth through contemporary teaching means toward knowing and experiencing God's purpose and plan through Christ in every aspect of living. It also equips them for effective ministry, with the overall focus on Christ the Master Educator's example and his command to make mature disciples.[16]

2. Christian education is the Christ-centered, Bible-based, pulpit-related process of communicating God's written Word through the power of the Holy Spirit for the purpose of leading others to Christ and building them up in Christ.[17]

3. Education is the re-creation and development of the true relationship between God and humans, between a human and his or her fellow human beings, and between humans and the physical universe.[18]

4. Education is the divinely instigated and humanly cooperative process whereby persons grow and develop in life, that is, in godly knowledge, faith, hope, and love through Christ.[19]

5. Christian education is the deliberate, systematic, and sustained divine and human effort to share or appropriate the knowledge, values, attitudes, skills, sensitivities, and behaviors that comprise or are consistent with the Christian faith. It fosters the change, renewal, and reformation of persons, groups, and structures by the power of the Holy Spirit to conform to the revealed will of God as expressed in the Scriptures and preeminently in the person of Jesus Christ, as well as any outcomes of that effort.[20]

The final definition I propose combines the descriptive dimensions of Cremin's suggestions with the normative dimensions fundamental to the Christian faith. While such a definition stresses intentionality, it recognizes

16. Werner C. Graendorf, ed., *Introduction to Biblical Christian Education* (Chicago: Moody, 1981), 16.
17. Roy B. Zuck, *Spiritual Power in Your Teaching*, rev. ed. (Chicago: Moody, 1972), 9.
18. DeJong, *Education in the Truth*, 118.
19. Ibid.
20. I am indebted to Lawrence Cremin's definition.

that learning can take place in situations in which human intentionality is not at all present.[21] Divine effort or agency is essential, as well as human agency, because God is the author and finisher of the Christian faith. God does not need to appropriate the faith as is the case with human beings.

This definition views education as a process more limited than socialization or enculturation, though it includes these important aspects of learning. It allows for personal study as well as interpersonal instruction, thereby embracing self-education. It envisions interactions across the generations with the intergenerational education of adults teaching children or children teaching adults; with the intragenerational education of peers within or across families and cultures; and with the self-conscious coming of age, which persons experience. Finally, this definition expands education beyond the school setting to a vast variety of persons and institutions that educate.[22] Christian education is much more than Sunday or church schooling, and Christian educators who grapple with philosophical questions can explore the contours of that "more."

Philosophical Questions

Before exploring the specific dimensions of philosophy, it is helpful to gain some perspective on the dimensions of the task in a larger framework. Norman DeJong suggests a philosophical ladder with corresponding questions that are best addressed in formulating a philosophy of education (see fig. 5):

1. *Basis or authority.* What is the basis upon which all thinking rests?
2. *Nature of persons.* Who are the persons involved?
3. *Purposes and goals.* What are the purposes and goals in education?
4. *Structural organization.* In what structures and by what agents are these purposes and goals to be realized?
5. *Implementation.* With what resources, tools, and methods will the purposes and goals of education be implemented?
6. *Evaluation.* How well are things being done?

DeJong rightfully contends that these questions are best addressed sequentially from the lowest to the highest rung, while striving for a consistency at all points with the underlying basis or authority.[23] Answers to these basic questions vary

21. Cremin, *Traditions of American Education*, 134.
22. Ibid., 134–36.
23. DeJong, *Education in the Truth*, 61–63. For a discussion of the question of authority, see Robert W. Pazmiño, *By What Authority Do We Teach? Sources for Empowering Christian Educators* (Eugene, OR: Wipf & Stock, 2002).

Figure 5
The Philosophical Ladder

Evaluation
Implementation
Structural Organization
Purposes and Goals
Nature of Persons
Basis or Authority

among Christian educators, and exploring the variety is important for those who regularly teach.[24]

The specific subject areas of philosophy can be detailed in the following manner. *Metaphysics* is the study of what constitutes the nature of reality and of what reality is constituted. Metaphysics addresses the question, "What is real?" and includes such disciplines as theology, anthropology, ontology, and cosmology. *Theology* is the study of God, which for theistic educators provides the essential foundation, while *anthropology* is the study of persons, societies, and cultures. *Ontology* is the study of being and life itself, and *cosmology* is the study of the world and material being.

A second subject area is *epistemology*. Epistemology, the study of knowledge, addresses the question, "What is true?"

Axiology, the third subject area, is the study of values and addresses the question, "What is of value?" It is concerned with ethics and aesthetics. *Ethics* is the study of value judgments and considers what is good or right. *Aesthetics* is the study of beauty and considers what is beautiful.[25] Each of these subject areas will be briefly considered with their implications for a philosophy of education.

24. One recent contribution to help in this exploration is Harold W. Burgess, *Models of Religious Education: Theory and Practice in Historical and Contemporary Perspective* (Wheaton: Victor Books, 1996).

25. I am using the outline suggested by George R. Knight in *Philosophy and Education: An Introduction in Christian Perspective* (Berrien Springs, MI: Andrews University Press, 1980), 14–37.

Metaphysics

Metaphysical insights affect each rung of DeJong's ladder, but in unique ways for the Christian educator. As was suggested in addressing theological foundations, theology has a particular contribution to make when addressing questions of authority, persons, and purposes with implications for questions of structure, implementation, and evaluation. Evangelical theology stresses the authority of Scripture, which functions as the basis for all other inquiry. Theology similarly contributes to understanding the nature of persons as creatures of God and therefore responsible to God. In the case of purposes and goals, theology suggests those that guide persons in all their efforts, including education. Thus theology provides the foundation for a thoroughgoing Christian philosophy of education.

Anthropology centers primarily on the nature of persons. From a Christian worldview, persons are viewed as created in God's image and therefore having responsibilities and obligations as image bearers. But they are also viewed as fallen and marred by sin with consequences at the personal and corporate levels of life. The implications emerging from the created and fallen aspects of human beings affect education. For example, persons are to be increasingly encouraged through education to act responsibly in all their interactions and relationships, thereby glorifying God their Creator. Persons are also to be encouraged to express their creative nature as endowed by God. Recognizing the effects of sin, Christian educators must also consider structure and discipline as important dimensions in educational planning and implementation. Structure and discipline are complemented by the effort to encourage actions that evidence the redemptive and restorative work of Christ. Every psychology has an implicit anthropology with which it operates that must be examined by the Christian educator.

Given the created nature of persons, students can be encouraged to be active participants in their own education and to interact with the world as the focus of their lives. Thus the study of anthropology forces consideration of more than individuals and the isolated classroom. Persons must be seen in relation to society and culture. Persons must also be seen in relation to their personal and corporate histories. This forces the Christian educator to consider interpersonal, intergroup, intercultural, and intersocietal questions beyond a comfortable preoccupation with personal life and piety. In relation to society, various forces, groups, movements, and institutions can be seen as being oppressive or liberating in terms of biblical norms and purposes. Likewise, cultures can be seen as reflecting or denying God in their various dimensions and Christians can be seen as called to preserve, redeem, or transform cultures

at various times in relation to gospel values. In this wider task, Christian educators are required to exercise careful analysis and discernment in enabling
others to consider the challenges of being in but not of the world. This is
possible only through the redeeming and renewing work of Christ in the lives
of persons and groups, as sustained by the Holy Spirit.

Ontology poses questions of being and life. Paul declared to the Athenians
that it is in God that "we live and move and have our being" (Acts 17:28). The
biblical worldview maintains that God's being is primary, with persons' being
secondary or derived from divine being. This is a natural consequence of the
creation. The purpose of existence is for persons to glorify and enjoy God forever. The Christian accomplishes this purpose through being actively engaged
in but not of the world, made possible through God's redemptive work.

The Christian is in the world as an exile and a pilgrim, as a member of
God's kingdom working for renewal and expressing the fruits of redemption
in Jesus Christ. Christians are called to work out their salvation with fear and
trembling while recognizing the work of God in them to fulfill God's purposes
(Phil. 2:12–13). As a new creature in Christ, the Christian has the vocation
of being Christ's ambassador, bearing the message of reconciliation (2 Cor.
5:17–21). The Christian's being necessitates the daily indwelling of the Holy
Spirit to fulfill God's purposes. Thus ontological inquiry has direct implications for the first two rungs on the philosophical ladder.

Cosmology raises questions concerning the nature of the cosmos, the universe, and the world. The world is perceived as a network of interdependencies
that emerge from the creation and God's continuing providence. In relation
to these issues the words of David are pertinent:

> The earth is the LORD's, and everything in it,
>   the world and all who live in it;
> for he founded it upon the seas
>   and established it upon the waters. (Ps. 24:1–2)

In relation to education, questions of proper stewardship of the earth and
ecology must be raised. Persons must remember that the cosmos has been
provided by God and must be cared for and shared. A difficult question is the
place of personal property in relation to the needs of others and in light of
the unity of creation. Cosmological inquiry explores the nature of humans as
inhabitants of the cosmos (rung 2) and the purposes and goals of education
(rung 3) in relation to human responsibilities for the cosmos. Howard Snyder
suggests a model for the church in the world that develops the idea of kingdom
ecology. This idea demonstrates sensitivity to cosmological issues and has

important implications for Christian education.[26] It is also possible to see the cluster of agencies that educate persons as an ecology of education.[27]

Epistemology

Questions of epistemology have a direct impact on one's conception of education regarding its basis, its view of persons, and its proposed purposes and goals (rungs 1–3 of the philosophical ladder). George R. Knight proposes an alternative way of exploring the impact of epistemology and other philosophical questions (see fig. 6).[28]

Knight indicates that a distinct metaphysical and epistemological viewpoint will affect one's stance on axiological questions. This stance on values, in conjunction with a corresponding view of reality and truth, will determine the choice of purposes and goals in the educational process.[29] Knight's scheme builds on DeJong's philosophical ladder and illustrates the various contextual factors (political, social, economic, communal, and familial) that influence educational practices beyond philosophy. At any point along this continuum, the actual influence varies in strength; there may not be a consistent relationship between one person's or group's position on philosophical issues and actual educational practice.

Cremin helpfully points out that in education, as in life, "there is inevitably a gap between aspiration and achievement, and between ideal and reality. And there is frequently a gap between stated intentions and revealed preferences."[30] This gap can serve to direct renewed efforts to be faithful to ideals. Nevertheless, the challenge for the Christian educator is to select and develop with discernment educational practices that are consistent with their beliefs and are, concurrently, feasible in their political, social, economic, and communal contexts.[31] Constant diligence is necessary if this is to be achieved along with the continual evaluation of educational practice in light of stated purposes and goals. The discernment of revealed preferences in relation to such stated intentions requires a predisposition and openness toward reform and renewal. Reform and renewal, in turn, often emerge through the reappropriation of original purposes and goals in light of changing contextual factors. Therefore, my stance is that a *reforming* rather than a *reformed*

---

26. See Howard A. Snyder, *Liberating the Church* (Downers Grove, IL: InterVarsity, 1983).
27. Lawrence Cremin proposed this understanding. See my description of his ideas in *Principles and Practices*, 59–90.
28. Knight, *Philosophy and Education*, 35.
29. Ibid., 34.
30. Lawrence A. Cremin, *Public Education* (New York: Basic Books, 1976), 36.
31. Knight, *Philosophy and Education*, 36.

Figure 6
The Relationship of Philosophy to Educational Practice

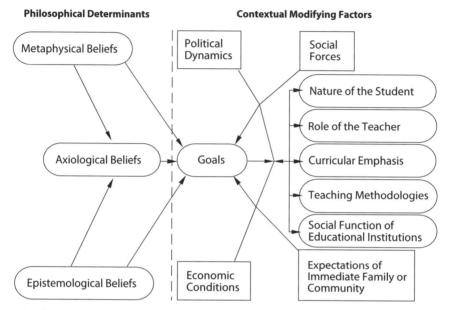

Taken from George R. Knight, *Philosophy and Education: An Introduction in Christian Perspective,*
4th ed. (Berrien Springs, MI: Andrews University Press, 2006), 34. © Copyright by Andrews
University Press. Used by permission.

perspective in education is needed, one that is sensitive to the continuing work
of the Holy Spirit in today's world and that addresses contemporary issues.
W. E. B. Du Bois, the great African American educator, observed this to be
the case. He saw education as a "necessary combination of the permanent
and the contingent—of the ideal and the practical in workable equilibrium,"
and this effort "must be in every age and place, a matter of infinite experi-
ment and frequent mistakes."[32]

In relation to substantive questions of epistemology, scholarship in the
field of religious education has reopened the consideration of the nature of
knowing and the validity of various ways of knowing.[33] This inquiry has
forced Christian educators to reconsider Scripture as the source for their efforts. The biblical view of knowledge is holistic in that it involves knowledge
in the cognitive sense along with feeling and action. Knowledge includes a

32. W. E. B. Du Bois, *The Souls of Black Folk* (New York: Bantam Books, 1989), 65.
33. An extensive discussion in this area is provided by Thomas H. Groome, *Christian Religious Education: Sharing Our Story and Vision* (San Francisco: Harper & Row, 1980), chaps.
7 and 8.

physical dimension that implies a personal commitment and intention to be one with the person or thing known. In the case of knowing God, this knowledge embodies a loving, obedient, and believing response to God and thus a relational/experiential/reflective way of knowing grounded in God's revelation as described in the Scriptures.[34]

Parker Palmer, in his search for a biblical epistemology, suggests that knowledge as understood in our societal context must be related to human interests and passions that are often ignored. In this analysis, Palmer suggests that knowledge can be tied to the three human interests or passions of control, curiosity, and compassion. The knowledge gained through applied empirical and analytical study generally seeks to gain control over a body of information. The knowledge gained through speculative, historical, and hermeneutical study generally seeks to discover knowledge as an end in itself to satisfy curiosity. The knowledge that liberates is described in 1 Corinthians 8:1–3: "Now about food sacrificed to idols: We know that we all possess knowledge. Knowledge puffs up, but love builds up. The man who thinks he knows something does not yet know as he ought to know. But the man who loves God is known by God." This type of knowledge is associated with the interest of compassion or love.[35]

Certainly the New Testament maintains that knowledge or truth must be related to love (Eph. 4:15; 2 John 1) and that all truth is God's truth, for he alone is the source of all knowledge, wisdom, and understanding (Col. 2:2–3). The problem facing the Christian educator is how to maintain in creative tension those truths discerned through study in various disciplines with the truths revealed in Scripture while at the same time being guided by love for God, others, and creation. It is Jesus's prayer that his disciples be sanctified by God's truth, recognizing that God's Word is truth (John 17:17). Christ declares that he incarnates truth (John 14:6).

In relation to this problem, George Knight has suggested six epistemological observations:

1. The biblical perspective holds that all truth is God's truth, which eliminates the distinction between secular and sacred truth.
2. The truth of Christian revelation is true to what actually exists in the universe so Christians can pursue truth without the fear of ultimate contradiction.

34. Ibid., 141–45.
35. Parker J. Palmer, *To Know as We Are Known: A Spirituality of Education* (San Francisco: Harper & Row, 1983), 6–10. Also see Jürgen Habermas, *Knowledge and Human Interests* (Boston: Beacon, 1971).

3. Forces of evil seek to undermine the Bible, distort human reasoning, and lead persons to rely on their own inadequate and fallen selves in the pursuit of truth.

4. The Bible is concerned not with abstract truth but with truth as related to life. Therefore, knowing in the biblical sense is applying the perceived knowledge to daily life.

5. The various sources of knowledge available to Christians (the special revelation of Scripture, the general revelation of the natural world, and reason) are complementary and should be used in light of the biblical pattern.

6. Given the unity of truth, the acceptance of a Christian epistemology cannot be separated from the acceptance of a Christian metaphysics.[36]

Knight's observations can be explored in relation to the particular challenge posed by contemporary scientism, which maintains that scientific inquiry is the only reliable way of knowing. Scientism, as contrasted with science, denies that truth can be discerned through the revelation of the Christian faith position and presupposes that empirically based reason is the only medium for understanding. Huston Smith points out the dangers of such a limited epistemology. Science values control, prediction, objectivity, numbers, and signs, while faith values surrender, surprise, subjectivity and objectivity, words, and symbols. Whereas science deals with the instrumental values of utility, usefulness, service, and control, faith deals with the intrinsic values of wonder, awe, reverence, creativity, imagination, and promise. Whereas becoming is the dominant focus of science, being/becoming is the focus of faith.[37]

The faith perspective of Christianity provides an alternative way of knowing that expands upon, but is not contradictory to, the truths of science, given that all truth is God's truth. Christians are free to explore the insights of science, which are discerned or discovered through reason and empirical observation in relation to the natural world of God's general revelation. But Christians must also beware of the potential forces of evil, which may seek to exalt science inappropriately.

A Christian view of the physical world and nature maintains that the creation is real and good and thus amenable to experimentation; empirical science can be affirmed. A Christian view also maintains that nature is ordered and intelligible; therefore, theoretical science is appropriate. Finally, a Christian view maintains

36. Knight, *Philosophy and Education*, 161–62.

37. Huston Smith, "Excluded Knowledge: A Critique of the Modern Western Mind Set," *Teachers College Record* (February 1979): 419–45.

that history and culture have meaning and purpose. Thus applied science and technology can be fully pursued.[38] But in each of these scientific areas

> a Christian view of the physical world sees nature in the light of Scripture and with a concern for culture. This involves a creative view of nature that recognizes the world as real and good. It includes a critical view of scientific ideas and methods that looks to Scripture for guidance, and for faith in the order and intelligibility revealed in creation. And it attempts a constructive view of culture that finds purpose and meaning in seeking to improve the world for the good of humanity and the glory of God.[39]

From the perspective of a Christian worldview and epistemology, it is helpful to see the potentials and dangers of science, as well as the Christian graces that can counter the dangers that emerge in scientism (see table 4).[40]

TABLE 4
Science and the Christian Graces

Potentials of Science	Danger in Scientism	Christian Graces
Explanation (knowing)	Misplaced worship	Faith
Prediction (choosing)	Unwarranted expectations	Hope
Control (changing)	Misuse of power	Love

The first potential of science is that of providing explanations for reality and contributing to human knowledge. But there is the potential danger of a misplaced worship that glorifies the scientific process or the human explanations derived from that process. Christian faith can help to focus worship on the God of all creation who is revealed to persons through the natural order. A second potential of science is that of predicting natural phenomena and contributing to human decision-making processes. But an inherent danger is that of unwarranted expectations in relation to future events and human capabilities to determine those events. The grace of a living hope alerts Christians to God's sovereignty and providential care along with the appropriate place of human responsibility in predicting and choosing the future. The third potential of science, which Palmer also identifies, is that of control and of changing the natural or human condition. The corresponding danger of this potential is the

38. Joseph Spradley, "A Christian View of the Physical World," in *The Making of a Christian Mind: A Christian World View and the Academic Enterprise*, ed. Arthur F. Holmes (Downers Grove, IL: InterVarsity, 1985), 59–69.

39. Ibid., 79.

40. I am indebted to Larry Martin, student at Gordon-Conwell Theological Seminary, for table 4.

misuse of power, something repeatedly witnessed in history. Complementing this danger is the quintessential Christian grace of love, which sets the glory of God, the welfare of others, and creation above the use of power.

This discussion of scientism illustrates the importance of a biblical epistemology and the usefulness of Knight's observations for considering epistemological questions. The truths of science can be integrated with a Christian worldview that affirms all truth as God's truth. The Christian can indeed pursue a scientific way of knowing that is subject at all points to theological evaluation. Biblical truth can address the dangers inherent in the misappropriation of science. A Christian epistemology is dependent on a Christian metaphysics and, in particular, a Christian cosmology, which sees the physical world as God's creation and therefore subject to God in all of its variety and unity.

Axiology

Questions of value involve both ethics and aesthetics. Ethics is the study of moral principles and practices. Christian ethics deals with the reality of sin and the Christian calling of service and sacrifice in the world. Aesthetics is the study of beauty and the creative dimensions in life. For Christians, aesthetics is based on the fact that God created a world of beauty; this implies a personal responsibility to both appreciate and create beauty.[41] The relationship between axiology and education can be explored by considering different value systems affecting the purposes and goals of education. Both metaphysical and epistemological issues interact with these axiological perspectives.

Paulo Freire emphasizes the need for a clear articulation of values in education and for critical reflection on and problematization of values.[42] Freire calls for intentionality, integrity, and honesty regarding those values that guide the entire educational process. Such intentionality, integrity, and honesty are fundamental to any educational efforts that claim to be Christian because the standards of truth apply to all levels of conception, planning, and action.

Values are generally conceived as conceptions to which worth, interest, and goodness have been attributed. Values are choices of ultimate concern that by their very nature embody theological considerations for Christians. They deal with what is desirable, meaningful, and enduring even within a given time span. Values identify the goals, ideals, and ultimate ends of human thought and endeavor that make up the very fabric of everyday life. They inherently involve belief in propositions and commitment to them (personal conviction

41. Knight, *Philosophy and Education*, 171–77.
42. See Paulo Freire, *Pedagogy of the Oppressed*, trans. Myra Bergman Ramos (New York: Seabury, 1970).

and full involvement).[43] To educate is to teach at every point the complex web of religious, moral, and intellectual values that ultimately define the arrangements of any community and society.

In our dealing with values in education, the struggle is often between that which is viewed as good and that which is viewed as better. This raises the question of priority and preference in values. Values for the educator thereby present the dilemma of choosing commitments involving one's thoughts, efforts, and loves. In dealing with the choice of values, Milton Rokeach suggests that each person holds many values arranged loosely and more or less flexibly in a hierarchy with different value systems having priority depending on the situation.[44]

In contrast to Rokeach's conceptions are those of Lynn White, who describes a changing canon of culture in considering value. According to White, the traditional hierarchy of values has, in fact, been turned at right angles to become a spectrum of values in which every human activity, including educational activity, embodies the possibility of greatness. No human activities are viewed by nature as being more profitable. The result is an equality of values. Though values imply a monetary metaphor that is scaled up and down rather than sideways, White suggests that the term "value" must be used in describing this spectrum of choices available to persons.[45] Whereas Christians have traditionally identified value hierarchies, White's insights are helpful because of the problems posed by change in educational planning where values must be reformulated and reapplied to new and varying situations. This is not to suggest that we support a situational ethics, but rather that we consider the various contextual modifying factors that Knight emphasizes in relating philosophy to educational practice (see fig. 6). With a spectrum of values, the Christian educator is called upon to regularly make conscious choices that will direct the actual practice of education.

Whereas with White's conceptions the scope of value choices is broadened and widened in dealing with a pluralistic society, the Christian educator must assert that some value systems better represent the totality of reality. This assertion is possible, given the nature of biblical revelation, supernatural realities, reason, and faith experiences. The Christian educator can propose higher values because he or she can answer questions such as What are human beings and their ultimate end? What is the meaning and purpose of human activity? What, or rather, who is God? These questions can be answered with a certainty and surety impossible outside revealed faith.

43. Daniel and Laurel N. Tanner, *Curriculum Development: Theory into Practice* (New York: Macmillan, 1975), 127.
44. See Milton Rokeach, *The Nature of Human Values* (New York: Free Press, 1973).
45. Lynn White Jr., *Frontiers of Knowledge* (New York: Harper & Bros., 1956), 312.

Before identifying specific value systems as they influence thought and practice, we can suggest four implications for Christian educators in this area of axiology.[46] First, Christian educators must be aware of the values undergirding their efforts in teaching, ministry, and life. Christian educators have too readily accommodated themselves to their culture in ways that deny the gospel and kingdom values. Considering values fosters the process of conscious identification and integration of biblical values in teaching and learning. Awareness of such values assumes a personal commitment to them.

Second, Christian educators must translate their values into the actual purposes and goals that guide educational practice. Values must be synthesized with and internalized throughout the actual educational enterprise so that persons can be encouraged to act consistently in accordance with stated values. This second implication assumes that values have prescriptive power and that they must consciously and unconsciously affect educational plans and their implementation.

A third implication emerging from this emphasis on values translation is that values must be pursued in communal and institutional contexts because we live in a communal and institutional world. Values too readily become privatized. A subjective preoccupation with self can plague Christians as a result of the psychologization of evangelicalism (*my* peace, *my* joy, *my* self-esteem, *my* self-worth, *my* health, and *my* . . .). Consequently, relatively little attention is given to the common welfare of all persons, especially those who are disadvantaged or oppressed. Given this situation, it is essential that Christian educators translate their values into communal and institutional goals. A fourth implication is that Christian educators must be aware of the constant need for renewal in relation to their values. Given the nature of persons, communities, institutions, and social structures, Christians must constantly reaffirm basic biblical values in the spiritual battle for persons' minds and lives. This need for renewal emerges from the reality of sin in its personal and corporate manifestations. Paul Tillich suggests that Christians are called to constantly live in relation to the Protestant principle, which maintains that reform and renewal is constantly needed in institutions given the changing needs, conditions, and issues of contemporary life. The Christian vocation is to protest against those efforts, forms, and structures that are no longer faithful to the gospel and to suggest alternatives consistent with Christian values.[47] This indeed is the task of Christian educators. While protesting,

46. See John W. Gardner's discussion in "Engagement of Values in Public Life," *Harvard Divinity Bulletin* (October–November 1984): 5–6.
47. Paul Tillich, *The Protestant Era*, trans. James L. Adams (Chicago: University of Chicago Press, 1948), 161–81.

the Christian recognizes the essential work of the Holy Spirit to actualize effective reform and renewal.

In considering questions of value, Dwayne Huebner has suggested five value categories that generally guide the practice of education in various settings: First, *technical valuing* emphasizes the importance of control and efficiency in education. This form of valuing maintains a means-end rationality that approaches an economic model and strives to mobilize material and human resources to produce ends. This valuing focuses on the elements in education that can be conditioned or controlled and therefore effectively manipulated.

Second, *political valuing* addresses questions of power that are usually covert in the process of education. Teachers or educators have a position of power and control over others and can influence them in various ways. Students also possess power to influence teachers and others. Education can be viewed as slow-fuse politics that attempts either to support a status quo or to work for change. Educators and students can raise questions about the ideologies and structures that maintain and legitimate injustice or unrighteousness in the wider society. Students and educators can be viewed as potential or actual change agents in the church and world.

Third, *scientific valuing* emphasizes the efforts in education that produce new knowledge with an empirical base. In this valuing category, scholarship and inquiry are emphasized along with the exploration of various options for meaning.

Fourth, *aesthetic valuing* focuses on activities having a symbolic or aesthetic meaning. Imagination, creativity, and dealing with the unconditioned or open-ended aspects of life are included in this educational category.

Fifth, *ethical valuing* considers the encounter among persons with education contributing to the realization of moral life. In this category, the teacher is called upon to influence students with their responsibility (or "response-ability") in various areas of life. This valuing generally emphasizes the need for conversation and for sharing a vision of a moral community among persons both within and outside the educational encounter.[48]

Huebner points out that education is seldom valued from within only one of these categories, and that all five influence the actual process of valuing in education.[49] In relation to these five categories, Christian educators might suggest a sixth category, "spiritual valuing," that would include a concern for

---

48. See Dwayne Huebner, "Curriculum Language and Classroom Meanings," in *Curriculum Theorizing: The Reconceptualists*, ed. William Pinar (Berkeley: McCutchan, 1975), 215–28.
    49. Ibid., 228.

freeing persons from the power of sin to live righteously and justly before God as God's adopted children. It would emphasize understanding and living in accordance with God's Word while encouraging a sense of wonder, awe, and worship in all of life. It would then be possible to view spiritual valuing at the apex of a hierarchy of values that in turn would influence the other valuing categories (see fig. 7).

Figure 7
Hierarchy of Values

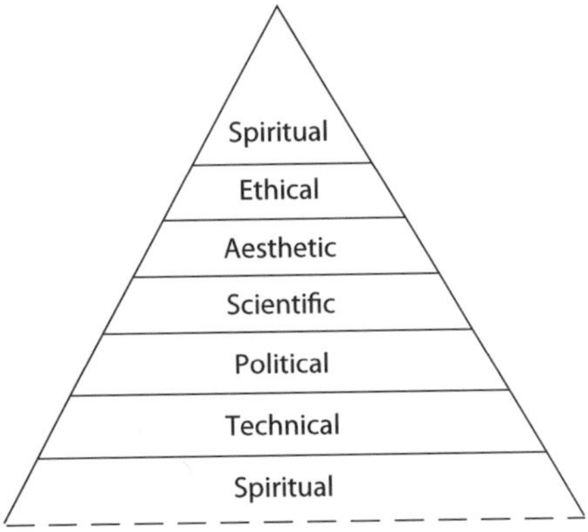

Spiritual
Ethical
Aesthetic
Scientific
Political
Technical
Spiritual

Spiritual values—the highest of values for Christians—must influence the other value options. In figure 7, spiritual valuing serves as the foundation as well as the apex of a values hierarchy, given the need for a clearly articulated basis for value decisions in educational questions, which is provided by a Christian worldview.

While these portrayals are real options, a reforming perspective on education suggests an additional alternative that might be diagrammed with ethical, aesthetic, scientific, political, and technical values of adjacent blocks encapsulated in the larger block of spiritual valuing (see fig. 8).

Figure 8
A Reforming Alternative

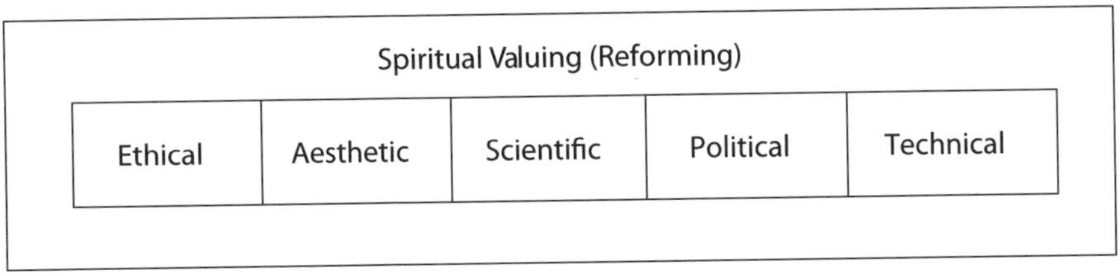

Spiritual Valuing (Reforming)				
Ethical	Aesthetic	Scientific	Political	Technical

Spiritual valuing is the entire domain in which educational values must be considered. Rather than seeing spiritual valuing as a sixth valuing category, spiritual values must impinge on each of the valuing categories suggested by Huebner, reforming them in five ways:

First, *technical valuing*, which emphasizes control and efficiency, can be reformed or renewed to emphasize the stewardship of God's resources. The life portrayed and values communicated in education can be seen in relation to God's ordered creation, reflecting God's harmony, providence, and sovereignty.

Second, *political valuing*, which emphasizes power and legitimation of that power, can be reformed in education to value the effort to free and empower others. This occurs as others are humbled before God and through redemption in Jesus Christ become vehicles of his transforming power in society. Being light and salt in the world and experiencing daily the resurrection power of Jesus Christ in one's personal and social life are then the focus of this valuing in education (Matt. 5:13–16; Phil. 3:10). There is power in the ministry of reconciliation, power in modeling love and service to others, and power in obeying God's will, which mitigates human power. Political valuing relates to the prophetic task of the church.

Third, *scientific valuing*, with its focus on empirical knowledge, can be reformed to focus on knowing God as the basis for better knowing God's creation. The challenge in all scientific inquiry is to "take captive every thought to make it obedient to Christ" (2 Cor. 10:5), seeing in him all the treasures of wisdom and knowledge (Col. 2:2–3). This provides the essential perspective for integrating the discoveries of all scientific disciplines. The challenge is to have knowledge of the very mind of Christ through Scripture and the guidance of the Holy Spirit as his thoughts relate to the natural and supernatural worlds.

Fourth, *aesthetic valuing* addresses concerns for freedom, creativity, and beauty. This category can be reformed to emphasize in education the disclosure of the beauty of Christ as revealed in creation and in humanity's creative expression and potential. Persons can give glory to God through all creative arts and crafts and see the beauty of God in the commonplaces of life. There is a need in education to enable persons to better image their God-given freedom within the structures and forms of God's creation.

Fifth, *ethical valuing* can be reformed in education to encourage persons to consider and actualize responsible action—first in relation to God, and then in relation to creation, others, and oneself. This necessitates grappling with the dimensions of a Christian lifestyle and ethical decisions in all areas of human endeavor. The Christian educator is challenged with the call for an integrity that addresses the contradictions of personal and social sin. This challenge must also be posed for students.

The five Christian values or, better termed, virtues that I identify to guide teaching follow from the integrated model that emerges in considering biblical foundations. Each of the virtues is related to the five educational tasks of the church and gifts of the Holy Spirit to God's people in the world. The five tasks of the church are proclamation, community formation, service, advocacy, and worship. The corresponding five virtues are truth, love, faith, hope, and joy. Related to each of these virtues is a call to educators for their consideration in the *e-value-ation* of teaching and learning. I suggest the following pairings of Christian virtues, which provide a basis for the evaluation of Christian education: truth—a call for integrity; love—a call for care; faith—a call for action; hope—a call for courage; and joy—a call for celebration.[50]

Specifics of an Educational Philosophy

The exploration of axiology has underscored the essential role of Christian values for decisions regarding the purposes and goals of education. A further consideration involves metaphysical, epistemological, and axiological concerns and how they affect a stated philosophy of education that strives to be Christian. To consider this issue, the Christian educator must adopt a model that identifies the key elements of an educational philosophy per se. Harold Burgess suggests such a scheme that includes purposes and goals, content, teacher, student, environment, and evaluation.[51] There are direct parallels between these elements and those of Knight: nature of the student, role of the teacher, curricular emphasis, teaching methodologies, and the social function of educational institutions. The "content" in Burgess's school can be equated with Knight's "curricular emphasis"; Burgess's "environment" category mirrors Knight's "teaching methodologies" and "social function of educational institutions." Burgess and Knight provide a comprehensive framework for the formulation of an educational philosophy.

Purposes and goals. How do proclamation, community, service, advocacy, and worship relate to the purposes of Christian education or education in general? The model in chapter 1 (fig. 2, p. 46) suggests a direct relationship between the purposes of the church and those of Christian education. This

50. See my discussion in Robert W. Pazmiño, *Basics of Teaching for Christians: Preparation, Instruction and Evaluation* (Eugene, OR: Wipf & Stock, 2002), 75–99.

51. Burgess's areas are standard for considering an educational philosophy or theory. See Harold William Burgess, *An Invitation to Religious Education* (Mishawaka, IN: Religious Education Press, 1975), 12–13, 167; and Burgess, *Models of Religious Education*, 19–21.

perspective does not equate Christian education with church education, but views the church as scattered in a multiplicity of settings and relationships. Nonetheless, it assumes that in homes, schools, communities, workplaces, relationships, and individual places of study a unity of purpose in Christian education can exist.

Some may raise serious questions regarding the dissolution of what traditionally has been viewed as a gap between the purposes of Christian education per se and secular education, and the participation of Christians in both spheres. What purposes can a Christian have in the area of vocational training in a public school? Others may maintain that the acquisition of knowledge, values, skills, sensitivities, and behaviors are ends in and of themselves. The additional purposes or goals of proclamation, community, service, and the like reveal a utilitarian or pragmatic emphasis that is foreign to the tasks of education in its purest and highest form. Why then suggest these additional purposes? A third area of concern may be raised by Christians who emphasize other scriptural foundations than those cited, or by those who place greater emphasis on experience or reason in the formulation of a Christian philosophy. Such alternative decisions at key points would affect what purposes and goals are identified. The need for clarity and consistency in the definition and implementation of whatever purposes and goals are selected obviates such questions.

In *Objectives in Religious Education* (1930), Paul H. Vieth offers a list of seven goals derived from the thought of leaders in the field at that time.[52]

1. Seek to foster a consciousness of God as a reality in human experience, and a sense of personal relationship to him through Jesus Christ.
2. Seek to develop an understanding and appreciation of the personality, life, and teachings of Jesus so as to lead persons to experience him as Lord and Savior, and to follow him loyally and obediently in daily life and conduct.
3. Seek to nurture a progressive and continuous development of Christlike character through the work of the Holy Spirit.
4. Seek to develop the ability and disposition to participate in and respond to the spiritual and social outworkings of the gospel, being about God's work in the world while not being of it.
5. Seek to develop the ability and disposition to responsibly participate in the Christian family when appropriate, and the extended Christian family, which is the church.

52. Paul H. Vieth, *Objectives in Religious Education* (New York: Harper & Bros., 1930), 70–78.

6. Seek to encourage the development of a Christian worldview that is contextualized in the life of each person.
7. Seek to educate Christians in the whole counsel of God as recorded preeminently in Scripture, which is the authoritative guide for all faith and life.[53]

Although the relative emphasis on each of these seven goals may vary with the actual teaching context, their general scope has an enduring quality. The careful articulation of such purposes and goals is the key element of an educational philosophy. The following general purpose for Christian education can be proposed:

> The general purpose of the church's educational ministry is that all persons know of, and develop a dynamic and growing personal relationship with, God (John 17:3) and his creation. This knowledge and relationship is to be grounded in God's revelation and self-disclosure in Scripture and centered completely and decisively in Jesus Christ as Lord and Savior (John 14:6; 17:7; 2 Tim. 3:16). Persons of all ages are to be enabled by the Holy Spirit to respond in faith, love, and obedience such that each person is continually growing as a member of the Christian community and living in the world as a representative of Christ, while abiding in the hope of his second coming. The goal of educational ministry is that persons become obedient disciples of Jesus Christ (Matt. 28:18–20), prepared for works of service and conformed increasingly to the image of Christ (Eph. 4:11–16).[54]

Content. Although the place of the Bible in Christian education has been emphasized thus far, Lois LeBar suggests an expanded perspective in which Christian education centers on both the living Word of God (Christ) and the written Word of God (the Bible).[55] This suggestion counters the danger of an emphasis on the Bible that fails to relate biblical content to the living Christ and to the lives of persons. Evangelical educators have been particularly susceptible to this danger. Another issue at stake is the place of the students' experiences and needs in the choice of content, because teachers present content to persons in the context of a particular setting. Some suggest that student needs, problems, and interests should have priority, while others maintain that

53. Ibid.
54. This statement is patterned after Kenneth L. Cober, *Shaping the Church's Educational Ministry: A Manual for the Board of Christian Education* (Valley Forge: Judson Press, 1971), 7–8.
55. Lois E. LeBar, *Education That Is Christian*, rev. ed. (Old Tappan, NJ: Fleming H. Revell, 1981), 212–15.

the logical and sequential order of the content should be the primary guide. Still others emphasize the place of social or communal responsibilities. Each of these three options is explored in the discussion of person, society, and subject-centered approaches.[56]

In a society that evidences an overwhelming preoccupation with human needs, evangelical educators must carefully distinguish the nature of those needs. This is important because one dictum of the common wisdom of the age is that student needs should be the primary determinant of educational content. A distinction must be made between persons' felt needs and their real needs. A corollary of this dictum is that the educator should initiate his or her efforts by addressing felt needs and then eventually disclose and address the real needs of students. Following such common wisdom may result in serious inattention to the demands of God on persons in various areas of responsibility. Abraham Heschel has described this scenario as the problem or tyranny of needs.[57] Christian educators must evaluate human needs making use of scriptural categories because a society or culture can actually distort perceptions of need.

One example of this problem is the tendency to define the better life through education in terms of progress measured by the increased accumulation of material resources. Thus the constant need is for increased possession and consumption of material goods of greater worth. Such a materialistic view has failed to adequately critique those areas of need as perceived through a particular culture that may conflict with a Christian worldview. This occurs because of human sinfulness. In fact, the educational task may be to challenge perceived needs with divine demands, which suggest alternative values beyond materialism. (This does not, of course, negate addressing appropriate or genuine human need as discerned from biblical categories.)

Another issue is the relationship between experience or action and content or reflection in education. Some educators who emphasize the transmission of accumulated wisdom suggest that content or reflection is primary and experience or action is secondary. Thus the agenda for educational efforts is to share content and subsequently address how that content can issue in action or affect experience. Other educators who emphasize the experiential dimensions of life suggest that effective integration in education occurs where experience is primary. Shared experiences or actions are subsequently reflected upon and evaluated in the effort to gain insights.

56. See pp. 119–21.
57. Abraham J. Heschel, *Between God and Man: An Interpretation of Judaism from the Writings of Abraham Heschel*, ed. Fritz A. Rothschild (New York: Free Press, 1959), 129–51.

The first approach can be described as a deductive agenda that moves from generalized and abstract knowledge to that which is particular and owned by individuals in the immediate context. The second approach can be described as an inductive agenda that moves from particular and experienced knowledge to that which is perhaps generalized and connected with other experiences through reflection. In many ways, both approaches can be viewed as complementary, but relative differences in emphasis imply a separate agenda in educational content.

Teacher. Wilbert J. McKeachie suggests that teachers assume six roles, each of which has corresponding goals. These roles and goals are expanded upon in a reforming perspective.

1. *Expert/neophyte.* As an expert, the teacher transmits information—the concepts and perspectives of the field or subject—while, as a neophyte, recognizing areas of inadequate expertise.
2. *Formal authority/subject.* As a formal authority, the teacher sets goals and procedures for reaching goals and as a subject is open to students' suggestions when appropriate.
3. *Socializing/socialized agent.* As a socializing agent, the teacher clarifies goals and options beyond the class or course and prepares students for them. As a socialized agent, the teacher is open to the suggestions and influence of students and others within and beyond the teaching settings.
4. *Facilitator.* As a facilitator, the teacher promotes creativity and growth in students' own terms and helps them overcome obstacles to learning. The teacher is sensitive to his or her own creativity and growth.
5. *Ego ideal in process.* As an ego ideal, the teacher conveys the excitement and value of educational inquiry in given areas and recognizes areas where ideals and practice are lacking.
6. *Person.* As a person, the teacher conveys the full range of human needs and skills relevant to and sustained by one's educating activity, to be validated as a human being, and to validate the students as persons.[58]

In relation to McKeachie's six roles, the Christian educator must ask himself or herself to what extent these roles can be affirmed or revised. The Christian teacher is called upon to transmit biblical information and the concepts and perspectives of the Christian faith. Also, she or he may be sharing additional

58. Wilbert J. McKeachie, *Teaching Tips: A Guidebook for the Beginning College Teacher,* 7th ed. (Lexington, MA: D. C. Heath, 1978), 81–82.

insights from any number of fields and subjects, with the proviso that they are either consistent with a biblical worldview or that they help students to grapple with possible inconsistencies. This poses the problem of integration for the Christian teacher and accountability in terms of the Christian heritage. The Christian teacher is an expert to the extent to which he or she manifests faithfulness to God and his or her discipline.

In relation to McKeachie's second role, the Christian teacher is the formal or nonformal authority, but final authority is always subject to God. Thus the Christian teacher is ultimately and finally accountable to God in all areas of endeavor. Second, the Christian teacher is accountable to a host of persons, groups, and institutions for the exercise of authority. The nature of the teacher's formal or nonformal authority is derivative, and the higher calling is to so exercise this derived authority that God is glorified. This perspective does not at all diminish the appropriate role of the teacher in setting goals and procedures for reaching those goals. The Christian teacher is also subject to insights offered by students when they are true and appropriate.

The Christian teacher's role as a socializing agent must be seen in relation to the complementary roles of parents, churches, communities, and governments in various areas of human life. In certain situations, the Christian teacher may also be a resocializing agent, depending on the nature of other socializing forces in the lives of students. This additional responsibility as a potential "resocializer" requires careful discernment regarding biblical values and the proper place of disenculturation. Neil Postman and Charles Weingartner allude to this role in their discussion of teaching as a subversive activity—one that poses questions and presents options for students to gain awareness of inappropriate socialization.[59] Postman has also discussed teaching as a conserving activity that affirms the teacher's roles as a socializing agent in terms of cultural and societal norms.[60] The Christian teacher is also socialized by the students through their interactions.

As a facilitator, the Christian teacher does indeed promote creativity and growth but not exclusively in the students' own terms. While recognizing McKeachie's focus on college students, the Christian teacher's perspective is informed by God's terms for understanding creativity and growth. This may not present a standard radically different from that of the students, but in many cases it will. This is the case because human creativity, growth, and freedom must be understood in relation to God's order, structure, and form

59. Neil Postman and Charles Weingartner, *Teaching as Subversive Activity* (New York: Delacorte, 1969).

60. Neil Postman, *Teaching as Conserving Activity* (New York: Dell, 1980).

for life. Within that order there is a tremendous potential for creativity and genuine growth, but also an equal potential for the manifestation of human sin with accompanying illusion and delusion. The Christian teacher must also be aware of his or her own need for continued growth and creativity.

In terms of McKeachie's fifth role, the Christian teacher is only a model to the extent to which Christ is a living reality in her or his life (1 Cor. 11:1). The excitement and value of Christian inquiry in all areas of life must be shared by Christian teachers. Too much of Christian teaching has settled for the mundane, lacking excitement and color.

An additional challenge is posed by the sixth role of being a person. Too many efforts in Christian education have denied the essential personhood of the teacher as created by God. The biblical model of teaching stresses a personal relationship and an appropriation of truth that results in sharing both doctrine and life as they reinforce each other.

Properly balancing these roles is a difficult task to accomplish in the various teaching settings. The need for competence and excellence in each of these roles is necessitated by the demand for Christian integrity in a world in need of teachers who reflect the glory of the Master Teacher. Further insights can be drawn for the role of the teacher through careful study of the teaching ministry of Jesus Christ. Christian educators have differed in the relative emphasis placed on each of these six roles.

From a Christian perspective, teachers are fellow human beings with students. They are fellow creations of God with unique strengths and weaknesses, and affected by the fall. In general education, they may or may not be believers in Christ but nevertheless can be instruments used by God to teach students. Scriptural standards for teachers include the following: a teacher must be (1) a believer in Christ (1 Cor. 12:27–28); (2) called by God and gifted for the teaching ministry (Rom. 12:7; 1 Cor. 12:28; Eph. 4:11–12); (3) faithful to true doctrine (1 Tim. 1:3–7; 2 Tim. 2:2); (4) a servant, an authority, and a mature and maturing disciple of Christ (1 Tim. 3:1–7; James 3:1); and (5) responsible before God for one's life and teaching (Matt. 23:10; 1 Tim. 4:12–16; James 3:1).[61]

Student. If one were to develop McKeachie's roles in terms of the student, the following could be suggested:

1. *Neophyte/expert.* As a neophyte, the student receives the information, concepts, and perspectives of the teacher and offers insights in areas of expertise.

61. Al Edeker, "A Philosophy of Christian Education" (unpublished paper, Gordon-Conwell Theological Seminary, 1985), 5.

2. *Formal subject.* As subject to the teacher's authority, the student accepts the goals and procedures set by the teacher, and/or suggests alternative goals and procedures in negotiation with the teacher.

3. *Socialized/socializing agent.* As a socialized agent, the student actively participates in the task of clarifying goals and options beyond the classroom in cooperation with the teacher. The student can also be a socializing agent by suggesting goals and options for the transfer of learning.

4. *Fellow facilitator.* As a fellow facilitator, the student identifies areas for creativity and growth and works to overcome obstacles to learning in cooperation with the teacher.

5. *Ego ideal in process.* As an ego ideal in process, the student shares in the excitement and value of the educational inquiry and recognizes areas where ideals are lacking.

6. *Person.* As a person, the student conveys the full range of human needs and skills relevant to and sustained by one's educating activity, to be validated as a human being, and to validate the students and teachers as persons.

In describing the roles of the student, we must move beyond an understanding of the student as passive or receptive and investigate areas for active participation. The extent of student participation and shared responsibility depends on the maturity and experience of the students, but wherever possible this is worth emphasizing given the nature of persons as created by God for total life responses. As suggested by Harold Burgess, "Even though Protestant traditional theorists do give some consideration to the student and to the teacher learning process, they appear to place little reliance upon these factors in their actual theorizing."[62]

Students are copartners with teachers in the educational effort, and any attempt to co-opt their active participation is a denial of their created humanity. Christian truth must be taught to human beings, and to neglect their humanity ignores half the equation. A reforming perspective recognizes the unique differences among individual students and encourages the place of dialogue, not to deny the need for teachers to share authoritative content and direct teaching, but to enable the active appropriation of truth in the lives of students. Otherwise, evangelical educators are perpetuating rote forms of learning that do not transfer beyond the educational setting or aid the process of integrating life in terms of a Christian worldview. Al Edeker suggests the following insights in understanding the student from a biblical perspective:

62. Burgess, *Invitation to Religious Education*, 49.

The view of the student within a Christian philosophy of education suggests several points. One is that the student is a creation of God and is created in the image of God. The student therefore has value in God's eyes. This means that the student himself or herself and others should value and respect the student. The student is not a second-class citizen or an empty container to be filled, but he or she is a person of value and potential.

A second point is that the student like all of humankind is fallen. Therefore, the student has limitations, faults, and destructive behavior that affect his or her growth and interaction with others.

Third, every human is potentially a child of God or is a child of God. This potential is realized in Christ.

Fourth, the student is capable of change and growth. The Christian view suggests that through the work of the Holy Spirit the destructive traits and behaviors of the student can be corrected or nullified through daily sanctification.

Fifth, the student is responsible before God for his or her actions, sinfulness, and response before God.[63]

This view of the student reflects both his or her potential and responsibility. The following roles suggest the possible response of the student of Christ. The student's ability to perform these roles may vary depending on the student's age and maturity in Christ.

1. Students should strive to grow into the likeness of Christ.
2. Christian students should worship and glorify God through their learning and the application of that learning.
3. Students should be good stewards of their talents.
4. Students should be diligent in all that their hands find to do.
5. Students should test all knowledge with Scripture and test spirits and teacher.
6. Students should apply their learning, being not only hearers but doers (James 1:22–25).
7. Students should remain open to the work of the Holy Spirit.
8. Students should value all of creation.
9. Students should be in community and encourage others (Heb. 10:24–25).[64]

Environment. Various factors of the environment, context, or settings for education must be considered. D. Campbell Wyckoff has insightfully named three interacting aspects of the environment.

63. Edeker, "Philosophy of Christian Education," 6.
64. Ibid.

The first factor is the *natural aspect*. This aspect entails the physical factors and material resources of the classroom, including room arrangement, decoration, aesthetics, and resource display, along with factors that affect visibility, mobility, and comfort. The *human aspect* is the second factor. It focuses on the teacher(s) and the student(s) and other human resources and factors. Also, the nature of commitments, interactions, and personal or shared concerns that are present overtly or covertly in the educational interaction are involved in this aspect. The last factor is the *divine aspect*. The Holy Spirit is the determinative environmental presence, and the challenge is to create those conditions in which the Spirit of God can work most fruitfully in the lives of persons.[65]

All three aspects require attention and intention in Christian education. An approach is needed that considers all three aspects of the environment, giving clear priority to the divine aspect. Every setting for education—formal, nonformal, and informal—involves these three aspects in varying degrees of consciousness and intentionality. The demands of a practical theology are reflected in the need to contextualize efforts of Christian education by carefully assessing these and other aspects of the environment. Knight's analysis suggests the need to consider the human aspects in terms of political, economic, social, communal, and familial forces.[66] The additional dimension of cultural factors must be recognized. These various forces will be considered in later chapters. But a perennial question for the Christian educator is how the three aspects of the environment interact and facilitate the most effective learning.

Evaluation. The final element of evaluation reintroduces the question of values because it is through the identification of values that one *e-value-ates*. In evaluation the Christian educator assesses formally and informally the extent to which stated or perhaps unstated purposes and goals have been addressed in actual practice. In evaluation the call is for responsibility and accountability. To a certain extent the outcomes of Christian education can be observed in terms of the change in knowledge, values, attitudes, skills, sensitivities, and behaviors manifested by both students and teachers. Evaluation is ultimately subject to divine assessment, yet Christian educators must devote the necessary time and energy to carefully observe and assess the results of their efforts and those of their students. The effectiveness of evaluation largely depends on the prior careful articulation of purposes and goals that can be reconsidered and

65. D. Campbell Wyckoff, *The Task of Christian Education* (Philadelphia: Westminster, 1955), 104.
66. See page 97, fig. 6.

measured after regular periods of time. Evaluation strives to combine both objective and subjective criteria for judgment.

Modern Philosophies of Education

Having considered the specifics of an educational philosophy, we now survey a number of modern philosophies to identify their distinctive elements. Burgess's first five categories (goals, content, teacher, student, and environment) will be used to outline the distinctive elements of each philosophy. The sixth category (evaluation) will be used to critique each philosophy. The following educational philosophies will be considered: perennialism, essentialism, behaviorism, progressivism, reconstructionism, romantic naturalism, and existentialism.[67] Some of these philosophies can be viewed as complementary in actual practice, but for the purpose of description they will be viewed as distinct.

Perennialism

Perennialism emphasizes the cultivation of rational powers along with academic excellence. It affirms intellectual, spiritual, and ethical purpose in education in guiding the individual to the eternal truths. Goals include the transmission and assimilation of a prescribed body of classical subject matter. Classical advocates of this philosophy include Aristotle and Thomas Aquinas and more recently Robert Hutchins, Mortimer Adler, Allan Bloom, and Jacques Maritain.[68]

The content for a perennialist education includes *Great Books of the Western World*, the classics, and the traditional liberal arts. The mind and reason are emphasized in exposing students to the great works of the Western intellectual past. The curriculum is subject centered, with stress on mental discipline and literary analysis.

Teachers are viewed as academic scholars, philosophers par excellence who have a grasp of vast areas of knowledge and wisdom. Corresponding to the teacher's role, students are viewed as rational beings who are to be guided by the first principles as revealed in the classics and liberal arts.

For perennialism, the primary settings for learning include the classroom or lecture hall, the study, and the library, where the classical heritage can be shared or acquired through diligent study.

67. See Knight, *Philosophy and Education*, 90–126, for a detailed description of these philosophies and theories.
68. Ibid., 102–8.

Perennialism can be affirmed for its sensitivity to the past, for its concern for rationality, and for its emphasis on excellence. This philosophy maintains that absolute truth exists and that human nature is consistent. Perennialists recognize the intellectual, spiritual, and ethical purposes of education. Perennialism can be criticized for its preoccupation with the past and a tendency toward rationalism. Its curricular uniformity may squelch creativity, and its totally intellectual and teacher-directed approach may not recognize the whole character of persons and the limits of human reason.

Essentialism

Essentialist educators stress academic excellence, the cultivation of the intellect, and the transmission and assimilation of a prescribed body of subject matter. The discernment of truths from this perspective is possible through the use of careful observation and reason. The primary advocates of this position are Arthur Bestor and Admiral Hyman G. Rickover.[69]

For essentialism the content of education includes the fundamental academic disciplines and the mastery of basic and advanced knowledge. Distinct from perennialism, essentialism considers modern scientific and experimental inquiry in addition to classical studies as being essential. Essentialism stresses a movement in education back to the basics along with the mastery of those basics defined broadly to include a variety of subject matter.

For essentialism, the model teacher is the person of letters and sciences who is in touch with the modern world and who has achieved the level of an expert in the area of her or his competence. Students are viewed as rational beings who are gaining command of essential facts and skills that undergird the intellectual disciplines in adjusting to the physical and social environment.

Like perennialism, essentialism centers on the primary settings of the classroom and library but also emphasizes the research laboratory. Students are to gain access to a wide array of academic disciplines through their study in these settings.

Essentialism can be affirmed for its emphasis on the mastery of basic learning skills and its recognition of the need for hard work and discipline in learning. This philosophy also recognizes the intellectual, spiritual, and ethical purposes in education. But distinct from perennialism, essentialism is not totally intellectual and manifests a greater concern for individual adjustment to the physical and social environment. Criticisms can be raised in relation to its teacher-directedness and its possible tendency toward rationalism. It

69. Ibid., 108–12.

can lead to exclusivism if the needs of exceptional persons are ignored in its emphasis on sharing exposure to broad fields of knowledge that may not relate to personal or corporate experience.

Behaviorism

Behaviorists strive to form persons who function with efficiency, economy, precision, and objectivity. Education serves to shape persons in prescribed behaviors and responses as determined by the educators. This shaping contributes to the end of a controlled or conditioned society that maintains equilibrium while reducing conflict. The person most closely associated with behaviorism is B. F. Skinner.[70]

A behaviorist philosophy incorporates a behavioral modification sequence to achieve desired student responses and skills and uses appropriate reinforcement. Clear and precise behavioral objectives are stated, and students are exposed to a rewarding environment with the possible use of programmed instruction and other instructional technologies.

Teachers are viewed as skilled technicians, sculptors of both persons and environments. A behaviorist approach strives to develop students as well-sculptured, conditioned persons who are responsive to a societal ideal. Students are viewed as highly malleable beings in need of clear and definitive direction for optimal functioning.

The appropriate setting for learning is a carefully controlled instructional environment where peripheral stimulation can be eliminated or unattended.

Behaviorism can be affirmed for its careful consideration of action and behaviors along with its conscious attention to environmental influences. This educational philosophy has been effective with some student populations and with certain discrete behaviors. The major critique of behaviorism is its reductionistic conception of human beings with an exclusive or limited focus on behavior. Persons are more than well-conditioned animals. Freedom and dignity have a place in a Christian view of humans, and transformation beyond the realms of conditioning is possible in a theistic perspective.

Progressivism

Progressivism fosters the development of reflective thinking for social problem solving, democratic relationships, and growth. Progressive educators strive to enable students to learn how to learn in order to adapt to a changing

70. Ibid., 118–23.

world. Life adjustment in terms of societal expectations is a key goal in this perspective. Progressive thinkers in education include John Dewey, William Kirkpatrick, Boyd H. Bode, and John L. Childs.[71]

The content of education for progressivism is a comprehensive, unified exposure to problem-focused studies. Curriculum centers on social problem solving through the reflective thinking of the scientific method and the use of democratic processes. Cooperative learning is stressed with a priority given to students' needs and interests. Wherever possible, students are permitted freedom of choice, and they should also consider the communal implications of their choices.

The teacher is not an authoritarian classroom director as is the case for perennialism, essentialism, and behaviorism. Rather, the teacher is a person concerned with progress, committed to society and democratic ideals, and sensitive to the growth of students. Thus the teacher is a fellow learner, traveler, and guide who facilitates the group learning process. For progressives, students are autonomously thinking and socially responsible individuals who are called to work democratically and cooperatively with others. Persons are viewed as organisms in ecological continuity with others and their social environment. Students are to be actively engaged in their own learning and that of others.

The preferred setting is the democratic classroom that is sensitive to and reflective of the wider society. In a real sense, the educational setting for progressivism is the world because the learning experience is a part of life, not a separated preparation for life.

Progressivism can be affirmed for its concern for persons, who are viewed as active participants in the learning process. This philosophy encourages a sensitivity to student experiences, needs, and interests, along with a concern for cooperative learning. It deals with issues of everyday life and breaks the dichotomy between academic formality and daily living experience. Progressivism can be criticized for its potentially optimistic view of humans, which does not recognize the effects of sin. Persons cannot solve their own problems without God. Progressivism also evidences relativist tendencies in terms of truth and values and an antisupernatural bias in the case of John Dewey, who has served as its major spokesperson.

Reconstructionism

A reconstructionist educational philosophy holds the goal of building an ideal and just social order. Efforts are directed toward the establishment of

71. Ibid., 91–97.

a practical utopia in which persons are liberated to be and become all they are intended to be. Reconstructionists include Theodore Brameld, George C. Counts, and Paulo Freire.[72]

The content of reconstructionist education centers on social problems and the development of corrective programs scientifically determined for collective action. Social flaws are critically analyzed in the effort to explore problems for consideration. The identification and analysis of problems can facilitate the corporate exploration of concrete alternatives.

Teachers are viewed as subversive educators, social critics, and community organizers who seek to raise the consciousness of others in the direction of needed change. Students are viewed as potential agents of change committed to and involved in constructive social redirection and renewal.

The settings for teaching are varied and include the classroom, the small cell or group meeting, the community center, the streets, and the fields.

Reconstructionism can be affirmed for its critical examination of current social, political, and economic orders and for its concern for social needs. Reconstructionists seriously grapple with human responsibility in the corporate and social realms. They recognize problems in current society and see possibilities for reform and change. Educators in this perspective are viewed as primary instruments for social change. Reconstructionists, while recognizing social sins, may ignore the realities of personal sin in the liberators and the oppressed as well as in the oppressors. Their preoccupation with the social order may result in ignoring personal responsibilities, and their emphasis on change may fail to see the need for continuity in personal and corporate life.

Romantic Naturalism

Romantic naturalism values individual freedom to develop one's potential with the goal of self-actualization. Self-fulfillment and realization are to be fostered through the various growth processes of education that stress creative expression. Those who have advocated this perspective include John Holt, Ivan Illich, A. S. Neill, and Carl Rogers.[73]

Learning activities are based on a person's felt and real needs, which are identified with the help of others. The curriculum provides for a free learning environment with the maximization of artistic self-expression and creativity.

Teachers are viewed as visionaries who provide the space for self-discovery and exploration by others. Teachers are sufficiently permissive and supportive to allow others their freedom in learning. Students are regarded as unfolding

72. Ibid., 112–16.
73. Ibid., 76–84.

flowers unencumbered by societal limitations. They are encouraged to learn in a variety of modes that best suit their individual dispositions.

The ideal settings for education include the free school, the open classroom, the open world, and the home, where students may be free from intense competition, harsh discipline, and the fear of failure. Such settings could be described as laissez-faire in climate or "deschooled" where schooling is associated with rigidity and imposition.

Romantic naturalism can be affirmed for its concern for individuals, human freedom, aesthetics, and creativity. It can be criticized for its negation of the teacher's responsibility and authority to share necessary wisdom and direction. In their stress on freedom, romantics can deny the realities of human sin and can negate the need for social responsiveness and discipline.

Existentialism

Existentialism as an educational philosophy emphasizes the inner search for meaning for one's own existence in the realization of authentic personhood. Advocates of existentialism in education include Maxine Greene, Martin Buber, and Carl Rogers.[74]

The content of an existentialist education centers on the themes of the human condition with learning activities free of rational constraints. These activities are designed to free the individual to find her or his own being. The curriculum includes opportunities for introspection and reflection in a free learning environment open to change.

Teachers are viewed as fellow inquirers with students and fellow travelers in the quest for meaning. They are authentic persons who are mature and deep in their understanding of life. Students are persons in search of the meaning of their own existence and open for inquiry and exploration.

The ideal setting for this in-depth learning should allow for the personal encounter that explores the inner world. A classroom where reflection and introspection are valued provides one such setting, but others can be imagined.

Existentialism as an educational philosophy can be affirmed for its concern for the individual and the place of personal choice. It values authenticity and integrity, emphasizes personal responsibilities, and encourages both the creativity and discovery of students. Existentialism revolts against the materialist and conformist tendencies of modern society and acknowledges the presence of alienation. But existentialism can be criticized when a focus on individuals

74. Ibid.

diminishes the authority of the teacher. It can lead to an overly introspective stance that reduces realities to experiential and relative categories devoid of absolutes or universals. The existential focus on personal existence and choice as primary may diminish the place of God's existence and choice. Truth may be ever-expanding and changing in this philosophy with little possibility for continuity in life or in the Christian heritage.

Postmodernism

More than an explicit educational philosophy, postmodernism can be considered an "educational impulse" representing a shift in the history of ideas.[75] My analysis of the educational implications of this impulse is explored in the appendices of this work. A description of this impulse or movement is warranted here. As Knight suggests, postmodernism draws on pragmatism, which influenced progressivism, existentialism, and reconstructionism through Marxist thought.[76] These influences question the claims of the Christian faith in relation to metanarratives, transcultural universals, and revelation. The claims of absolutes for all creation and truths applicable to all persons are refuted by postmodern critiques of historic Christian beliefs. Nevertheless, the invitations implicit in such critiques require that Christians carefully interpret authoritative texts and be aware of both educational contexts and processes in new ways with new audiences influenced by cultural and ideational changes.

The antifoundationalism of postmodernism calls Christian educators to revisit foundational issues and questions with new eyes and perspectives. Such a revisitation does not discount the need for stability and direction along with points of continuity. The shifts in the educational landscape have been compared by Leonard Sweet in his works *Aqua Church* and *Post-Modern Pilgrims* with launching a ship on changing waters. Sweet proposes an *epic* model for education that stresses *e*xperiential instead of rational learning, *p*articipatory rather than representative strategies, *i*mage-driven rather than word-based methods, and a *c*onnected rather than an individual focus.[77] In contrast to Sweet, I would opt for both-and approaches to the categories that he proposes: both experiential and rational, both participatory and representative, both image-driven and word-based, and both connected and individual. To extend Sweet's metaphor, Christian pilgrims still must construct a seaworthy ship to

---

75. See George R. Knight, *Philosophy and Education: An Introduction in Christian Perspective*, 4th ed. (Berrien Springs, MI: Andrews University Press, 2006), 89–102.

76. Ibid.

77. Leonard I. Sweet, *Aqua Church: Essential Leadership Arts for Piloting Your Church in Today's Fluid Culture* (Loveland, CO: Group, 1999); and *Post-Modern Pilgrims* (Nashville: Broadman & Holman, 2000).

navigate turbulent waters and to survive storms with options. The articulation of a viable Christian philosophy proposes to assist Christians in their ship construction, building on the insights shared by the apostle Paul to the Christians in Corinth. The insights from 1 Corinthians 3:10–23 are as applicable to ship construction as they are to more permanent land construction: "Each builder must choose with care how to build . . ." (1 Cor. 3:10 NRSV). Those who construct seaworthy ships attend to the sources of the raw materials used in their work. Educational theorists and practitioners who propose postmodern visions must draw upon trustworthy sources in their shipbuilding and must have sufficient food and water on board for their journeys. While in port, educators who travel on postmodern seas must secure replenishable sources as guided by their philosophies for educational ventures. Those who venture into educational thought and practice must exercise discernment in their choice of the nautical maps and celestial visions to guide their efforts.

The Choice of Philosophies

A careful blending of the various philosophies described above best contributes to educational practice. This can be appreciated by locating these philosophies or approaches in a framework suggested by Hollis Caswell, educator and curriculum theorist (see fig. 9).

Caswell's framework distinguishes three different foci for education: student interests, social functions, and organized knowledge.[78] In other words, educational philosophies may center on persons, communities or societies, or content as their primary focus while recognizing the place of the other two foci. Thus perennialism and essentialism can be seen as philosophies that are content-centered, while behaviorism and reconstructionism are society-centered. Romantic naturalism and existentialism are primarily person-centered. Progressivism emphasizes both the society and its democratic processes and persons in need of growth, but it is primarily society-centered.

With these various foci or centers, educators are challenged with the need for a choice. But as John Dewey asserts in *The School and Society* and *The Child and the Curriculum*, education embodies teaching content to persons in the context of their community and society; extremes in any approach limit a holistic perspective.[79]

---

78. Hollis L. Caswell and Doak S. Campbell, *Curriculum Development* (New York: American Book Co., 1935), 141–89.

79. See Martin S. Dworkin, *Dewey on Education: Selections* (New York: Teachers College Press, 1959), 33–111.

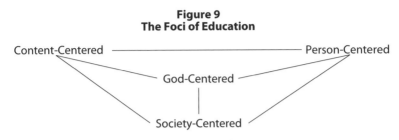

Figure 9
The Foci of Education

These three approaches to education—person-centered, content-centered, and society-centered—might be roughly likened to the considerations in the preparation of a meal. The content-centered advocate is primarily concerned with the detailed preparation and serving of the food itself. The society-centered advocate is primarily concerned with the choice of the food in relation to the group assembled and the nutritional content of the menu in terms of preparing the guests for the activities during and following the meal. The person-centered advocate desires to please and is sensitive to the individual tastes of each of the guests and their unique needs. Hollis Caswell contends that the educator can act like a chemist, processing the various elements of students' interests, social functions, and organized knowledge in effective teaching.

Using Caswell's framework, we can conceive of various combinations of emphases that involve the three centers. It is also possible to conceive of a change in emphases within a particular class or group over time. Given the variation and combination of emphases, the educator's problem is how to maintain an adequate balance in her or his class, curriculum, or educational program. Evangelical educators have proposed that a God-centered education offers an alternative and that a Christian life view provides distinctive elements to guide the entire educational process. What, then, is a God-centered approach to education, and how is it related to Caswell's framework?

A God-centered approach establishes as its starting point the authority of God as revealed through Jesus Christ and illumined by the Holy Spirit within Scripture. From the Bible, viewed as the guide for Christian faith and practice, essential principles are derived that impact educational efforts. One such guiding principle is the affirmation that all truth is God's truth, which implies a unity in truth and a correspondence between scriptural truth and reality. This principle calls for a joyful acceptance of truths in Scripture without subjection to a rigid literalism.

As was previously stated, the evangelical is not exempt from the tasks of hermeneutics and the challenge to contextualize biblical truths in contemporary settings. A God-centered approach subjects all truth claims to scriptural scrutiny while recognizing that the Bible is not an exhaustive source of truth and knowledge. Thus, any truth claims are initially judged in terms of their consistency with a Christian world and life view. A God-centered approach, with its recognition of the primacy of biblical authority, does not neglect knowledge discerned through nature, rationality, tradition, history, intuition, and even imagination. But insights derived from these sources are always secondary to Scripture. This approach recognizes that certain educational issues are not resolved by a flippant proof-texting or referral to biblical principles that ignores adequate grappling with the questions. Such a grappling recognizes the context of life that is explored with five cities in global perspective.

A Tale of Five Cities in Global Perspective

The question of a philosophy of education can also be addressed in relation to the question posed many centuries ago by Tertullian in his work *Against Hermogenes*: "What has Jerusalem to do with Athens?" Tertullian contended that philosophy was to be denounced and that Athens, symbolizing the intellectual and philosophical life, had nothing to do with Jerusalem, which symbolized the religious life. My perspective, expressed in this chapter and throughout this book, disagrees with Tertullian's response but suggests that his question is significant. In fact, Tertullian's comparison between two cities can be expanded to include five cities or ports of call in a more contemporary global perspective. The five cities are Jerusalem and Athens along with Nazareth, Rome, and Prague.

Nazareth can be identified with Galilee, which was a center of multicultural life that even in Jesus's day elicited the scorn of those who preferred cultural purity, contending that "nothing good" could come from this region. Yet it was in Nazareth of Galilee that Jesus lived most of his life and invested a large portion of his public ministry. The multicultural life symbolized by Galilee and the city of Nazareth is an important aspect of life in a globalized society, where cultures daily collide. The relation of multicultural life to both the intellectual life and the religious life is a current issue for discussion among Christian educators.[80]

Prague, in the area of the Czech Republic known as Bohemia, can be identified with the artistic or aesthetic life. As will be explored in chapter 4, the place of the arts and imagination (or *poesis* in Greek terms) has

---

80. See my work *Latin American Journey: Insights for Christian Education in North America* (Eugene, OR: Wipf & Stock, 2002) for a discussion of these issues.

reemerged in educational thought and practice. This suggests the emergence of a new Middle Ages with a postliterate culture that is highly dependent on various media as an alternative to the written word as a means to convey the faith to current and future generations. The relation of aesthetic life to the religious, intellectual, and multicultural dimensions of life thus becomes a current issue to explore in developing one's educational philosophy and in the choice of educational methods that engage the imagination and foster creativity. Increased interest in the arts and music as vehicles for teaching can be observed.

Finally, the inclusion of Rome raises the question of institutional and political life. In the first century Rome symbolized the center of the political power of the Roman Empire as well as its economic and social power. In current use Rome can also symbolize that arm of the Christian church that models an explicit concern for institutional and political life, the Roman Catholic Church. In an institutionalized world, Christian educators must attend to the relationships between and among the political, religious, intellectual, multicultural, and aesthetic dimensions of life in their teaching. In formulating their philosophies, Christian educators can ask a host of questions: What does Athens have to do with Jerusalem? What does Prague have to do with Rome? And so on. Certainly additional cities and symbols can be suggested to pose issues and questions of educational import. For example, Hollywood, California, could be another city to include because of the global influence of media and entertainment and the curriculum embodied in this impact. But these five cities and the relationships they symbolize serve to underscore the need for Christian educators to wrestle with philosophical foundations that can guide practice.

This survey of philosophical foundations has identified essential issues that demand the continuous attention of Christian educators who seek to be diligent in the task of thinking after Christ in the area of Christian education. Careful thought is not anathema to the faithful practice of Christian education, and it is essential to meet the challenges of the modern world. All Christian educators, even those most enamored with practice itself, have philosophies or theories that guide them. Without attention to philosophical foundations, Christian educators have wandered into the deserts of cultural accommodation or cultural irrelevance and have failed to provide the vision necessary to guide their generation and those to come in relating God's truth, in its beauty and wholeness, to the tasks of Christian education. It is no longer possible to affirm this irresponsible approach and claim to be faithful. The call to be faithful also applies to a careful consideration of one's place in history, which is the focus of the next chapter.

Points to Ponder

- Write your own definitions for both education in general and Christian education in particular to share with others.
- Which of the philosophical questions named by DeJong are most important for you and why?
- What authorities guide educational thought and practice in your Christian community and why?
- How do you see metaphysics, axiology, and epistemology influencing each other and which has priority for your community's educational practices?
- Which of the educational philosophies identified most resonate with your perspective and why? To which educational philosophy are you most opposed, and how do educational experiences influence your view?
- Identify additional global cities to consider besides the five noted and suggest their importance for your educational perspective.

4

Historical Foundations

The first three chapters of this book have explored the biblical, theological, and philosophical foundations of Christian education. Through the study of these foundations, Christian educators seek to identify transcultural and cultural universals or principles to guide their thought and practice. In investigating historical foundations, educators are forced to consider aspects of education that are more subject to change and various contingencies in different times and places. These aspects, though evidencing points of continuity, can be identified as cultural variables over against the transcultural and cultural universals discerned through biblical, theological, and philosophical study.

Vigilance is necessary to avoid an ahistorical mind-set. In dealing with the challenges of educational ministries, Christians can learn from the past to gain insights for current and future needs. The dominant North American culture values the present and the future and all too frequently ignores principles from the past worthy of continued emphasis. To remedy this situation, Christian educators can affirm the educational principles embodied in the orthodox faith and evidenced through the study of history. A consideration of historical foundations can also identify aspects of historical particularity that require careful attention if one is to address one's unique time and location.

History and Historical Method

Marc Bloch has helpfully defined history as "the science of persons over time."[1] History is a *science* in the sense that it is a disciplined and objective

1. Marc Bloch, *The Historian's Craft*, introduction by Joseph R. Strayer, trans. Peter Putnam (New York: Alfred A. Knopf, 1953), 20–47.

inquiry concerned with the analysis of documents and other evidence. History is a science *of persons* in the sense that it is concerned with individuals and groups of persons in a concrete sense and with understanding persons in their concrete situations. History is a science of persons *over time* in the sense that historical time is not a mere abstraction but a concrete and living reality with a constantly changing and developing character. Thus the task of historical understanding is a continuous one as time progresses and provides new perspectives on the past. History focuses on a concrete and living reality with a constantly changing and developing character.

The historical method in a narrow sense centers on a pursuit of truth based on careful investigation and cross-examination of documentary evidence. The object of history in this sense is to discover and set forth facts. In a broad sense, the historical method involves a methodology that uses the data and facts accumulated through the critical examination of documents to understand the past. Such an understanding requires interpretation, and Christian educators can avail themselves of those insights gained through the historical method in both its narrow and broad senses.

R. G. Collingwood maintains that the historian is concerned to deal with both the outside and the inside of an event and to view past actions as a unity of both dimensions.[2] The outside of an event consists of those facts discovered through investigation. The inside of an event comprises the thoughts, intentions, motives, and beliefs of persons of which actions, institutions, and all other expressions are embodiments. The historian's goal is to understand persons' consciousness, thoughts, values, beliefs, and intentions, and their expressions in time and space. The historian also considers the changes of these dimensions over time and in different contexts. Following Collingwood's perspective, Christian educators can appreciate both the inside and the outside of events, which are explored through the use of the historical method in its dual sense.

Historians are interested in the unique, the individual, and the particular in the past. All historians seek to maintain an essential tension between the universal and the particular, between the general and the unique. Given this perspective, they are concerned with development and change over time. Aspects of persons' lives that change over time include their ideas, beliefs, intentions, and commitments. As a result of such changes, other dimensions of life are transformed, including laws, institutions, programs, and views of life. Thus the historian has a particular interest in the potentiality, the mutability, and diversity among persons over time. In fact, the claim can be made that

2. R. G. Collingwood, *The Idea of History* (Oxford: Clarendon Press, 1946), 210–31.

to adequately understand anything human, one must recount its history and grasp the particularity revealed in such a recounting.

The historian views the past from an individualizing, rather than a generalizing, point of view. This distinguishes history from the social sciences, though historians have increasingly made use of the social sciences. Social scientists primarily have nomothetic concerns (*nomos* refers to a law or standard) in formulating generalizations, norms, and laws based on abstraction and application to general phenomena. Historians are primarily concerned with an idiographic perspective (i.e., they are concerned with inquiring into unique and particular phenomena). The historian assumes the uniqueness of each person and affirms that meaning is context dependent.

Historical understanding is dependent on specific situations or settings. The historian views the similarities or continuities and points of discontinuity in which the particular stands in relation to the universal, in which the specific stands in relation to the general. For example, the educational historian can make use of a sociology of education and yet not be dependent on sociological explanations that tend to reduce the complexities of persons and human interactions to corporate relationships. Rather than being limited to a sociological perspective, the educational historian views realities not readily observable from a scientific viewpoint. The historian considers the pervasive spirit of a particular age or culture and the varied intentions and interests of persons, groups, and institutions.

History and Education

History cannot serve as a search for quick and easy solutions to present and future problems. History does not disclose particular and concrete answers for dilemmas in the field of education. Rather, history provides an awareness of both the possibilities and the complexities of education. It also helps persons to discern the continuity or carryover of the past into the present and the future along with points of discontinuity.[3] From historical inquiry it is possible to discern the persistent and recurring interests, concerns, problems, and issues in the field of education.

But vestiges of education's past—which include not only physical objects, such as textbooks and school architecture, but also mental attitudes, values, institutional structures, and ideologies—must be appropriated critically

3. Arno A. Bellack, "History of Curriculum Thought and Practice," *Review of Educational Research* 39 (June 1969): 291.

because of the greater emphasis on the "search for the usable past."[4] There is a danger that persons will absolutely reject the tradition represented by such vestiges. Such a response may fail to recognize the stability of tradition and its sustaining nature, which can ensure a moderate rate of change and lend orderliness to transitions in a rapidly changing world.[5]

Even beyond points of continuity, history serves to outline points of discontinuity with the past. For example, educational questions may be similar to those of the Middle Ages, yet those questions may be asked in a different way. Thus historical investigation must explore additional contextual factors beyond the educational matrix. For example, the question of how to share the Christian faith with children is a recurrent one, but as it is posed in the twenty-first century with the rise of the new media is quite distinct from a first-century context.

In addition to stimulating our awareness of continuities and discontinuities, history can broaden understanding beyond a limited focus on the past and provide inspiration for current and projected educational efforts.[6] History reveals not only the ecology of education in the past but also the pathology of education. The ecology of education is the interactive network of factors and forces that result in effective and positive educational experience. The pathology of education reveals forces of indifference, apathy, ignorance, and vested interest that result in miseducation or the lack of needed education.[7]

An understanding of both the ecology and the pathology of education is needed to gain a critical assessment of the history of education. Education must be seen in terms of both its liberative and its oppressive effects on persons, groups, and society at large. The past is a mixture of both good and bad, and this must be recognized in the area of education. The history of the great expansion and popularization of education in the United States portrays a complex ecology of institutions that teach persons, but it also reveals the pathology of those excluded and ignored.

A third contribution of history to education is enabling persons to see the broader stream of cultural and intellectual history of which education is just one facet.[8] In studying and practicing education, educators must explore

4. Edward Shils, "Tradition and Liberty: Antimony and Interdependence," *Ethics* 68 (1958): 153–65.
5. Kenneth Charlton, "The Contribution of History to the Study of the Curriculum," in *Changing the Curriculum*, ed. John F. Kerr (London: University of London Press, 1968), 70.
6. Bellack, "Curriculum Thought and Practice," 291.
7. Charlton, "Contribution of History," 75.
8. Bellack, "Curriculum Thought and Practice," 291.

the wider societal context and consider those economic, political, and social interests and ideologies that affect efforts to pass on wisdom and knowledge to other persons. Different views of history exist, and it is important to ask which values and orientations guide a particular historical explanation and interpretation. Without asking this question and others, the readers of history may not be able to assess the validity of the suggested interpretation. History must be more than a political statement. Careful consideration must be given, for example, to the impact of science on the life and worldviews of those making and writing history in the twentieth century.

History and Christian Education

Martin Luther considered history the story of divine providence and a practical guide for life. He praised historians for aiding the understanding of worldly events and for noting the wonderful acts of God.[9] The Christian educator can regard accounts of earlier efforts in Christian education as sources of key insights and lessons. In response to such lessons, educators can take a stance of affirmation and/or criticism in light of both the liberating and the oppressive effects of past efforts. Thus the past serves as an ever-present tutor for present and future Christian education.

Christian educators do not have to reinvent the wheel. Through the study of history, they have the potential to identify principles, purposes, and goals of education that may be eternal and unchanging. They may also adapt educational strategies and methodologies that were effective in the past to present realities. Several key questions can be posed in affirming the past: (1) What caused an awakening, renewal, or growth in godliness and how did educational efforts foster this development? (2) How did Christians effectively relate their faith to their cultures, and how did they educate for this living faith? (3) How were persons' needs effectively addressed, and what biblical demands were formative in this response? How were biblical virtues and demands interpreted or applied in this particular setting? (4) What vision, conceptions, and rationale grounded effective educational work, and how were these communicated to and owned by others?

George Santayana's oft-quoted insight is worth repeating: Those who ignore the mistakes of the past are bound to repeat them.[10] Christian educators must

9. Harold J. Grimm, "Martin Luther (1483–1546)," in *A History of Religious Educators*, ed. Elmer L. Towns (Grand Rapids: Baker, 1975), 114.

10. George Santayana, *The Life of Reason; or The Phases of Human Progress*, vol. 1 (New York: Charles Scribner's Sons, 1905–6), chap. 12.

carefully assess how social, economic, political, technological, and religious factors in the larger culture or a subculture have hindered effective educational efforts and renewal. In this assessment they must be aware of the effects of classism, racism, sexism, ageism, and other forms of coercion, imposition, and oppression that have prevented the formation of whole persons, that is, persons created in God's image and reflecting that reality and potential in all areas of their lives. Much can be learned from the mistakes of the past if persons are willing to rely on God's grace and seek the forgiveness of God and others in owning the past.

Beyond these areas of affirmation and criticism, the Christian can appropriate history with a sense of appreciation and inspiration—despite warnings that history should not be used exclusively for political purposes or as a form of evangelism that focuses solely on inspiration.[11] Inspiration is a secondary result of the pursuit of truth through historical investigation because a Christian worldview affirms God as an active agent in the historical process. Christians can appreciate God's transcendent intervention in the world and God's immanent working through persons and all creation. The Christian educator can discern how God has revealed and transmitted truths through various educational processes in the past.

Christian educators can compare and contrast past developments in Christian education from those in general and ask these questions: (1) How were Christian philosophies of education formulated, and how did they differ among different persons and groups? (2) How was the actual practice of education affected by new light and vision from Christian sources? (3) What was the extent of cultural accommodation of the faith as compared with cultural renewal in the area of Christian education? Through such study, Christians may be inspired by the realization that others have trod a similar path, encountering and overcoming obstacles through their faith in God. History reveals that persons make history and can be used by God to redirect historical developments in significant ways.

History also reveals that God is active through all persons who retain the image of God, though marred, and who are sustained divinely in their efforts. All persons discover truths of God's creation, providence, and/or redemption, but the particular challenge for Christians is to discern which "truths" apply to the thought and practice of Christian education or which "truths" are in fact consistent with a Christian worldview. This is a constantly challenging and arduous task from which no Christian is exempt in his or her sphere of responsibility and calling. Two basic questions are at stake in this task from

11. Bellack, "Curriculum Thought and Practice," 291.

the perspective of the history of Christian education: To what extent were truth, love, peace, and justice practiced in the previous Christian education effort? And how does this understanding and appreciation challenge and/or warn us? As was noted in the case of history in general, the responses to these questions will reveal a varied record of faithfulness and sin, of obedience and disobedience to God's will for persons and the entire creation.

Every community has a heritage or memory that can serve to guide its life. The Christian community is one such community, and the heritage or history of Christian education can help guide present and future ministries. Christian education and education in general have depended on what Bernard Bailyn has identified as the great axles of society in his study of education in colonial North America: family, church, community, and economy.[12] In the context of contemporary society, education also depends on the school, the media, and various social and community agencies and groups. As these fundamental social institutions or agencies have shifted over the generations in their relative impact on persons, the forms of education have also shifted.[13]

In colonial New England, the family and the church were the dominant educational agencies in persons' lives. Input from the family and church generally confirmed and complemented each other, with the church being a gathering of families or households. Households represented a more inclusive group than the nuclear family, for it included multiple generations and extended family members. In contemporary North American society, the school and the media are dominant influences in the educational experiences of persons. Furthermore, input from the media may often contradict the values and commitments stressed by the family and the church. The conflict resulting from such contradiction has necessitated the development of strategies to resolve or avoid the conflict.

Through various epochs of history, the church has developed different agencies and instruments by which it has sought to fulfill its educational task in relation to the other axles or institutions of society. Education has been the means most often utilized for initiating both adult converts and the young into the practices and beliefs of the Christian community. This goal is partially,

---

12. Bernard Bailyn, *Education in the Forming of American Society* (New York: W. W. Norton, 1960), 45. For a discussion of these educational agencies or structures, see Robert W. Pazmiño, *Principles and Practices of Christian Education: An Evangelical Perspective* (1992; Eugene, OR: Wipf & Stock, 2002), 59–90.

13. William Bean Kennedy, "Christian Education through History," in *An Introduction to Christian Education,* ed. Marvin J. Taylor (Nashville: Abingdon, 1966), 21. Kennedy draws heavily on the work of Lewis J. Sherrill in *The Rise of Christian Education* (New York: Macmillan, 1944). See the table of contents in Sherrill's work for an outline of the historical periods Kennedy suggests.

though indirectly, addressed as the community participates in worship, shares its common life, and follows ethical teachings. Christian groups have also almost universally developed institutions, programs, and methods to directly pursue the goal of initiating others in the Christian faith and in encouraging their discipleship as Christians.[14]

Douglas Sloan, an educational historian, points out that churches, beyond their particular educational agenda, have given expression to many of the core values and life views of the larger community. They have also borne the prime responsibility for certifying, preserving, transmitting, and transforming those values and views from generation to generation. In this effort the church has employed all the traditional means of education: teachings of the Christian faith; teachers (ministers, theologians, Sunday school workers, and spiritual guides); textbooks (Scripture, confessions, creeds, and commentaries); and teaching aids (rituals, sermons, catechisms, and spiritual disciplines). In a broader sense, too, as the outward expression of the ideas, values, convictions, and prejudices of a culture and its subcultures, Christian faith has often furnished the very material and the matrix of education. Moreover, Christian movements have at various times had an impact on defining reality, sanctioning and rationalizing behavior, and developing social visions and goals that can be described as educational.[15] Such a broadened view of the role of the Christian church provides the context in which to consider the Christian education heritage. We will survey this heritage from the pre-Christian sources of Old Testament and Greek education to post-Reformation developments in the United States. Only key issues will be highlighted with an emphasis on areas of continuity.[16]

The Old Testament

Old Testament teaching included instruction and admonition. Instruction involved informing persons about God's truths and demands; admonition entailed challenging persons in their way of life. Education centered on

14. Marvin J. Taylor, ed., *Religious Education: A Comprehensive Survey* (Nashville: Abingdon, 1960), 11.

15. Douglas Sloan, *Historiography and the History of Education*, Occasion Paper no. 3 (New York: Institute of Philosophy and Politics of Education, Teachers College, Columbia University, n.d.), 16.

16. More detailed accounts are available in other sources. For example, see Kenneth O. Gangel and Warren S. Benson, *Christian Education: Its History and Philosophy* (Chicago: Moody, 1983); and John H. Westerhoff III and O. C. Edwards Jr., eds., *A Faithful Church: Issues in the History of Catechesis* (Wilton, CT: Morehouse-Barlow, 1981).

the Torah, the law of God, first communicated orally, then written in the Scriptures, which contained the very moral and spiritual revelation of God. God was the measure of all things; all of life was dedicated to God. The purpose of education in the Old Testament accounts was to lead persons to holiness and transformation. The Torah served to reveal God's demands of or expectations for persons. Persons were to be trained in the very ways of God, and the focus was on godly character and wisdom that would issue in moral action. The law was to be lived; obedience was the fruit of a faithful response to education.

The primary context for this education was the home, and parents were responsible for instructing their children in the law, bringing them into marriage, and teaching them a trade.[17] Beyond the centrality of the home as a house of worship, participation in communal religious life served to educate persons. Priests were experts in ritual life bridging the gap between persons and God, and prophets spoke God's Word, protesting the violation of it in personal and corporate life. Wise persons addressed ethical questions and shared guidance for practically working out dedication to God.[18] During and subsequent to the exile, synagogues and schools were developed to teach the Hebrew language, oral tradition, and the written Scriptures.

Teaching methodology depended on oral communication aided by various memory aids, including poetry, wordplay, and acrostics. Teaching was conducted at scheduled times and also on spontaneous occasions (Deut. 6:7), with significant time devoted to instruction (Neh. 8:3). Visual aids were used in teaching (Exod. 12:1–28; Deut. 6:4–9; Josh. 4:1–24), along with music and psalms. The guiding principle in all these teaching efforts was that persons should bring honor and credit to the name of God and their families through their lives. God was honored through one's obedient life, which was an expression of worship and reverence. David Ng and Virginia Thomas's account of how the Hebrew child learned to worship describes the spirit of the Old Testament educational heritage:

> How did the Hebrew child learn to worship? First through a relationship with a worshiping parent, a member of a worshiping community; through intentional education built into the rituals of home and community worship; through a multitude of sensory experiences and vivid, thought-provoking symbols and dramas; through a life of ethical actions growing out of worship; through a pattern of recurring sabbath and festivals that recreated the Hebrews' story;

17. William Barclay, *Educational Ideals in the Ancient World* (Grand Rapids: Baker, 1974), 16.
18. See also the discussion of the Old Testament in chap. 1.

and eventually through a form of public, community gathering which made teaching an essential part of the liturgy.[19]

The Greek Heritage

In his discussion of Western education, Freeman Butts, an educational historian, makes this observation: "We think the way we do in large part because the Greeks thought the way they did. Thus, to understand our own ways of thinking we need to know how the Greeks thought."[20] Given this dependence on Greek thought in the West, educational thought and practice reflect distinctive features of the Greek intellectual heritage. Socrates maintained that knowledge itself was a virtue. For Socrates, to really know what is good is to prohibit one from doing evil. He stressed the place of reason and logic, with thinking itself viewed as objective reasoning. Human reason was the means by which one discerned divine revelation and its implications for all of life. Socrates stressed the importance of moral life, but not in terms of the God of the Hebrews.

Of greater subsequent influence in the Christian community was Plato. Plato defined education as the training in excellence from youth onward, which makes a person passionately desire to be a perfect citizen and teaches him or her how to rule with justice. He viewed only the ideal as real with actualities regarded as mere copies of the transcendent and perfect ideal. This aspect of Plato's thought was particularly attractive to Christian thinkers like Augustine, who later synthesized these insights with the Christian faith. Plato's idealism fostered a concern for social and political reform as a fruit of education in the lives of those who grasped the ideals.

In contrast to Plato's emphasis was that of the Sophists. The Sophists advocated the use of reason and believed that metaphysical questions were beyond solution. Therefore, they stressed human nature and human relations, which resulted in the belief in the relativity of all truth. Ultimately, persons, not God, who was beyond knowing, were the measure of all things. Their concern was with the world of the senses and with the effective use of reason. The perspective of the Sophists is associated with skepticism and individualism, which are dominant philosophies in the postmodern world.

Representing a mediating position between Plato and the Sophists was Aristotle. Balancing Plato's idealism and the Sophists' this-worldliness, Aristotle

19. David Ng and Virginia Thomas, *Children of the Worshiping Community* (Atlanta: John Knox Press, 1981), 52.
20. Freeman Butts, *A Cultural History of Western Education* (New York: McGraw-Hill, 1947), 45.

viewed matter as purposeless with form emerging as the mind or spirit transformed matter into something with life and purpose. Aristotle is associated with scientific empiricism and realism in emphasizing control of oneself and one's environment. Aristotle's golden mean stressed that nothing is to be done in excess, assuring discipline and control in the entire life process. Education was viewed as a means by which persons, through the use of reason and experience, could achieve balance and moderation in life through making right choices. Human virtue was based on knowledge of the world and its rational principles and was evidenced by appropriate behavior in all dimensions of life.

A Greek concept of particular significance is that of *paideia*. *Paideia* represents a culture's consensus about what constitutes human excellence. It reflects a culture's ideals and shared vision that shapes the calling of a nation-state as well as that of its individual citizens. Socrates, Plato, the Sophists, and Aristotle all had different visions and ideals. Further differences were apparent in their distinct visions of the city-states of Athens and Sparta. In Sparta the male ideal was the well-conditioned military leader with a courageous and bold character. In Athens the male ideal was the citizen developed both in mind and body with a strong intellect. Therefore, in considering any educational heritage, one must consider the controlling *paideia* in any particular community or effort. The ancient Greeks used the term to refer to "education," "culture," or "social, political, or ethical aspiration." But significantly, as Lawrence Cremin notes, some have considered the concept of *paideia* incompatible with individual freedom and growth, in that it entails the imposition of a corporate or communal vision on individuals. Nevertheless, he points out that individuality is impossible to define apart from some sort of community life.[21]

Paideia, communal vision, is a major challenge in the pluralistic society of the West. There exists a genuine quest for community on the part of many persons who do not relate that quest to a continuing and exclusive emphasis on their private and individual lives. A renewed awareness is needed in the Christian community in affirming the public and communal dimensions of life. Apart from such awareness, individuality and private life are truncated. Also, effective educational planning requires the articulation of a shared *paideia* within a particular faith community. For example, Ephesians 6:4 encourages fathers to bring up their children in the *paideia*, the discipline or instruction, of the Lord.

The biblical use of the term *paideia* refers to nurturing, chastening, and character formation, implying that persons are genuinely committed and

21. Lawrence Cremin, *Public Education* (New York: Basic Books, 1976), 39.

vitally related to one another in community. It also implies the existence of a vision for excellence within that community that directs the process of forming character and chastening and nurturing persons. Frank Gaebelein maintains that in Christian education those responsible have a duty to direct everyone "to the highest examples of excellence—namely, the most excellent of all books, the Bible, and the most excellent of all persons, Jesus Christ."[22] This duty demands the best efforts to pass on a Christian *paideia*, a Christian world and life view that addresses one's role in society.

 In addition to *paideia*, other issues emerge from the consideration of the Greek educational heritage. What is the nature of knowledge in a Christian perspective, and how is knowledge related to life? How is reason related to faith? What has Jerusalem to do with Athens? To what extent can Christianity be wed to a particular philosophy, or does Christianity itself imply a general philosophy and an educational philosophy? What Christian virtues should be fostered in Christian teaching? How does one balance commitments to the community with personal needs and aspirations? How does one fulfill Christian commitments in both the private and the public spheres of life and educate others in these responsibilities?

Abraham Heschel, a Jewish educator, has suggested a comparison of the insights from the Greek heritage with those of the Old Testament and today: "The Greeks learned in order to comprehend. The Hebrews learned in order to revere. The modern man learns in order to use."[23] Whereas comprehension and the use of learning are important, the challenge remains for Christian educators to enable persons to revere, to appreciate, to stand in awe of and worship God as a result of their teaching. This challenge applies to those who teach in homes as parents and family members; in churches, schools, and communities as teachers, pastors, and fellow Christians; and in all other settings of life. Heschel points up the need for Christian educators to transcend the persistent pragmatism prevalent in the United States.

The New Testament

Beyond the biblical foundations presented in chapter 1, additional observations can be made regarding the practice of education during the New Testament period. The disciples of Jesus followed the Jewish pattern of worship and

---

22. Frank E. Gaebelein, *The Christian, the Arts, and Truth: Regaining the Vision of Greatness*, ed. Bruce Lockerbie (Portland, OR: Multnomah Press, 1985), 144.

23. Abraham Heschel, *Between God and Man: An Interpretation of Judaism from the Writing of Abraham Heschel*, ed. Fritz A. Rothschild (New York: Free Press, 1959), 37.

learning. Several New Testament books evidence the use of different methods of education, most reflecting earlier Jewish customs. In many ways the New Testament, written in Greek, weds the educational ideals from both the Old Testament and Greek heritages.

Some persons in the New Testament learned of their Christian faith in family settings. Timothy was influenced by both his grandmother, Lois, and his mother, Eunice (2 Tim. 1:5; 3:15). The Ethiopian eunuch was instructed by Philip before coming to faith and presumably received some instruction subsequent to his conversion (Acts 8:36–40). Still others assimilated their faith into pagan and Jewish backgrounds. Paul, for example, was thoroughly trained in the law under the tutelage of Gamaliel in Jerusalem (Acts 5:34; 22:3).[24] He made use of his training to become an effective advocate for the faith among Gentiles and Jews.

Education gradually came to emphasize a distinctive way of life for God's chosen people. Christians were identified as followers of the Way (Acts 9:2; 24:14). Education emphasized the teachings by and about Jesus, for in his very person he represented the way, the truth, and the life (John 14:6). The disciples of Jesus were commissioned to teach others to obey everything Jesus had commanded (Matt. 28:20). Education emphasized the Old Testament background for interpreting the meaning of Jesus's lordship (Luke 24:25–27; John 5:39). Creedal summaries and hymns (such as 1 Cor. 15:3–8; Phil. 2:5–11; 1 Tim. 3:16; 2 Tim. 2:11–13; Titus 3:4–7) suggest essential truths that the early Christians felt were important for converts to learn. In time, certain official teachers arose after the rabbinic pattern whose responsibilities included the preservation, transmission, and interpretation of essential truths to the Christian community.[25] They were called and held responsible for the stewardship of their ministry (James 3:1). Teachers were to ensure the perpetuation of the Christian beliefs that were essential for the identity of the Christian community in the midst of a hostile and pluralistic world.

The way of knowing and life as perpetuated in the New Testament called for active engagement in the world in obedience to Christ's reign and in response to the experience of Christ as Lord in the midst of life.[26] This active engagement included the need for careful reflection on the teachings of the Old Testament Scriptures and the words of Christ as shared and elaborated by his disciples and later recorded. Such reflection was to enable a faithful response to God's calling on the part of followers of Jesus. Their faith was to be expressed in

24. Kennedy, "Christian Education through History," 22.
25. Ibid.
26. Thomas H. Groome, *Christian Religious Education: Sharing Our Story and Vision* (San Francisco: Harper & Row, 1980), 157.

their way of life. The miracle of the incarnation was to be repeated in the lives of the disciples through the person and work of the Holy Spirit.[27] Education should help persons reflect the renewed image of God through the presence of the risen Christ. In light of this New Testament perspective, one issue posed for current and future efforts is the extent to which educational efforts foster the head, heart, and hand response of persons to the very revelation of God in Jesus Christ. Such a response is to embody in fresh ways the reality of the living Christ in the world.

Early Christianity

In the early church there was an emphasis on the faithful transmission of the Christian heritage. Up until the fourth century, the church did so in a hostile society and thus held a largely countercultural stance of contending for the faith. External and internal challenges had to be addressed in carefully reflecting on the faith. In this context the community was maintained by stressing the canon, a rule of faith, and church order. The canon identified the accepted sources that were to ground the faith and be its final authority. The rule of faith included the confession of Jesus's lordship, the Apostles' Creed, and summaries of biblical history that were to be believed by those faithfully following Jesus. Church order specified the organization and discipline necessary to define the true church and those with valid authority in directing the church's shared life.[28] These three elements served to maintain continuity as the faith addressed itself to a Hellenistic-Roman world marked by cultural and religious pluralism.

Various educational forms emerged to meet the challenges of interpreting the faith in light of unfulfilled eschatological expectations. In particular, catechesis arose as an essential component of passing on the faith. John Westerhoff points out that the Greek source for this term refers to resounding or echoing, to celebrating or imitating, to repeating another's words and deeds. The term *catechesis* originally referred to instruction by oral repetition in which persons were taught by having them sing out the answers to posed questions.[29] To fulfill the need for catechesis, catechumen classes emerged in various localities

---

27. See my discussion of this process in Robert W. Pazmiño, *So What Makes Our Teaching Christian? Teaching in the Name, Spirit and Power of Jesus* (forthcoming, 2008).

28. William Bean Kennedy, "Background Historical Understanding for Christian Education" (unpublished course handout, Union Theological Seminary, 1980), 1.

29. John H. Westerhoff III, "The Challenge: Understanding the Problem of Faithfulness," in *A Faithful Church: Issues in the History of Catechesis*, ed. John H. Westerhoff III and O. C. Edwards Jr. (Wilton, CT: Morehouse Barlow, 1981), 2.

to support home training and worship services. The form and length of this catechesis varied, but generally the training continued for three years.[30] This period served as a time of training and probation before a person was fully accepted into the church. Among the catechumens were the "hearers" who were considering Christianity, the "kneelers" who remained for prayers after the hearers withdrew, and the "chosen," or actual baptismal candidates, who were given intensive doctrinal, liturgical, and ascetical training in preparation for baptism and full participation in the life of the church. Following baptism, additional instruction was provided regarding the meaning of the sacraments and other mysteries of the church that had been experienced by new members. A process to form Christian disciples was sustained over time.

In addition to catechumen classes, catechetical schools were formed. Christianity soon found itself needing highly educated apologists to interpret the faith in the Hellenistic ways of thinking and to defend it against cultured attackers. At catechetical schools, like the university at Alexandria, future leaders of Christian thought and life were instructed in the various disciplines and philosophies of Hellenistic culture. Some leaders, such as Tertullian, maintained that to use the thought forms of Greek philosophy to express the gospel was dangerous and even heretical. Other leaders, such as Origen, believed that it was essential to synthesize the Christian faith with contemporary thought forms in order to address the world on its own terms.[31] An issue of continuing concern for a faith community is how it relates its perspective to the wider social and cultural context.

The curriculum for Christian education included the reinterpretation or interpretation of the Old Testament Scriptures. Many converts were not Jews and thus were being exposed to the Old Testament for the first time; they needed an interpretation of how Jesus's life and ministry related to God's dealings with people and creation prior to the incarnation. For those converts who were Jews, the Old Testament had to be reinterpreted in light of the claims of the Messiah. In addition to the Old Testament, the Gospel accounts of the life and teachings of Jesus were shared. Following the death of eyewitnesses to these events, the accounts and their implications were codified to provide an authoritative standard. It is noteworthy that four Gospels were canonized honoring a diversity of perspectives disclosing the wonders of Jesus's life, death, and resurrection. The book of Acts can also be seen as a Gospel of the Spirit.[32] In addition to the Scriptures, the curriculum was comprised of the confession

---

30. Michael Dujarier, *A History of the Catechumenate: The First Six Centuries*, trans. Edward J. Haarl (New York: Sadlier, 1979), 94.

31. Kennedy, "Christian Education through History," 23.

32. See Justo L. González, *Acts: The Gospel of the Spirit* (Maryknoll, NY: Orbis, 2001), 8.

of faith and teaching of "the Way." The confession of faith was the affirmation of Jesus's lordship, which was elaborated upon in the Apostles' Creed. "The Way" specified moral expectations for a follower of Christ that were clearly outlined in the *Didache*, the earliest extant form of catechetical instruction.[33] Beyond these explicit curricular components, the common life of the Christian community provided the implicit curriculum as nonformal and informal teaching and learning occurred.

As has been suggested for other historical periods, certain issues emerge from the general distinctive elements of the educational heritage during early Christianity. A recurring issue is continuity. An alternative to this emphasis is one that focuses on the adaptation of the faith in light of a rapidly changing world and in some cases drastically distinct conditions. A second issue relates to the maintenance of the Christian community. In the early church the constant threat of annihilation required an emphasis on order, discipline, and clear guidelines, but in a more accommodating societal and cultural context an emphasis on ardor rather than order may be appropriate. Certainly the loss of community rather than its maintenance may be more of a contemporary concern, but the need to balance both concerns for continuity and discontinuity is posed in each historical setting of the Christian church. The task of education in the midst of these issues is to raise such questions and to suggest possible ways of resolving the inevitable tensions.

Membership in the early church implied costly discipleship and serious commitment in stark contrast to many congregations in the West. Church membership must be made to mean something more than occasional attendance and financial giving or even the mere appearance of one's name on a church roll. The radical demands of following Christ must be made explicit through educational efforts that move the church beyond a faithless cultural accommodation to a faithful response. A final issue is posed in terms of the inclusion of definite ethical demands as a part of the curriculum where "the Way" is specified and persons are actually expected to fulfill their ethical responsibilities, allowing for the place of forgiveness and the operation of God's grace in the midst of human frailty and sin.

The Middle Ages

After Constantine and the establishment of Christianity, the role of Christian education changed. The church no longer required intensive preparation

33. Kennedy, "Background Historical Understanding," 2.

for those joining its numbers. Church leaders had to find new ways to nurture large numbers of persons and lead them to a deeper understanding and appreciation of the faith.[34] Subsequently, with the fall of Rome and the collapse of imperial power, the church became the social institution with continuing influence. As a result of a power vacuum, ecclesiastical interest increased in all areas of human life. The emerging dominance of the church had a profound impact on education.[35] The dominance that emerged in relation to scholasticism resulted in reactions expressed during the Renaissance and the Reformation.

Worship emerged as the chief medium of Christian education.[36] Although worship was directed toward God, the developing richness of symbolism in architecture, art, and music taught lessons of the faith to participants. The elaborate character of worship included the Mass, which was celebrated daily; the various Christian festivals associated with the liturgical calendar; and the religious drama of the morality and mystery plays.[37] Along with drama and architectural and artistic symbolism, penitential literature guided priests in addressing contemporary ethical concerns.[38] All of these nonformal vehicles functioned to convey the Christian message to a largely illiterate population who for the most part had no access to formal Christian education. The very fabric of the shared life of the church with its sacraments provided cognitive input to supplement the affective input of drama and counseling and the visual input of architecture. Thus socialization, acculturation, and enculturation provided the vehicles for educating the masses.

During this time the family declined in its relative importance in educating for the faith. Celibacy, or the single life, emerged as a viable option and manifested a redefinition of the Christian faith. Those intensely committed to spiritual formation in some cases could opt for life in monasteries and convents, which sought to foster community and a sense of order through common discipline, manual labor, and spiritual exercises.[39] The rise of alternative communities to the family as the center for Christian education must be seen in relation to economic developments in which survival was an all-consuming concern. Energy was devoted primarily to economic sustenance, and for the

34. Kennedy, "Christian Education through History," 23.
35. Marvin J. Taylor, "A Historical Introduction to Religious Education," in Taylor, ed., *Introduction to Christian Education*, 14.
36. See a contemporary discussion of the centrality of worship for Christian education in Debra Dean Murphy, *Teaching That Transforms: Worship as the Heart of Christian Education* (Grand Rapids: Brazos, 2004).
37. Ibid.
38. Kennedy, "Background Historical Understanding," 2.
39. Ibid.

common folk opportunities for reflection and learning were extremely limited outside of the worship experience.

Formal education was conducted in monastic and cathedral schools as well as in universities (beginning in the twelfth century). Such education was reserved primarily for training a few young men entering the orders. These schools eventually broadened their curricula after AD 800 to include the seven liberal arts and were the forerunners of later universities. From approximately AD 500 to 1000 monastic schools were centers of intellectual activity, but as large cities grew, collegiate church schools or cathedral schools emerged. Their curricula stressed the liberal arts and humanities, in addition to theology; the focus was not on personal piety. In the twelfth century, universities grew out of the cathedral school movement; they sought to produce both a professional and a scholastic mind. Their origin reflected the growth of cities, the rise of a middle class, and new intellectual interests stimulated by contacts with Muslims. The universities were not narrowly religious in their focus, and most of their students studied law, medicine, and other secular subjects in preparation for careers outside the church. Increasingly the church, government, and theology itself were subjected to critical inquiry in the universities despite their rigid and formalized instruction.[40]

In *Children without Childhood*, Marie Winn suggests that North American society is moving toward a "New Middle Ages" in how it relates to and educates children.[41] She notes a shift in focus from children being protected and differentiated from adults in the past century to a current emphasis on the preparation of children for adult life, which places them in an undifferentiated position. Her provocative suggestion is that this move reinstitutes a view popular in the Middle Ages. Winn's analysis, if correct, maintains that current educational efforts have focused on children gaining awareness of the responsibilities and realities of the adult world. Such an exposure assumes that children need to know about both the positive and the negative dimensions of life, often in areas they are not mature enough to handle.

The issue for Christian educators is whether they should maintain a guarded environment for children and youth or expose them to societal realities with adequate opportunity for dialogue and reflection. One youth worker, for example, was faced with the dilemma of being invited to view an R-rated video with young people with the possibility of discussing its portrayal of life with them or opting to refuse their invitation and to discourage the viewing. In

---

40. Taylor, *Religious Education*, 14–15.
41. Marie Winn, *Children without Childhood: Growing Up Too Fast in the World of Sex and Drugs* (New York: Penguin Books, 1981), 205–10.

this case he chose to view the video and was able to discuss the debasement of human sexuality and the alternatives suggested by the Christian faith.

Beyond this issue of children being protected or prepared, the increase in the options of a celibate or single life have resulted in persons opting out of marriage, childbearing, and parenting within marriage. These developments raise the issue of the place of the family in local church efforts. Because a large proportion of the population is single, the local church must consider educational programming that is inclusive of singles, childless couples, and others, and that is sensitive to their needs. Jesus, who was himself a single adult, may not be welcome in some churches that exclusively emphasize the nuclear family.

Paralleling medieval developments of increased anomaly and a plurality of visions for life, the local church in modern times must address the need for a unifying center in corporate and communal life. Without an understanding of the Christian call to corporate life that affects the public and wider society, a narrow concern for personal survival needs and a fortress mentality can emerge, which isolates persons. Certainly the church must address the genuine needs of food, clothing, and shelter, but an educational agenda must emphasize the Christian responsibility to care for the world as God's creation and the stewardship of resources beyond the maintenance of any personal, familial, or national fortress. Beyond the walls of present-day monasteries and convents are vast areas of human enterprise that require the presence and work of Christians who can make a difference by the grace of God.

Two additional issues are suggested by the educational heritage from the Middle Ages. The increased interest in spiritual disciplines and formation that characterized monastic developments can be affirmed as they foster necessary communion with God and reflection in a rapidly paced world. Christian education efforts must seriously evaluate the extent to which persons are encouraged to grow in their personal relationship with God—provided a concern for the private sphere does not neglect the public and corporate responsibilities of Christians. An emphasis on personal piety can easily degenerate into a pietism devoid of concern for the wider community and culture. Evangelicals have been particularly delinquent in this area as they have neglected Jesus's call to work for justice and peace.

A second issue is posed by the extensive use of visual communication during the Middle Ages. The decline of the impact of the written word can be noted in a media-oriented society like the United States, paralleling the limited availability of the written word and formal education in medieval times. To what extent should Christian educators adapt or supplement visually oriented technologies and forms to teach the Christian faith? Fewer people are reading books in the United States, and the rise of various visual media demands a critical and appropriate response by Christians in order to effectively address persons without diluting the message of the gospel.

The Renaissance

The Renaissance was a reawakening, a rebirth, a renewal of learning that took place in the fourteenth, fifteenth, and sixteenth centuries. A reawakened interest in the classical sources originated in Italy but spread to other parts of Europe. Corresponding to this classical interest was a rise in humanism, with persons and their world rather than God and heaven as the focal point for human interest. A new emphasis on individualism began to develop, reflecting a break with traditionalism and a reaction to the ecclesiastical despotism that characterized medieval society. These shifts occurred in the context of chaotic societal change with great ferment in the political, social, economic, cultural, and intellectual dimensions of life.

Various areas of life affected by the Renaissance in turn influenced education. Education became important to individual cities, with rich merchants and powerful banking houses supporting and sponsoring learning. Political tensions between the papacy and various princes and rulers resulted in an emphasis on education as serving the state and society at large. A scientific revolution, beginning with Roger Bacon's inquiries, fostered a focus on the created world rather than its Creator. This new interest in science resulted in shifts in the curricula of schools. Much experimentation developed in music, architecture, literature, and the arts. In the area of religion, increased interest in differing perspectives was fostered through the printing of religious books, which, though expensive, were in demand. Many Renaissance leaders and thinkers saw the chief purpose of persons as glorifying human life and enjoying the world to the fullest.

A broadening aim characterized Renaissance education, with more emphasis on individual development. Individuals were increasingly viewed as identities separate from their community but possessing sufficient personal influence to affect those communities. The great technological advance of printing made self-education possible. Greek and Roman classics were reappropriated through Muslim and Jewish scholarship, which provided vast resources for curricular expansion along with increased scholarship and study in the areas of the humanities, the arts, and the sciences.

Issues emerging from the Renaissance reintroduced questions identified from the Greek educational heritage, in particular, the place of human reason in relation to the Christian faith. For some Renaissance thinkers, reason was enthroned above faith. There was a tendency to place the humanities, science, and arts on an equal footing with the revealed truths of Christianity.

Evangelicals, in contrast, maintain that all truth is God's truth, but not all truth is of the same order or on the same level. The question of priority is important, and evangelicals have maintained that only the truth revealed in Christ and in Scripture comprises the ultimate and unifying perspective for learning and life. Anything less can make persons the measure of all things.[42] This faith in Christ and reliance on Scripture are to have a higher priority than those insights gained through human reason and experience.

Augustine maintained that if one did not believe in God, that person would not come to know the essential truth. Anselm of Canterbury in the eleventh century stated, "Believe that you may know." Evangelicals suggest that this principle also extends beyond religious faith to other endeavors in the sense that believing, as commitment, leads to the knowledge of truth.[43] This stance in Christian education implies the need to emphasize personal belief in Christ and Scripture as the essential foundation for inquiry in all areas of knowledge and truth.

This reliance on Christ and Scripture follows from the recognition of the presence of sin and the fallen nature of persons, which affects the use of unaided reason, not subject to divine revelation. Given the presence of personal and corporate sin, Christian education must address the areas of moral, ethical, and character formation to supplement intellectual training, but not in a way that violates the worth and dignity of persons as God's creatures. How this balance is achieved presents a continual problem in the actual practice of education. For example, what is the place of doubt and questioning? The use of reason implies posing questions and having doubts, even about various truths that Christianity has historically defended. Posing questions becomes the very occasion for discovery, using the capacities of human reason created by God.

The Reformation

Medieval patterns of education (home training, worship, pastoral teaching, and guidance) continued past the schism of the church.[44] Home training made use of several catechisms, a major educational innovation, written for

42. Gaebelein, *Christian, the Arts, and Truth*, 252.
43. Ibid., 86.
44. Kennedy, "Christian Education through History," 24.

both children and adults, and parents were held responsible for the religious training of their children. Worship included the liturgy, but the sermon also took on new importance as a primary vehicle for teaching. Pastoral preaching and teaching were revised to encourage the active participation of laity as learners; pastors were to assume the educational leadership of their congregations. Guidance was provided by church leaders and parents who sought to encourage personal appropriation of the Christian faith. An additional educational form for Roman Catholics was the confessional, which provided personalized guidance and teaching.

The authority of the Bible was emphasized with a return to the sources of the Christian faith. Historical-grammatical exegesis of the texts in their original languages resulted in a new appreciation of biblical truths. *Sola scriptura* affirmed the sole and final authority of the Scriptures over that of the church.

The Reformation emphasized justification by faith (*sola fide*). A distinction was made between faith and belief. Faith emphasized with whom one walked, whereas belief emphasized content and creed. Both faith and belief were important, but salvation was seen in terms of personal faith, a personal commitment to and trust in Jesus Christ as Lord and Savior. Hence, there was a new concern for the evangelistic dimension of the Christian faith; salvation centered in personal response in addition to participation in the church's life. Another principle operative was the priesthood of all believers.[45] Each and every person had access to God through Christ and had significance in Christ's body, the church.

These three principles fostered a new vision for Christian education cast in terms of universal education. The aim of Christian education was to train all Christians to be priests of the living God. This was to be realized in part through translating the Bible into the vernacular. One could know God directly through reading Scripture with the eyes of faith. For education this implied that each individual was important and that reading was an essential skill for each and every person. Preaching was revitalized as well and viewed as teaching persons to assume their personal responsibilities before God. Preaching was not primarily evangelistic but expounded the biblical tradition in a didactic manner to foster its personal reappropriation by all of God's people. The home was viewed as an extension of the church for instruction of all its members.[46] Luther stressed the centrality of home instruction by writing catechisms for children and regularly encouraging parents to assume their teaching responsibilities.

45. Kennedy, "Background Historical Understanding," 3.
46. Ibid.

Because an educated citizenry was valued and domestic training was inadequate, state-supported schools arose. These schools were supported by those in political power, often in cooperation with the church. State-supported education generally developed along two tracks or levels. On the lower level, elementary schools sought to teach children how to read. On the upper level, elementary and Latin grammar schools and the universities sought to teach those with promise to become future societal and church leaders. Despite these efforts, the realization of compulsory universal education awaited later historical developments.[47] Noteworthy in the efforts of the Reformers is the inclusion of girls along with boys in the schools established by John Calvin in Geneva, Switzerland, and John Knox in Scotland.

Given the potential impact of a revived Christian education, teachers had an essential role demanding both dedication and training. Calvin, for example, stressed the need to train pastors as teachers because of their place in the community. As the significant educated person in the community, the pastor became the chief teacher or school supervisor, and the importance of right doctrine required that teaching be a high priority in pastoral ministry.[48]

During the Reformation, education for the sake of the community of faith—for its protection, its enhancement, or its extension—began to share primacy with education for the development of the individual. Christian education was first for one's personal response to God, but increasingly also for the fulfillment of one's individual potential as God's unique creation with a contribution to make to the larger community. Thus there emerged an increased appreciation of the nature of the Christian calling or vocation to be in the world serving God and others. This responsibility belonged to each priest, each faithful believer in Jesus Christ.

By comparing and contrasting developments in the Renaissance and the Reformation, it is possible to identify issues for educational thought and practice. A number of similarities between the Renaissance and the Reformation can be noted. Both movements were expressions of societal renewal: in the case of the Renaissance, this renewal was cultural and intellectual; in the Reformation, it was primarily theological and ecclesial. In both periods the individual was affirmed: in the Renaissance the autonomy of individuals was stressed; in the Reformation a new sense of individual faith fostered personal reading of Scripture and the personal responsibilities of persons to be God's priests in the Christian community and the world. In terms of education, both movements expanded the curriculum beyond traditional areas of study. Finally, both

47. Kennedy, "Christian Education through History," 25.
48. Ibid., 24.

movements represented a break with tradition and a questioning of existing authorities. In the Renaissance a questioning of the political power and mind-set of the state and the church developed; in the Reformation serious questions were raised about established religious norms and church traditions. These similarities indicate the potential for renewal and change that can significantly affect all dimensions of life. They also indicate the potential costs of implementing change and the need to raise questions about the limits of that change.

By way of contrast, the Renaissance and the Reformation represent distinct commitments and worldviews. The following contrasts can be noted:

1. Whereas the Renaissance generally focused on persons, the Reformation centered life and education on God, evidencing a renewed consideration of persons as God's creatures with definite privileges and responsibilities.
2. Whereas the Renaissance centered primarily on the elite, the Reformation included the masses of society as well.
3. In the Reformation spiritual renewal was primary, whereas the Renaissance centered on cultural and intellectual renewal. But spiritual renewal and cultural or intellectual renewal are not mutually exclusive. In Reformation thought, human reason was viewed as fallen and subject to God's revelation in Scripture, whereas in certain Renaissance developments human reason was perceived as perfected. Given the Reformers' sensitivity to human depravity, their primary source for understanding was the Bible, but biblical truths were integrated with insights gained through reason and experience.
4. In contrast to a Reformed focus on the Bible, Renaissance thinkers relied primarily on extrabiblical classical literature.
5. Reformers stressed the expanded use of the vernacular in disseminating knowledge in contrast to the exclusive use of classical languages by Renaissance scholars, who were not necessarily committed to universal education. Nevertheless, many of the Reformers were schooled in classical studies and used classical languages in their scholarship.
6. A final contrast might be stated in terms of the ultimate goal of education. In the Reformation knowledge was viewed in relation to the higher goal of commitment to and communion with God, whereas in the Renaissance traditional knowledge itself was a goal, largely irrespective of God's revelation.

In relation to each of the above contrasts, choices must be made and priorities set in relation to basic educational thought and practice. Each contrast can best be thought of as representing a possible continuum of responses embodying emphases on divine and human centeredness. A Christian worldview must remain faithful to God's revelation while being sensitive to human realities.

John T. McNeill maintains that the Reformers differed from Christian humanists in that they emphasized the majesty and holiness of God, the sinfulness of human beings, and the gulf between God and persons, which is only reconcilable in Jesus Christ.[49] But the Renaissance humanists can be identified as moderate, radical, or Christian. Erasmus best typified the Christian humanist who influenced the Reformers. The young John Calvin hoped to see humanism contained within the bounds of decent responsibility. Thus the Renaissance and the Reformation pose the issue of the relationship between theism and humanism in the context of the very human enterprise of education that seeks to be faithful to God. Certainly the roots of the Reformation were in the Renaissance, but subsequent historical developments posed many questions regarding the central emphases of educational commitments.

The United States

In dealing with the increasing complexity of the post-Reformation, we will consider developments in the United States while recognizing that significant changes have occurred in other national contexts as a result of a host of intellectual, political, economic, and social factors that include the Enlightenment, the Industrial Revolution, and increased urbanization and plurality. In addressing these complex developments, Lawrence Cremin proposes a network or configuration of institutions that educate, also identified as an educational ecology. These social institutions include the family, the church, the community, the school, various agencies, the media, and others. Each institution interacts with the others and with the larger society. Each institution has its own values, assumptions, and agenda, which are either explicit or implicit in teaching its members or participants.[50] Well beyond the United States, developments in the southern hemisphere, where the Christian faith is dynamic and growing, calls for a writing of a history by Christians living in those contexts.

49. John T. McNeill, *The History and Character of Calvinism* (New York: Oxford University Press, 1967).

50. Lawrence A. Cremin, lecture given at Teachers College, Columbia University, New York, December 18, 1978. See also Lawrence A. Cremin, *American Education: The Colonial Experience, 1607–1783* (New York: Harper & Row, 1970); Lawrence A. Cremin, *American Education: The National Experience, 1783–1876* (New York: Harper & Row, 1980); and Lawrence A. Cremin, *American Education: The Metropolitan Experience, 1876–1980* (New York: Harper & Row, 1988).

Awareness of educational configurations forces the evangelical educator to consider a vast array of institutions and their interrelationships far beyond parochial concerns. For example, those primarily concerned with church education via the Sunday school cannot neglect the educational impact of families, schools, communities, media, and the larger society in planning and implementing programs. Such influences must be considered in identifying purposes, developing strategies, implementing programs, and evaluating efforts. Also, networks must be established with other institutions or vehicles for processing their messages if the church is to be effective. To neglect to do so is shortsighted and resigns evangelical efforts to cultural backwaters.

The relationships among the institutions or agencies constituting an educational configuration can be described as confirming, complementing, and/or contradicting one another.[51] Institutions confirm one another by supporting the same message and encouraging compliance with certain guidelines. For example, the church can confirm the role of the family by encouraging children to honor and obey their parents and to heed the truths passed on by parents. Likewise, parents can confirm the role of the church by encouraging children to learn from, respect, and obey Sunday school teachers, pastors, and other adults in the church setting. Parents can also confirm the church's message through their active participation and support of the church and by modeling the church's teachings.

Relationships between institutions can also be described as complementing one another in the sense of having input and impact that supply areas lacking in the other compatible institutions. For example, schools can complement families in certain settings by supplying lunches for children from homes that cannot supply them. In a similar way, parents can complement the schools by tutoring their children in school subjects that teachers cannot address. Parents may also be able to complement or supplement the emphases in Sunday school curriculum through family devotional times, elaborating themes and concepts shared by teachers.

A third possible relationship is contradictory in the sense that institutions may have distinctly different messages that create dissonance and conflicts for participants. A contemporary example of this is the relationship between the agenda of certain segments of commercial television and the values supported by the Christian church or family. Commercial television generally defines the good life in terms of the abundance of goods a person possesses. This stance contradicts Christian concerns for stewardship and service in a

---

51. Lawrence A. Cremin, *Traditions of American Education* (New York: Basic Books, 1977), 128.

world of declining resources. Another example of a contradictory relationship is the perception of some Christian parents that the public school's secular humanism directly opposes Christian values and truths. This perception has resulted in the increased development of Christian private and home schools that confirm and/or complement a Christian worldview held by the family.

In addition to these three designations describing the relationships among institutions in an educational configuration, configurations as a whole or in part interact with the larger society. An example of this is a Christian family that takes a strong countercultural stance and as a result decides not to own a television, attend movies, frequent public schools, or relate to local public communities. The Amish and Bruderhof communities represent guarded Christian enclaves that opt for a more cloistered and separated life in relation to the larger society.[52]

Using this concept of an educational configuration, we can trace the shifting relationships and perspectives of the constituents of Christian education efforts. Rather than attempt to recount a vast and diverse array of shifts, the following discussion describes developments in general education in the United States as traced by Cremin with implications for Christian education.

Cremin identifies five major thrusts characterizing American education. First, there is a multiplicity of institutions. The impact of these institutions differs with the individual. Some people gain their education through self-education rather than through the direct efforts of a traditional educational agency or program.[53] For example, persons may be educated primarily through personal study, observation, and reflection, using resources available through libraries or other information storage agencies. An implication for Christian educators is the need to carefully assess the particular educational configurations of the persons with whom one is ministering. Persons who are primarily self-educated may need increased access to resources and opportunities to share with others what they have gained through their study and experience.

Christian educators must also assess the extent to which the input from other social institutions and society in general confirm, complement, and/or contradict the truths and values of a Christian worldview. On the basis of this assessment, decisions must be made regarding possible Christian responses to the particular historical context. The allocation of personnel, material

---

52. For a study of a fundamentalist private school that represents a guarded community, see Alan Peshkin, *God's Choice: The Total World of a Fundamentalist Christian School* (Chicago: University of Chicago Press, 1986). Also see Yaacov Oved, *The Witness of the Brothers: A History of the Bruderhof* (New Brunswick, NJ: Transaction, 1996).

53. Cremin, lecture, December 18, 1978.

resources, and time requires a reading of the times in light of the past and the projected future. Christian educators must ask about the ways in which teaching in any institution, agency, or program were or are educative in terms of specified purposes. One challenge posed for current Christian education efforts is how parents, pastors, teachers, and others should respond to the increased impact of the media.

Cremin's second point in assessing developments in the United States is that at different times society has emphasized different institutions. During the colonial period (1607–1783), the family and the church were the educational institutions of primary importance, and society was to be saved and bettered through their teaching efforts. Colonial developments did evidence distinct configurations in New England, the Middle Colonies, and the South, but the efforts of the family and the church generally confirmed and complemented one another. During the national period (1783–1876), the school (in particular, the public school) along with the church were to educate persons and save society. This occurred in the context of a rapidly expanding nation and the increased separation of church and state. During the metropolitan period (1876–1986), the school and various child-rearing or rehabilitative institutions were to make for an educated and good society. Each of these efforts had varied success and has been viewed differently by historians from various perspectives. Each general societal configuration was intended to save all, but their efforts were varied.[54] Some people were significantly served and bettered through their educational experiences in the dominant educational configuration, whereas others were not served. Cremin's account notes the decreased role of the church amid the increasing secularization of life, but does not indicate that Christians cannot influence the educational efforts of society in general. This scenario suggests that the church has a key role to play in raising critical questions about the dominant educational configuration and in proposing alternatives from the perspective of a marginal status. This marginal status is suggested by the decreased impact of Christian values in the wider society.

Third, in the United States a concerted effort has been made in the schools to balance the societal ideals of liberty, equality, and fraternity. Liberty can be viewed as the right to strive for educational, social, political, and economic achievement. Equality traditionally has been viewed as equality of opportunity for all, but in the twentieth century it has been defined in terms of results. Fraternity can be defined as the concern for human community and the desire to build a new and good society with education at its heart. Given the ever-present plurality of persons in the United States, the realization of community

54. Ibid.

has necessitated an interaction and mix of persons and groups.[55] In such a mix, a constant tension exists between maintaining one's distinct identity and entering the mainstream of society. This tension has been particularly acute for those coming from cultural and racial backgrounds other than that of northern Protestant Europe. Also, the two primal crimes of the United States, namely, the genocide of American Indians and the system of chattel slavery of blacks, have perpetuated a struggle with racism and discrimination. Thus the ideal of liberty must address the liberation of persons currently excluded from society along with a commitment to the responsibilities liberty entails; the ideal of equality must address the fact that some are perceived as more equal than others; and the ideal of fraternity must assess the nature of the community that has excluded some from full membership.[56]

Christian educators can relate to the ideals of liberty, equality, and fraternity in terms of the Christian gospel. Liberty can be defined in terms of the freedom made available in Jesus Christ. Yet this freedom must not be viewed in isolation from the corresponding obligation of covenant, with responsibilities to God, other persons, and creation. Equality can be defined as equal access to God through Jesus Christ. The gospel embodies a commitment to view each person as having infinite worth and dignity by virtue of being created in God's image. Fraternity can be defined in terms of the common humanity of all persons and the unique relationships that exist in Christian community. Christian educators can affirm these three ideals in their educational efforts, but they must always be related to the whole counsel of God as revealed in Scripture. A particular challenge is posed for Christians when these societal ideals are in conflict. For example, should Christians support the busing of school children to achieve greater racial equality in public schools?

Fourth, there has been a persistent effort to popularize education, to make it more readily available to all persons. This popularization has included the areas of access, content, and control. The advantages and disadvantages in popularization can be cited in terms of the inevitable tensions between quantity and quality. Popularization may result in the vulgarization of knowledge and truth, while the lack of popularization results in an elitism that is inherently prejudicial.

Cremin's fifth and final observation is that the historical record of education in the United States reveals that efforts have been both oppressive and/or

---

55. Ibid.
56. See Robert N. Bellah for an analysis of the polarities revealed by the history in *The Broken Covenant: American Civil Religion in the Time of Trial* (New York: Seabury, 1975).

liberating depending on the persons or groups involved.[57] Christians have been both faithful and unfaithful in sharing the faith, and though the prospects of popularizing the faith are not an option, the concern is to enable every person to hear the claims of Christ in a way that enables a knowledgeable response. Christians are called to faithfulness over against a popular accommodation of the faith, while sharing the Christian worldview in ways that others can understand and respond to. In relation to Cremin's fourth and fifth points, we must ask if evangelical communities have vulgarized the gospel in an effort to be popular in society and have therefore oppressed those persons who need to hear the whole counsel of God. This may be the case if an emphasis on personal transformation has neglected the call for social transformation.

Postwar Evangelical Educators

The contributions of evangelical educators following World War II must be viewed in relation to the earlier fundamentalist-modernist controversy.[58] The term *fundamentalist* emerged from a series of booklets distributed from 1909 on titled *The Fundamentals*. These booklets sought to affirm orthodox Christian doctrines in response to critical and evolutionary views of Scripture and theology that were popularized through the modernist or liberal movement. One expression of the liberal movement in education was its emphasis on progressive education, supported through the efforts of the Religious Education Association founded in 1903.

During the twentieth century, parallel organizations gradually emerged that supported either liberal or mainline groups or evangelical constituencies. The National Association of Evangelicals was established in 1942 in protest against some of the theological and social concerns of the Federal Council of Churches (now the National Council of Churches). Similarly, the National Sunday School Association was begun in 1946 to stimulate growth in Christian education among evangelical or conservative groups.[59] From commissions of

---

57. Cremin, lecture, December 18, 1978.

58. Three works that explore the evangelical heritage are Anthony A. Koyzis, "Evangelical Christian Education in America: The Ideas, the Institutions and the Enterprise," *Christian Education Journal* 15 (Winter 1995): 70–87; Kevin E. Lawson, "Marginalization and Renewal: Evangelical Christian Education in the Twentieth Century," *Religious Education* 98 (Fall 2003): 437–53; and Ronnie Prevost, *Evangelical Protestant Gifts to Religious Education* (Macon, GA: Smyth & Helwys, 2000).

59. Kendig B. Cully describes further developments in *The Search for a Christian Education—Since 1940* (Philadelphia: Westminster, 1965), 94–112.

this body the current National Association of Professors of Christian Education and National Association of Directors of Christian Education emerged, parallel organizations to the Religious Education Association in providing leadership for conservative constituencies. These developments set the context in which to explore the work of Frank E. Gaebelein, Lois E. LeBar, Lawrence O. Richards, and Gene A. Getz.[60]

Frank E. Gaebelein

Frank E. Gaebelein guided the efforts of the National Association of Evangelicals in the formation of its statement on Christian education, *Christian Education in a Democracy*.[61] In 1954, Gaebelein's perspective was further elaborated in *The Pattern of God's Truth: Problems of Integration in Christian Education*.[62] As the title suggests, Gaebelein addresses how a Christian faith commitment and a Christian world and life view might be integrated with the teaching and learning of various school subjects. Gaebelein quotes Edwin H. Rian's insights on the task he undertakes: "A Christian theory of education is an exposition of the idea that Christianity is a world and life view and not simply a series of unrelated doctrines. Christianity includes all of life."[63]

Gaebelein sets out to reaffirm the perspective espoused by Augustine of Hippo. Augustine maintained that all truth is God's truth and that the Christian educator is called to the task of "spoiling the Egyptians," to the task of discerning truth as revealed in all areas of human knowledge and discovery. The discernment of truth requires a constant reference to biblical truth and to the person of Jesus Christ. Therefore, Gaebelein proposes that Christian educators adopt as their unifying principle Christ and the Bible.[64] Gaebelein acknowledges that areas of truth not fully addressed in Scripture are part of God's truth and therefore crucial for consideration. But primacy must ultimately be given to spiritual truth revealed in the Bible and incarnate in Christ.[65] This was the inherent pattern of God's truth,

60. The four educators highlighted here are cited in Gangel and Benson, *Christian Education*, 338–45.
61. *Christian Education in a Democracy: The Report of the N.A.E. Committee* (New York: Oxford University Press, 1951).
62. Frank E. Gaebelein, *The Pattern of God's Truth: Problems of Integration in Christian Education* (New York: Oxford University Press, 1954).
63. Edwin H. Rian, *Christianity and American Education* (San Antonio: Naylor, 1949), 236.
64. Gaebelein, *Pattern of God's Truth*, 20.
65. Ibid., 23.

which must be explicitly shared with students and related to every aspect of their lives.

Gaebelein's position was liberating for those who were accustomed to compartmentalizing spiritual truth in that it encouraged thinking "Christianly." He was criticized for being rationalistic in this approach.[66] But Gaebelein reminded evangelical educators that they were to do more that just *know* the truth—they were to *do* the truth in their efforts. The challenge inherent in Gaebelein's thought is that education be effectively integrated with the truth of God and thus consciously stand under the authority of Scripture. Gaebelein's four main principles are: (1) Christian education must be done by Christian teachers; (2) the Bible is the very heart of the curriculum; (3) education may be integrated with a Christian worldview through excellence; and (4) Christian education, broadly considered, must be democratic in a scriptural sense.

Harold Burgess aptly observes that "the heart of religious education, for Gaebelein, is the communication of biblical truths by teachers who are able to lead students to an understanding of these truths."[67] Gaebelein is idealistic about the advance of Christian education and in his expectations that the transmission of biblical truths will lead to personal and communal appropriation.

Lois E. LeBar

Lois LeBar's primary work is *Education That Is Christian*, written originally in 1958 but revised and updated in 1981.[68] In this work, LeBar outlines methods that consistently emphasize biblical content and the centrality of Christ. She maintains that Christian education must be centered in both the living Word of God (Christ) and the written Word of God (the Bible).[69] She exemplifies Gaebelein's vision that Christian educators would stand under Scripture in their formulation of educational theory. LeBar consistently refers to Scripture for her insights. In doing so, she places a significant emphasis on the work of the Holy Spirit as the human teacher consciously seeks to work with the Divine Teacher in all aspects of teaching.[70]

LeBar is distinct from Gaebelein in her conscious effort to include experiential aspects of learning, drawing on the insights of John Amos Comenius

---

66. Cully, *Search for a Christian Education*, 109.

67. Harold W. Burgess, *An Invitation to Religious Education* (Mishawaka, IN: Religious Education Press, 1975), 27.

68. Lois E. LeBar, *Education That Is Christian*, rev. ed. (Old Tappan, NJ: Fleming H. Revell, 1981).

69. Ibid., 212–15.

70. Ibid., 238–54.

and his educational realism. Comenius emphasized the place of "nature" and the impact of education on society. Comenius's hope was that education would transform or reform society because teaching would grapple with the practical applications of truth. Comenius was sensitive to the world of the needs, interests, and motivations of students.

LeBar identifies three goals for Christian education, stated in terms of student outcomes: (1) to lead students to Christ; (2) to build students up in Christ; (3) to send students out for Christ.[71] In other words, the three goals of education are transformation, formation, and service.

Following in the tradition of Comenius, LeBar emphasizes both authoritative content and the actual experience of students. This is distinct from Gaebelein's subject-centered approach. She also seeks to wed emphasis on the Sunday school with emphasis on the home and the community. In some ways she is not unlike the progressive educator John Dewey, though she comes from a distinctly theistic and supernatural faith commitment. Dewey sought to synthesize child-centered and content-centered approaches in education. He also sought to emphasize both the school and society in the hope that the school would become a microcosm of the society.[72]

LeBar affirms the distinctive historical, revelational, and soteriological elements of Christianity, while accomplishing that which Dewey sought to achieve in his synthesizing efforts in general education. Although LeBar traces her roots to Comenius, her ideas are a sensitive Christian complement to those of Dewey in the areas of educational practice and curriculum formation. LeBar can be criticized, however, for her lack of sensitivity to some of the wider social implications of the Christian faith and for her emphasis on the formal structures of education, namely, the school, to the relative exclusion of nonformal education.

Lawrence O. Richards

Lawrence O. Richards is a well-known contributor to the literature on evangelical Christian education. His most comprehensive and definitive work is *A*

---

71. Lois E. LeBar, *Children in the Bible School* (Westwood, NJ: Revell, 1952), 193–94.

72. The best introduction to Dewey's educational thought is provided in Martin S. Dworkin, *Dewey on Education: Selections* (New York: Teachers College Press, 1959). From a Christian perspective, Dewey must first be criticized for his ahistorical pragmatism and presentism. Christianity is a historical faith. Second, Dewey must be criticized for his antisupernatural bias that discounts the place of revelation. Christianity is a revealed religion. Third, Dewey must be criticized for his excessive faith in progress and education and for his assumption that education can result in the salvation of people. Christianity recognizes the reality of sin and maintains that salvation comes through faith in Jesus Christ by the grace of God. Beyond these criticisms, much can be gained from a study of Dewey.

Theology of Christian Education.[73] In contrast to Gaebelein and LeBar, Richards is an enthusiastic advocate of nonformal education, which, he maintains, better fosters change and development in the total personality of students as compared with an exclusive focus on formal education.[74] Richards opposes a formal school approach to Christian education that depends exclusively on a subject-centered method to nurture persons in the Christian faith and life. As an alternative, he recommends a socialization/enculturation approach that includes a self-conscious intention to develop a community of faith in which the Christian life is modeled and more "caught than taught." Richards's approach does not exclude a concern for revealed truth but encourages persons to consider the implications of truth for life and the response to truth in life.[75]

Richards is a visionary who calls the church to renew its educational efforts by stressing training and discipleship. He advocates a whole-person focus that requires students to be active rather than passive participants in the learning process. He sets high ideals for leadership, growth, relationships, and home nurture in the effort to encourage the ministry of all believers.

Richards can be criticized, however, for his lack of sensitivity to various contextual factors. He appears to be insensitive to liturgical structures and distinctive denominational elements in stressing renewal. He limits the place of authority in emphasizing servant leadership and assumes the ready availability of models and disciples in the local church setting. He fails to recognize the multiple factors that can limit effective nurture in the home, including the presence of non-Christian parents. His emphasis on nurture fails to adequately stress the need for evangelism and service as equal concerns in the educational program of the local church.

Despite these criticisms and the potential limitations of Richards's perspective, his thought represents an alternative to a dead orthodoxy that fails to impact the lives of its adherents with the life that is Christ. His theology embodies a concerted effort to grapple with biblical foundations for Christian education outside the confines of formal education. Richards suggests an alternative paradigm for renewal in Christian education in the local church, providing essential insights for developing nonformal education and for the socialization and enculturation processes of Christian communities. Richards reminds educators that significant educational experiences are the relationships established and the modeling communicated.

73. Lawrence O. Richards, *A Theology of Christian Education* (Grand Rapids: Zondervan, 1975).

74. Ibid., 68.

75. This emphasis is expanded in Lawrence O. Richards, *Creative Bible Teaching* (Chicago: Moody, 1970).

Gene A. Getz

Like Richards, Gene A. Getz is another spokesperson for the renewal movement in evangelical education.[76] He shares Richards's concern to provide an alternative vision to guide the church in its educational efforts. Basing his insights on the educational commission of Matthew's Gospel, he emphasizes the tasks of evangelism and edification in the development of disciples of Jesus Christ. Getz proposes a model that incorporates three lenses for discerning an appropriate philosophy of education.

From the first lens of Scripture, Getz identifies biblical principles essential for evangelism and edification. From the second lens of history, he suggests lessons from previous educational attempts in the evangelical church. For example, he points out that the strength of emphasizing Scripture has diminished the importance of the active participation of individual members in the church. Getz questions whether current church activities are actually contributing to mature discipleship among all church participants. The third and final lens is that of culture. Getz discusses the element of culture, whereas Gaebelein, LeBar, and Richards do not devote much attention to this factor in their theorizing. Cultural considerations helpfully confront the Christian educator with the need to distinguish cultural and biblical values and to struggle with questions of contextualization.

The focus and characteristic stance of each of these four evangelical spokespersons are summarized in table 5. An examination and understanding of each of the perspectives of these four educators discussed in this section is valuable in the attempt to appreciate the evangelical heritage of Christian education.

TABLE 5
Evangelical Educators

Educator	Focus	Stance
Frank Gaebelein	Quality formal education Academic excellence under the authority of Scripture	Wise scholar/headmaster
Lois LeBar	Spirit-filled formal education Teaching sensitive to student needs	Inspired teacher
Lawrence Richards	Nurturant nonformal education Discipling and modeling in the body of Christ	Enthusiastic visionary
Gene Getz	Faithful local church education (formal and nonformal) Evangelism and edification	Discerning pastor/guide

76. See Gene A. Getz, *Sharpening the Focus of the Church* (Chicago: Moody, 1974) for an introduction to his work.

Other educators such as Findley B. Edge could be cited, but these four serve as representative spokespersons.[77] These four theorists share a concern for the authority of Scripture and the need for faithfulness and excellence in any education that claims to be Christian. Gaebelein calls for consistency with biblical truth, LeBar for cooperation with the Holy Spirit, Richards for impact on life and the church community, and Getz for accountability in relation to ecclesiastical purposes. Building on this heritage is the task of evangelical educators today and in the future.

Continuity and Reaffirmation

In addressing the question of continuity, we would do well to recall what C. S. Lewis has termed the "chronological fallacy." This fallacy dismisses ideas and values simply because they are not new and thereby makes the calendar the criterion of truth.[78] An evangelical theology implies an affirmation of basic truths or essentials on the basis of revelation and their correspondence with reality as evidenced through the study of history. These insights serve as helpful guidelines for current educational thought and practice.

While these insights provide for continuity, they also require adaptation to specific contexts. A Christian world and life view must be sensitive to historical developments. The development of an educational theory is an art that includes creativity, subjectivity, and risk. Risk is inherent in our human condition. It involves the recognition that persons are embedded in the fabric of history and have responsibilities as makers of history to live out their values and commitments.

Christians have not chosen the timing for their historical journeys, but being in a particular historical time requires learning from the past and living in the present with a concern for God's future. Viewing the past provides a rootedness from which to address the challenges of the present and the future world in which the Christian vocation is to be expressed. In appreciating the light and shadows of the past, Christians can reappropriate an all too forgotten heritage, resulting in rejoicing, repentance, and renewal. In moving from the past to address the present, Christian educators have relied on the social sciences to gain insights. Chapter 5 will explore sociological and anthropological foundations, and chapter 6 will consider psychological foundations that serve educators in their practice.

77. See the work of Findley B. Edge, *The Greening of the Church* (Waco: Word, 1971).
78. Frank E. Gaebelein provides this insight in "The Idea of Excellence and Our Obligation to It," *Gordon Review* (Winter 1962): 137.

Points to Ponder

- What lights and shadows in terms of educational ideas and ideals from the history of Christian education are most prominent for you and why?
- From the historical overview in this chapter, which specific insights have you gained for the current practices of Christian education in the home, the church, the school, the community, or the nation of your particular setting and calling?
- Who serve as educational exemplars for your educational visions and why? Identify persons from the past who most inspire you as teachers and learners and suggest how they serve as models for your life.
- Outside the United States, which Christian education efforts are most outstanding for current ministries?
- Identify additional exemplary women and men, still living, who have served as Christian educators in your particular faith tradition. Consider sharing their ministries in writing with others.

5

Sociological Foundations

In their work *The Social Construction of Reality: A Treatise in the Sociology of Knowledge*, Peter Berger and Thomas Luckmann maintain that reality is socially constructed. They define reality as "a quality apertaining to phenomena that we recognize as having a being independent of our own volition."[1] The task of a sociology of knowledge is to analyze those processes by which reality is socially constructed. This task is particularly important for Christian educators to consider because education is concerned with the production and distribution of knowledge. In the case of the Christian faith, educators intend to share a knowledge of God, as revealed in Jesus Christ, and a knowledge of the Christian faith itself. This is the reality they hope others will embrace as a result of their teaching.

Christian educators seek to share with their students not only that which is real for them but also that which the Christian community down through the ages has identified as real. Berger and Luckmann define knowledge as "the certainty that phenomena are real and that they possess specific characteristics."[2] Christian educators seek to share knowledge that is essential for life as it is offered in the person and work of Jesus Christ. They strive to share a knowledge of God, a knowledge of God's Word, and reality as viewed from the perspective of the Christian faith community in its various expressions.

1. Peter L. Berger and Thomas Luckmann, *The Social Construction of Reality: A Treatise in the Sociology of Knowledge* (Garden City, NY: Doubleday, 1966), 1.
2. Ibid.

It is essential to recognize that the Christian community is a social entity in both its historical and its contemporary expressions. As a social entity, the Christian community manifests variety along with an underlying unity. Both its variety and unity have an impact on the thought and practice of Christian education. Thus careful attention must be given to the sociological foundations of Christian education.[3] These sociological foundations include insights drawn from both sociology and anthropology, and, in particular, cultural anthropology. To understand the process of Christian education, one must refer to culture and society. The very practice of Christian education assumes a cultural context. This is a given in our created world. God created persons with the capacity to create culture and to form societies. Without culture, Christianity is an abstraction unrelated to human life. In relation to education the matter of culture is essential, as suggested by Bernard Bailyn's definition of education discussed in chapter 3, namely, that education is "the entire process by which a culture transmits itself across the generations."[4] Given the variety of Christian cultures today, the task of Christians is to transmit a viable faith to present and future generations that allows for both continuity and change as suggested by the last chapter's discussion of historical foundations. But a crucial issue is to understand the nature of culture itself in which persons in general and Christians in particular live their lives together.

The Social Construction of Reality: Culture

There are various ways to regard culture in relation to education. G. H. Bantock, for example, sees culture as sharply divided into two kinds, high and low culture, relative to social-class designations. High culture is associated with the sophisticated elite class, while low culture is associated with the working class. From Bantock's perspective, education for different classes would be distinct in that each class has a distinct culture. For Christian education this distinction might imply a different educational agenda depending on the social class of participants. In contrast to Bantock, a second perspective is advocated by P. H. Hirst, who ignores historical and social

3. My stress in this chapter on a constructionist perspective is related to my interest in a reforming perspective. The insights of structuralism for education are explored in Robert W. Pazmiño, *Principles and Practices of Christian Education: An Evangelical Perspective* (1992; Eugene, OR: Wipf & Stock, 2002), chap. 3, "Educational Structures," 59–90. The school of thought of structuralism in cultural anthropology is sometimes criticized for its lack of attention to historical and cultural distinctives. This also holds for structuralism in the field of psychology.

4. Bernard Bailyn, *Education in the Forming of American Society* (New York: W. W. Norton, 1960), 14.

differences in cultures and subcultures. Instead Hirst sees education in terms of "culture-free" knowledge, which implies sharing knowledge interculturally and transculturally. For Hirst, culture is a way of life, independent of the educator's primary tasks. From Hirst's perspective, the task of Christian education would be consistent for all participants regardless of historical, class, or social differences. An essential core of content is to be sustained regardless of the cultural context. A third perspective regarding culture is that of Raymond Williams. Williams sees culture in terms of its historical setting and examines cultural change taking place over various periods of time. His analysis indicates that educational change has not kept pace with social and cultural change. Thus the task for educators is to make their teaching contextually as updated and relevant as possible in order to impact the lives of students within emerging cultures.[5] For Christian educators this would require the use of the most updated approaches and technologies in light of recent research developments and trends. It would also require a critical and careful analysis of every cultural context before an educational agenda could be proposed.

To discern the relative truths of these three perspectives, we must define culture in general and consider a possible Christian perspective on culture, which makes up the fabric of our lives. Clifford Geertz, a cultural anthropologist, provides a helpful general definition. He defines culture as a historically transmitted pattern of meanings embodied in symbols. It is a system of inherited conceptions expressed in symbolic forms by means of which persons communicate, perpetuate, and develop their knowledge and attitude toward life. Culture integrates both the ethos and the worldview of a particular people. The ethos of a group is the tone, character, and quality of its life. It is the moral and aesthetic style and mood that characterizes the group's way of life. A worldview is the picture one has of the way things in actuality are, the most comprehensive idea of order.[6] Using Geertz's conception of culture, educators should consider the ethos and worldview of the folk they intend to teach.

5. Denis Lawton, *Class, Culture, and the Curriculum* (London: Routledge & Kegan Paul, 1975), 9–26. For a further discussion of Williams's perspective, see Raymond Williams, *Culture* (London: Fontana, 1981), in which he seeks to develop a sociology of culture. Williams discusses the problem of definition on pp. 10–14. One definition sees culture as a distinct way of life with a distinctive signifying system. A second definition encompasses artistic and intellectual activities, which include signifying practices. For a fuller definition of culture, see Raymond Williams, *Keywords: A Vocabulary of Culture and Society*, rev. ed. (New York: Oxford University Press, 1985), 87–93.

6. Clifford Geertz, *The Interpretation of Cultures* (New York: Basic Books, 1973), 126–27.

Geertz's comprehensive definition enables the Christian educator to view the Christian faith in its particular expression as one cultural system. The Christian world and life view is a historically transmitted pattern of meanings that is embodied in symbols. It is much more than this system, given the Christian claim to supernatural realities, but for the purposes of considering the educational task of transmitting Christian truth it is at least this. Also, there is an ethos that characterizes the Christian community. One aspect of this ethos is the hope that the community actually manifests love in its various relationships. (Of course, there are additional cultural aspects that characterize any given group of Christians relative to their historical and sociological situation. A first-century Christian community in Asia Minor is distinct from a twentieth-century Christian community in Latin America, though there may be some remarkable similarities.)

How, then, does culture operate in the lives of Christians and in their efforts to teach? As N. H. Beversluis suggests, culture for Christians can become piety expressing itself in honesty, fairness, and righteousness. It can become participation in the world's work, making things or changing things, and doing this as an image bearer in conformity with what is understood to be God's will and particular call. Culture is working with the givens, the "materials," in the world of nature or in society. Christians can do this work with sensitivity and accountability, with creative imagination and self-expression giving glory to God.[7] Thus, what may distinguish Christians' cultural activities is their commitment, values, and sensitivities that focus on the revelation and will of God for human life. Herein is the potential of a Christian culture in the midst of a pluralistic and multicultural society.

While Bantock recognizes the existence of social classes and different cultural expressions, a Christian worldview implies the necessity of sharing the whole counsel of God with all social classes. This does not negate the need for cultural sensitivity in sharing Christian truth and the consideration of the readiness of the participants, but suggests a reconciliation in Christ that unites persons of high and low culture in a common community, namely, the church. The cosmic Christ has shattered cultural walls that promote division at the expense of humanity's unity but has also honored the gifts that diverse cultures bring. The apostle Paul in writing to the Galatians makes explicit the extent of Christ's shattering of walls: "There is no longer Jew or Greek, there is no longer slave or free, there is no longer male and female; for all of you are one in Christ Jesus" (Gal. 3:28 NRSV).

---

7. N. H. Beversluis, *Toward a Theology of Education*, Occasional Papers from Calvin College, vol. 1, no. 1 (Grand Rapids: Calvin College, 1981), 15.

The first-century church as described in the book of Acts (4:32–5:11; 6:1–7) wrestled with finding a common ground, a unity despite the tensions created by class differences.

Hirst's "culture-free" knowledge necessitates careful evaluation. The Christian faith lays claim to a body of knowledge that is true by virtue of its being God's revelation. This truth is transcultural in the sense of having significance for all cultures, for all historical contexts. Yet this truth was initially communicated with very specific cultural situations in view, and the task of Christians in a contemporary context is to discern the implications for current life. Herein is the task of hermeneutics, which calls for the interpretation, explanation, and application of the transcultural truths of Scripture for the present. The work of hermeneutics takes place within various cultural contexts, and the application of transcultural truths requires a careful reading of both the cultural situation in which one ministers and the cultural situation initially addressed by biblical writers. In one sense, freedom from culture is not possible given the created nature of persons as cultural beings, yet in another sense Christ enables persons to be free from those aspects of culture that limit or oppress them and prevent them from becoming all God has intended them to be.

Williams's perspective on the historical character of culture must be affirmed from a Christian worldview. As explored in chapter 4, Christianity is a faith rooted in history that emphasizes the significance of persons in time as God interacts with them. God, in the person of Christ, entered into time and space to accomplish redemptive purposes, and the historical process gives evidence of God's continuing creative and providential activities through the person and ministry of the Holy Spirit. But we should question Williams's emphasis on educational change keeping pace with social and cultural change. All social and cultural change may not reflect the will of God, and thus Christians are called to be critical of change for its own sake. For Christians, growth implies not only change but also continuity, not only change but also conformity to God's will in the midst of change. Thus Christians must be aware of cultural change and support those changes that represent closer approximations of God's will for humanity and all of creation.

Is there a Christian culture that Christian educators should perpetuate through their teaching? There are many cultures, and each can embody the Christian faith in ways that glorify God. The culture in which persons are born provides them with windows on the world. But this culture can also erect walls, walls that can isolate and separate people.

Each person's culture serves as a lens through which he or she sees and understands other people. All information is filtered through that lens—beliefs about the world, people, life, God, and ultimate reality. Each person's lens can be viewed as liberating and/or oppressive to the extent to which it provides knowledge that is true in relation to God's general and special revelation. The challenge for Christians is to be discriminating about the nature of that lens. In certain areas, each culture must be affirmed and preserved given the unique understanding it provides for human life. In other areas, the lens distorts things, and the Christian task is to apply the redemptive fruits of Christ's work. In some situations, the lens is so faulty, as was the case in Nazi Germany, that a total transformation is necessary if human life is to continue. Making such judgments requires spiritual discernment and a serious grappling with Christian values.

What *is* the relationship between the Christian faith and human culture? What *has* Jerusalem to do with Athens? The responses to those questions have often been described by comparing the perspectives of two early church fathers, Tertullian and Origen. It will be recalled from chapter 3 that Tertullian first posed that question as the Christian church related to a Hellenized world.

Tertullian essentially maintained that Jerusalem had nothing to do with Athens. He saw the need to affirm the place of piety in the Christian faith because Christians were called to be set apart, distinct, holy, and sanctified in relation to a culture he viewed as directly opposed to God. Tertullian's stance, while affirming piety, has the potential of fostering pietism. Pietism can be defined as an otherworldly, subjective, withdrawn, and legalistic religious stance in relation to the wider culture. Pietism is neither of the world nor in the world. By comparison, piety can be characterized as being not of the world while being engaged in it. Beversluis describes piety as living between doubt and faith, between guilt and renewal with hope. Piety is "the practice and celebration of the presence of God in the midst of life."[8] A sense of God's presence in all of life leads to a love of and devotion to God.

Origen, in contrast to Tertullian, essentially maintained that Jerusalem had everything to do with Athens. He saw the need to affirm the place of cultural obedience in the Christian faith because Christians were called to be actively engaged in the world, given that it was God's creation and the locale for Christian life and vocation. Origen's stance, while affirming engagement, has the potential of becoming cultural accommodation and secularism. Cultural accommodation is this-worldly, undiscriminating, undiscerning, and profane. By comparison, cultural obedience or engagement can be characterized as being in the world while not being of it. Beversluis describes cultural obedience as

8. Ibid., 12–13.

doing the world's work with discrimination and accountability. He sees this involvement as part of Christian sanctification, which takes account of sin and affirms the world while seeking to transform it.[9]

Tertullian's and Origen's perspectives represent two extremes of answers to the enduring question regarding the relationship between Christ and culture. H. Richard Niebuhr's typology, introduced in chapter 2, provides a helpful vehicle for further consideration. Each model has strengths and weaknesses for dealing with the wider society and culture, and each community response may vary with the issue in question. Each model also implies a distinct approach to the task of Christian education. Evangelicals have usually opted for types 1, 4, and 5 of Niebuhr's models (Christ against culture, Christ and culture in paradox, and Christ the transformer of culture).[10]

Tertullian represents the model of Christ against culture. The strength of such a model is the obedient emphasis on being set apart for God, on being not of the world, on fundamental allegiance to the holiness and righteousness of God. The weakness is its withdrawal, its ghettoism of the mind and heart from the world. Educational practice under this model tends to be guarded, disciplined, protected, purist, and isolated. Some Christian day schools and home schooling efforts attempt to stand over against the culture with its pagan philosophy and lifestyle. Such an education is also polemic and apologetic.

The model of Christ and culture in paradox necessitates a careful assessment of the claims of Christ and those of the culture. The claims of both domains must be addressed, resulting in inevitable tensions for Christians who want to faithfully exercise their responsibility. The primary call is for loyalty to Christ, yet responsibility for culture cannot be ignored. Life is lived between a rock and a hard place. The rock is that of Christian faith, and the hard place is the world with its many demands.

The strength of this second model is its realistic portrayal of the dimension of conflict in the lives of Christians and of the radical work of God in Christ. But its weakness is that such conflict may never be resolved or resolvable. Such a stance can imply an acceptance of the status quo, and antinomianism, or an incipient cultural conservatism.[11] Given the inevitability of paradox or conflict, Christians may become disinterested and distant from further engagement in the world while negotiating a reasonable peace within their personal lives. Educational practice under this model tends to be challenging, introspective, and conserving.

9. Ibid., 15–17.
10. David J. Hesselgrave, *Communicating Christ Cross-Culturally* (Grand Rapids: Zondervan, 1978), 79–80.
11. H. Richard Niebuhr, *Christ and Culture* (New York: Harper & Row, 1956), 185–87.

The model of Christ as the transformer of culture highlights the need for Christians to promote renewal and revival in the wider culture as a means by which to promote God's will in human life. This model promotes the extension of Christ's redemptive work to the whole of creation. Such an approach assumes the personal appropriation of salvation in Christ and the expression of personal faith in the works of culture. The strength of this model is its conscious attempt to relate the claims of Christ's lordship to all of life and to struggle with the implications of this. The weaknesses of this model are its failure to seriously grapple with the extent of sin and its misspent energies in seeking the conversion of culture, which may rarely happen.

Educational practice under this model would stress the need for a careful reading of the wider culture focusing on opportunities for renewal. There is a constant effort to relate Christian truth claims to study in all areas. Such an effort is inevitably optimistic while recognizing the realities of sin and human fallenness. A constant challenge in this model is the effective use of Scripture to discern the whole of God's truth as discovered in general revelation. Unlike the first two models, this model holds a greater potential for compromise and cultural accommodation. To be discerning of their relationship with the wider culture, Christian educators can consider the role of contextualization and decontextualization in their ministries.

Contextualization and Decontextualization in Culture

In the discussion of theological foundations in chapter 2, contextualization was defined as the continual process by which truth is applied to and emerges from concrete historical situations.[12] Harvie Conn, a Reformed missiologist, defines contextualization as "the process of the conscientization of the whole people of God to the hermeneutical obligations of the gospel."[13]

Stephen Knapp identifies contextualization as the "dynamic process through which the church continually challenges and/or incorporates–transforms elements of the cultural and social milieu of which it is an integral part in its daily struggle to be obedient to the Lord Jesus Christ in its life and mission in the world."[14] All three of these definitions point to the need for Christians to recognize and address the wider culture in which they are called to live.

12. See page 64.

13. Harvie M. Conn, "Contextualization: Where Do We Begin?" in *Evangelicals and Liberation*, ed. Carl E. Armerding (Nutley, NJ: Presbyterian & Reformed, 1977), 104.

14. Stephen Knapp, "Contextualization and Its Implications for U.S. Evangelical Church and Missions" (paper presented at Partnership in Mission, Abington, PA, 1976), 15.

The first definition emphasizes the translation of the gospel as truth into relevant social and cultural forms or symbols. Both Conn's and Knapp's definitions imply not only such translation but also the additional dimension of decontextualization. Decontextualization is the judgment of the Word of God, which transforms personal, political, economic, social, and cultural spheres of life.[15] This stance is representative of the prophetic tradition and a concern for advocacy noted in chapter 1. Thus two processes are important in relating the Christian faith to culture. The first process is contextualization, which requires dialogue between the Christian educator and the immanent context of ministry. This process requires a hermeneutic of the world in its social and cultural particularity that honors the incarnation. The second process is decontextualization, which necessitates dialogue between the Christian educator and the transcendent Scriptures. In this second process a hermeneutic of the Word is required. Both processes complement each other and are necessary for a faithful response to the gospel demand of being in but not of the world. This is the distinctive Christian calling and vocation.

Evangelical Christians on occasion have recognized these processes and their complementarity. This new interest has been largely facilitated by those involved in missions because they address the outworkings of the Christian faith in the global context. Prior to this recent interest, evangelicals, while addressing the hermeneutics of the Word, have all too readily dismissed the various dimensions of the world. Ignoring contextualization, evangelicals have often reduced God's agenda to souls instead of the entire cosmos. Individual souls are of eternal significance, yet they represent but one dimension of human beings and but one sphere of God's creation.

In contrast to evangelicals, liberal Christians and liberationists have tended to address the hermeneutics of the world. In so doing, they have too readily dismissed the various demands of the Word. Overlooking decontextualization, liberals, and in some cases liberationists, have on occasion baptized the world's agenda as God's agenda. The world is of great significance, but it represents God's creation, not the Creator. God the Creator has been revealed in the Word, created, written, and living.

In terms of contextualization, the Third Mandate Programme of the Theological Education Fund has posed some significant questions for seminaries, churches, and schools to consider in their educational efforts.

What about *missiological contextualization*? Is the seminary, school, or program focusing on the urgent issues of renewal and reform in the church,

15. Conn, "Contextualization," 104–5.

and on the vital issues of human development and justice in its particular situation? (A liberationist perspective would question the notion of reform and renewal in the face of injustice and would instead propose revolution and complete transformation.)

What about *structural contextualization*? Is the church, school, or program seeking to develop a form and structure appropriate to the specific needs of its culture in its peculiar social, economic, and political situation? (A liberationist perspective would require that the form or structure be liberating and transformational at points where the culture is oppressive.)

What about *theological contextualization*? Is the church or seminary seeking to do theology in a way appropriate and authentic to its situation? Does it seek to relate the gospel more directly to urgent issues of ministry and service in the world? Does it move out of its own milieu in its expression of the gospel?

Finally, what about *pedagogical contextualization*? Is the seminary, school, or program seeking to develop theological training that attempts to understand the educational processes as a liberating and creative effort? Does it attempt to overcome the dangers of elitism and authoritarianism in both the method and the goals of its program to release the potential of a servant ministry? Is it sensitive to the widespread gap between the academic and the practical?[16]

There are no simple answers to these questions, but these and others must be addressed in responding faithfully to Christ in the midst of various cultures and in wrestling with the sociological foundations of Christian education. These questions serve to promote the thoughtful efforts of Christian educators to contextualize their teaching. In this contextualization, educators can consider insights gained from the sociology of knowledge for how they structure their teaching.

The Sociology of Knowledge

Lawrence Stenhouse aptly observes that the sociology of knowledge treats knowledge (or what counts as knowledge) as socially constructed or constituted. It also examines how subjects or disciplines are socially constructed as sets of shared meanings. The idea that knowledge is represented in culture implies that knowledge can be socially determined by the needs of both groups and individuals. Stenhouse goes on to point out that the determinations of groups and individuals may be deliberate departures from truth,

---

16. Theological Education Fund, *Ministry in Context: The Third Mandate Programme of the Theological Education Fund (1970–77)* (Bromley, Kent, England: Theological Education Fund, 1972), 31.

though not necessarily intentional departures. A sociology of knowledge, then, does not deal with tests of truth, but its perspective implies a relativism of truth.

Given the tradition of aspiration toward absolutes, toward a notion of warranted knowledge,[17] evangelicals might readily dismiss such an inquiry or any insights that might be derived from this seemingly relativistic perspective. This would be unfortunate because, as Denis Lawton suggests, sociological inquiry must be supplemented by both philosophical and psychological research.[18] Philosophy and theology are disciplines that explore truth claims and their validity. The viewpoints of philosophy and theology can be complementary rather than contradictory to those of sociology.

Berger and Luckmann, in *The Social Construction of Reality*, propose a dialectical relationship between persons as producers and the social world as their product. From their perspective the social world has three functions in relation to knowledge.

First, knowledge programs the channels through which an objective world is produced. Persons are the agents of externalization who express themselves in various activities and forms just as God is expressed in creation.

Second, knowledge objectifies this world through language and the cognitive apparatus based on language; that is, it orders the world into objects apprehended as reality. Adam named the creation and in that naming objectified its reality. God is revealed initially as the Word who spoke and brought forth all life and creation.

Third, knowledge is internalized again as objectively valid truth in the course of socialization. The world as named by God and Adam was then passed on to Adam's offspring and internalized by them as objective truth.[19]

Despite Berger and Luckmann's critical interest, their analysis can lead to an acceptance of dominant social knowledge and religious norms as functional necessities to be perpetuated. This is not a problem when continuity and the preservation of cultural forms are necessary, but if change and transformation are required, difficulties arise. This analysis can foster a sense of powerlessness for Christians; it lacks a moral perspective from which to critique the functional requisites of any given society in light of gospel values that Christians claim are of perennial and eternal significance.

Berger and Luckmann's portrayal of religion is one-sided in its emphasis on the role of religion in legitimating existing cultural forms. It fails to

17. Lawrence Stenhouse, *An Introduction to Curriculum Research and Development* (New York: Holmes & Meier, 1975), 14–15.

18. Lawton, *Class, Culture, and the Curriculum*, 58–59.

19. Berger and Luckmann, *Social Construction of Reality*, 57–58.

adequately consider the prophetic dimension of religious faith that questions the legitimation of social structures. Such a viewpoint reduces religious concerns to merely social and psychological factors. It emphasizes enculturation to the relative exclusion of disenculturation.

Evangelicals have been criticized for their support of the status quo in various societies, for failing to affirm the prophetic and radical dimensions of biblical faith. Although evangelicals may be attracted to Berger and Luckmann's perspective, they must also assume responsibility for the definition and perpetuation of the knowledge that analysis reveals. In other words, if the selection of knowledge tends to exclude other realities equally embodied in biblical revelation but not valued by evangelical communities, then corporate guilt must be recognized and addressed. Failure to do so represents a lack of faithfulness and brings into question integrity and consistency. One example of this oversight is the emphasis on redemptive themes to the relative exclusion of the implications of creative themes in biblical revelation. These themes can be recovered through direct attention to their significance in the biblical record. The Bible begins with the account of creation and ends with the vision of a new heaven and earth restored by God in the consummation.

A second perspective on the sociology of knowledge is represented by Jerry Gill in *The Possibility of Religious Knowledge*. Gill maintains a functional view of knowledge based on the thought of Michael Polanyi. Gill's functionalism has a positive correspondence with structuralism, which is identified at the beginning of this chapter. With this perspective, the experience of knowing is understood as composed of dimensional and contextual awareness, together with committed, functional response. The interaction between these two aspects calls attention to the tacit and mediated aspects of knowledge, as well as to its more direct and explicit aspects. Polanyi and Gill attempt to bridge the domains of fact and value, which have been viewed as separate in much of modern Western thought.[20] This bridging of domains serves to connect knowledge to life and the response of persons to what is shared as valuable knowledge.

Gill proposes simultaneously interpenetrating dimensions of knowledge that include (1) physical awareness of the material world; (2) moral awareness of other persons; (3) personal awareness of oneself as a person; and (4) religious awareness of transcendent reality. Gill's contextual factors include intentionality, purpose, activity, response of the knower and known, and social and perceptual conventions. Gill situates knowledge

20. Jerry H. Gill, *The Possibility of Religious Knowledge* (Grand Rapids: Eerdmans, 1971), 7–8, 13.

along a continuum, with explicit and tacit knowledge at opposing poles. Explicit knowledge exhibits characteristics such as precise analysis, verbal articulation, descriptive identification, observational objectivity, and an absolute distinction between the knower and the known. Tacit knowledge is characterized by intuitive awareness, bodily expressions, holistic recognition, embodied subjectivity, and a contextual distinction between the knower and the known.[21] Although Gill does adequately explicate the contextual dimensions of his scheme, he does expand upon an understanding of knowledge within a biblical perspective. Knowledge is not to be limited to explicit knowledge discerned through facts, but must include values, intuition, and personal response. Gill's perspective fosters a more holistic appreciation of all that Christian educators can attend to in their teaching with some exceptions.

Gill does not offer a clear analysis of power relationships that operate in societal contexts. He appears to tacitly accept as valid knowledge that is posited by disciplines, societies, or institutions. He speaks of contextual concerns but does not radicalize them in terms of considering their roots, relating these concerns to social, political, and economic structures that sustain any teaching effort. Whereas he considers personal and religious dimensions, he does not broaden the individual focus to include corporate and global concerns that are recognized in the current global context of corporate life. Beyond persons and their face-to-face encounters, structures and institutions must be reckoned with and cannot be collapsed into Gill's moral dimension. Gill's insights, while valuable, must be expanded upon in light of the corporate and social dimensions of life, which are also addressed in the Scriptures. Evangelicals are called to recognize the wider global and cosmic implications of the gospel in relation to social, political, and economic structures and must develop a theology of institutions to address the realities of an institutionalized world. This work is not easily undertaken, but it is essential in considering the sociological foundations of Christian education. These sociological foundations require that Christian educators wrestle with the implications of Christ's lordship for all of life.

A third viewpoint on knowledge is that of Jürgen Habermas, a leading spokesperson of the school of critical theory at the Frankfurt Institute in Germany. Habermas proposes three approaches to knowledge: (1) the approach of the empirical-analytical sciences, which incorporates a technical, cognitive interest and yields information; (2) the approach of the historical-hermeneutical sciences, which incorporates a practical interest and yields

21. Ibid., 119–36.

interpretations; and (3) the approach of the critically oriented sciences, which incorporates an emancipatory interest and yields analyses.

A key concern for Habermas is to maintain all three approaches in dialectical tension. The first two approaches yield nomological knowledge, while the third yields critical and transformational knowledge through self-reflection. The three possible categories of knowledge are: (1) information that expands one's power of technical control; (2) interpretations that make possible the orientation of action within common traditions; and (3) analyses that free consciousness from its dependence on hypostatized powers.[22] It is noteworthy that these three categories have parallels with the three major divisions of the Old Testament canon that Walter Brueggemann calls *ethos*, which provides norms; *logos*, which provides guidelines for action; and *pathos*, which breaks patterns in a critical and liberating fashion.

Habermas's concern for responsibility and the corresponding ethical concern for responsible decisions in engagement with the world can be affirmed, but his autonomous stance is inadequate from a Christian perspective. Autonomy is an independent stance that inevitably excludes an adequate consideration of others. The danger of this exclusive autonomy is that it fails to recognize other autonomous individuals. Theonomy, in contrast, affirms a shared humanity with others that is grounded in God. This moves beyond an individualistic, introspective, and personalistic stance. In a theonomous stance, one sees oneself realistically in relation with other persons in community. In this stance one affirms one's personhood as part of God's creation.

This theonomous aspect of knowledge must be superimposed on Habermas's categories. The ideal emancipated society of which Habermas speaks finds actualization in the covenant community of God approximated in the church as a remnant of God's choosing. The Bible proposes a prophetic stance of knowing that would enlarge Habermas's critically oriented approach to include personal and corporate responsibility to God and a knowledge that is personal. Human interest would embody commitment and engagement with appropriate and corresponding affective and volitional elements. Evangelicals can engage in the critical dialogue suggested by Habermas's work while maintaining a distinctly theonomous center for their understanding that raises questions for Habermas and any other social theorist.

A fourth viewpoint is articulated by Paulo Freire. Freire maintains that persons can never be understood apart from their relationships with the world through thought-language. For Freire reality implies constant interaction between persons as thinking subjects and history and culture. Persons are both

22. Jürgen Habermas, *Knowledge and Human Interests* (Boston: Beacon, 1971), 308–15.

the cause and the effect of history. Persons can shape culture in liberating ways. Knowing is a form of praxis, a process in which a person begins to reflect on her or his orientation to the world by objectifying actions and reflecting upon them in order to return to new action and reflection. Freire, like Gill, seeks to maintain both subjectivity and objectivity in a true act of knowing. True knowing also involves active engagement in the political process of transforming the world to realize liberation as he defines it, as the humanization of persons.[23] Freire hopes that persons will become all that God intends them to be, actively engaging the world and fostering the liberation of all creation.

Freire moves beyond the critique of Habermas to include an incarnated concern for the social activity of knowledge that includes co-intentionality. He addresses the political aspect of knowing that makes joint use of analysis, reflection, and critical consciousness to realize new potentials in society. But Freire can be criticized for his failure to deal adequately with the depth of sin, which distorts the continuing process of conscientization or transformation that he envisions is possible.

The sociology of knowledge demands that Christian educators attend to some important considerations:

Knowledge cannot be separated from a person's being in the world, and knowledge, as proposed by societies and faith communities, embodies and conditions the tasks of naming, creating, critiquing, and transforming that world by particular persons and groups.

Knowledge implies its actualization and its expression, but what of knowing without certainty and knowing only in part, which is implied by God's hidden nature beyond revelation? Christians must acknowledge the place of mystery and incomplete knowledge in both doctrine and life, which counters any stance of arrogance in relation to one's own perspective on life, theology, and education. Christians can recognize the place of paradox and always be open to new light and truth.

What is the relationship of knowledge to speaking, thinking, listening, and interpreting? How is knowledge embodied in each of these activities? How is knowledge assumed in those activities that largely mark personal commitments and value decisions? Christians are called to be explicit about their commitments and values in light of key societal issues and ethical questions.

What of a person's need to know, to realize a *nomos*? Is this quest a human given? Are persons socialized to question, and when does questioning transcend

23. See Paulo Freire, *Pedagogy of the Oppressed*, trans. Myra Bergman Ramos (New York: Seabury, 1970); and Denis E. Collins, *Paulo Freire: His Life, Works, and Thought* (New York: Paulist Press, 1977).

a society's accepted knowledge? What about anomie and acceptance of a state of not knowing or suspended knowing? Evangelical Christians are called to engage in the process of serious questioning and dialogue with nonevangelicals and persons from other faith perspectives.[24]

Is all knowledge part of a larger whole? In that God is the source of all knowledge, what implications are there for a person's quest for knowledge? Evangelicals can affirm their distinctive God-centered focus in response to these questions, recognizing God as the source of all truth.

Knowledge is conditioned by the context, by the questions being asked, and is therefore always knowledge from a certain perspective or position. The recognition and ownership of one's perspective is important for all communities.

Knowledge is also socially distributed. It is an instrument in the struggle for survival and power and has the potential for the liberation and actualization of persons. Knowledge can be a tool for oppression or liberation, depending on its distribution and perpetuation. Knowledge as distributed by evangelical communities must be evaluated in these terms.

There are different ways of knowing. A person may only draw upon an established authority or tradition (heteronomy). Through the use of human reasoning and thought, a person may ask questions, critique ideas and situations, assemble data, and use what appeals to reason and thought in light of experience (autonomy). Personal or corporate experience may provide knowledge (autonomy). However, while Christians use reason, experience, and authority to make sense of the factual world, they acknowledge the beyondness known only by revelation. They accept both the supernatural and the reality of the concrete and practical, giving priority to the place of revelation (theonomy). Christians are to actively listen and interpret within their historical context, combining conviction with tolerance, commitment with openness.

It is possible to view knowledge as a union with the person or thing known. It does not mean that there must always be union with the object of knowledge in order for knowledge to exist. The highest knowledge possible for persons is knowledge of God, which is discussed today in terms of spirituality. This knowledge is conditioned by faith and obedience, by a willingness to know and submit to the will of God that flows from a loving heart. The known in this case is God, but God is also unknowable and unknown beyond revelation. Christians recognize the place of mystery and allow for the working of the Holy Spirit. As the Holy Spirit encounters human spirits, life and growth are possible.

---

24. For a discussion of the nature of this dialogue, see my work *By What Authority Do We Teach? Sources for Empowering Christian Educators* (Eugene, OR: Wipf & Stock, 2002), 119–46.

The Bible regards knowledge as arising from personal encounter, and knowledge of God is related to the revelation of God in the historic past and the promised future. Yet God is also revealed in the present earthly sphere in which God's creatures have their being and live out their history. The knowledge of God is inseparably bound up with God's revelation in time and space, in historical contexts. In the Bible, knowledge implies the awareness of the specific relationship in which the individual person and corporate community stand with the person or object known. Just as the individual is considered a totality rather than a being composed of body and mind, knowledge is an activity in which the whole individual is engaged.

The exploration of insights from the sociology of knowledge brings Christians to a fuller appreciation and understanding of the various dimensions of knowledge. But the words of the apostle Paul directed to the issue of food sacrificed to idols in Corinth serve to warn Christians: "We know that we all possess knowledge. Knowledge puffs up, but love builds up. The man who thinks he knows something does not yet know as he ought to know. But the man who loves God is known by God" (1 Cor. 8:1b–3). Human knowledge is transcended by being known by God and encountering God's love. Paul's warning does not negate the quest for knowledge but rather sets that quest in a wider context of biblical faith and commitment. Grappling with the sociology of knowledge can enable Christian educators to identify the distinctive elements of their teaching that build on faith perspectives.

The Sociology of Education

Beyond considerations of knowledge itself, sociological inquiry can also be directed to the larger effort of education itself. The works of Émile Durkheim, John Eggleston, and Rolland Paulston, among others, provide helpful insights for the Christian educator in understanding how education functions in the wider society and culture. This can assist Christian educators in relating their efforts to what other persons, agencies, and institutions teach in the wider society. These other influences include the home, the community, the church in general, the economy, the media, political bodies, various schools, and social agencies.[25]

Émile Durkheim

In Western Europe, sociology developed as a response to the problems of rapid change. Émile Durkheim was concerned with the breakdown of

25. For an exploration of these various influences, see Pazmiño, *Principles and Practices*, 59–90.

social life following the loss of customary norms and values that had in the past been provided by the church or the personal bonds of a society based on mechanical solidarity. Therefore, his sociology centers on the themes of social order, social control, and consensus.[26]

Durkheim viewed education as a vehicle to restore equilibrium. The sociologist was to study generic types of education corresponding to different types of societies, seeking out the conditions on which each type of education depended and how they emerged from one another. One would thus obtain the laws that govern the evolution of systems of education.[27]

In his analysis of education, Durkheim views education on three levels: the science of education, pedagogical theories, and the practice of education. The science of education involves research, the description of present or past phenomena, and inquiry into their causes or the determination of their effects. Such a science of education provides descriptions and analyses, and it encourages exploration and divergent thought. It proposes working hypotheses, and it draws upon various sources for its scientific content. These sources include psychology, sociology, anthropology, biology, economics, and political science, some of which are discussed in this work.

Of these sources, psychology and sociology share a privileged position along with the study of philosophy in understanding education.[28] At this level of inquiry, the Christian educator can participate in research and make use of the descriptions gained as working hypotheses for pedagogical theories at the second level. In making use of these hypotheses, the guide for the Christian is her or his worldview. A Christian worldview centers on the living and written Word of God and discounts any insights that are not consistent with or complementary to God's truth. Thus the constant challenge at this level is for the Christian to be discerning of any proposed insights.

The second level of Durkheim's analysis is the level of pedagogical theories or practical theories. The objective of this level is not to describe or explain what is or has been the case in education, but to determine what should be the case. Pedagogical theories are oriented neither to the present nor to the past, but to the future. They propose and advocate prescriptions and syntheses for education. Such theories inform persons what must be done and are by their nature speculative, creative, and imaginative reflections. In contrast to the divergent thought of a science of education, pedagogical theories are engaged with convergent thought.[29] Most Christian educators in

26. Lawton, Class, Culture, and Curriculum, 56.
27. Émile Durkheim, Education and Sociology (New York: Free Press, 1956), 95–98.
28. Ibid., 99.
29. Ibid.

the academic world have devoted their primary energies to the development of pedagogical theories on an ad hoc basis, selectively incorporating insights gained from the science of education. Fully elaborated pedagogical theories have not been developed by evangelical Christians until recently.[30]

The third level of Durkheim's analysis is the level of practice. Practice in education describes what must be done, the procedures. Practice is concerned with the art of education and is a system of ways of doing education oriented to special ends. These ways of doing education are products of a traditional experience communicated by a community and/or the product of personal experience. Practice is creative and as an art may be illuminated by reflection. Nevertheless, reflection is not an essential element of the practice of education.[31] Evangelical Christian educators have generally emphasized the practice of education, given their commitments to persons and various local church and parachurch ministries. This has often been done without adequate consideration of Durkheim's first two levels.

From the above analysis, it is possible to suggest an agenda for evangelical Christian educators. The strength of evangelical education is its commitment to the practice of education, and this commitment should not be lost. But evangelical educators must more seriously engage the challenges of formulating pedagogical or practical theories. These theories are better described as practical theologies, given the concerted effort to relate all work to one's theology in evangelicalism. Without such practical theories or theologies, evangelical educators become context bound and unresponsive to important critical issues while being dependent on either traditional strategies or the latest educational trend. This need not be the case if adequate time is devoted to reflection and evaluation amid the urgent demands of ministry.

John Eggleston

In contrast to Durkheim, John Eggleston is a proponent of a "new" sociology of education that considers how knowledge is defined, selected, organized, transmitted, and distributed in schools themselves. His perspective can be applied to Sunday or church schools. He considers how knowledge is valued and the relationships of power and control among those in the knowledge business, namely, among those in schools. But his inquiry is not limited to schools or classrooms, for he looks beyond them to see how they are connected to the larger structures of society, including economic and political systems.

---

30. Warren Benson confirms this analysis in "Evangelical Philosophies of Education," in *Changing Patterns of Religious Education*, ed. Marvin J. Taylor (Nashville: Abingdon, 1984), 53.
31. Durkheim, *Education and Sociology*, 99.

With this larger view it is necessary to consider questions of the legitimacy of current arrangements and commitments.

In his analysis Eggleston suggests five key questions for exploring values and commitments in the particular educational work or ministry:

1. What will be regarded as knowledge, understanding, values, attitudes, and skills (the elements of education)?
2. How should these elements be ranked in importance and status?
3. On what principles will these elements be distributed? To whom and at what times will they be made available and from whom will they be withheld?
4. What is the identity of the groups whose definitions prevail in these matters?
5. Is it legitimate for these groups to act in these ways?[32]

These questions are implicit in every educational endeavor, and Eggleston is helpful in making explicit those areas often assumed or even neglected in the discussion of education. Regarding knowledge, understanding, values, attitudes, and skills, it is important to consider those areas that are neglected or forgotten—the "null curriculum." Careful consideration of excluded knowledge can identify the criteria used in determining the appropriate content. Given the wide possibilities of knowledge, understanding, values, attitudes, and skills, some choice is necessary.

The determination of priorities is inevitable in education, given that the limited resources of time and energy force both personal and corporate evaluation. This evaluation may occur in both private and public domains. In either domain careful discernment is needed to maintain an adequate exposure along with balance. Posing Eggleston's first two questions indicates the essential need for planning and periodic evaluation that wherever possible includes all participants in a particular educational work. Often these choices are not subject to public consideration and the input from all constituencies in a community. A board or committee of persons involved in Christian education can explore the nature of their choices using Eggleston's questions.

Eggleston's third question requires that educators and others who provide direction in educational work carefully articulate principles for distributing content and be aware of the persons involved and their readiness to receive such

32. John Eggleston, *The Sociology of the School Curriculum* (London: Routledge & Kegan Paul, 1977), 23.

content. Such principles are derived from various values and commitments. In the case of the evangelical church, biblical and theological commitments have generally served as normative categories for the derivation of guiding principles. Also, increased attention has been paid to the insights from educational and social science research to discern the characteristics and needs of students and their readiness for learning. But beyond these areas, evangelical educators need to carefully assess their philosophical commitments and how they affect explicit or implicit principles. This assessment cannot be ignored in responding to ever-present needs.

Christian educators must address areas that have not received adequate scrutiny. This has been the case in part because of a conservative stance that has extended beyond theological categories to include all areas of life. In such a stance, persons are generally reluctant to question the identity and legitimacy of those who direct and control various educational ministries. Eggleston's questions guide evangelicals into radical and uncharted waters by raising questions about those who wield power and the legitimacy of the uses of that power. Eggleston's perspective suggests that those who are called to positions of responsibility and power must be questioned and evaluated by those who are served. This is a necessity, given the fallen nature of persons and the inevitable consequences of leadership that is other than moral. Examples can be cited where evangelical leadership has assumed authoritarian stances and has resisted the acknowledgment of weaknesses as well as strengths.

Rolland Paulston

A third contributor from the perspective of a sociology of knowledge is Rolland Paulston, whose work is in the area of international studies. He has developed a general conceptual framework for comparative and international educators. His major contribution is in relating different commitments in social and educational change to their underlying conceptual frameworks or ideological orientations. Table 6 summarizes Paulston's insights.[33]

Paulston notes that educational reform theories are rooted in systematic ideological orientations concerning social reality and the social-change process. Such ideological orientations or biases constrain the abilities of educational planners and reformers to explore the full range of potentially effective strategies for educational reform. For example, a predisposition toward an equilibrium paradigm may ignore insights gained from the perspective of conflict.[34]

33. Rolland G. Paulston, *Conflicting Theories of Social and Educational Change* (Pittsburgh: University Center for International Studies, University of Pittsburgh, 1976), vi–vii.
34. Ibid., v.

Paulston's insights challenge Christians who are concerned for educational reform or renewal. Which of any of these theories are consistent with a Christian worldview in light of Paulston's observation that these orientations are "not random or eclectic but rather follow from personal bias concerning theoretical and ideological orientations to social reality and social-change process"?[35] Lest evangelicals totally avoid conflict models, one must recall the revolutionary beginnings of the United States and other nations that have resulted in a better life for a majority of persons.

These various orientations have some parallels with Niebuhr's Christ and culture scheme. For those Christians who opt for the Christ and culture in paradox, Christ the transformer of culture, and Christ above culture stances, an equilibrium paradigm would seem consistent with their commitments. By comparison those Christians who opt for a Christ against culture would be more likely to opt for a conflict paradigm and, in particular, the theory of cultural revitalization. It is also possible to see how Christians who opt for a Christ the transformer of culture stance might be attracted to a cultural revitalization theory if it were focused on working within the existing system rather than opting out of it. The challenge would be for Christians to be agents of fundamental change within society at large, revitalizing it through their presence and service in diverse ministries.

Paulston reminds evangelical Christians that they must be aware of their ideological commitments. Intellectual integrity and consistency are at stake along with the need to understand various perspectives on social and educational change. Each of the eight theories Paulston outlines contributes insights that must be carefully assessed. Paulston also reminds us that Christians may be called to ministry at various points in society, some working within the system seeking an equilibrium more in line with gospel demands, while others are called to oppose the system or society and through creative conflict to offer new possibilities. Spiritual discernment is crucial in order to distinguish at what points the equilibrium can be supported and at what points radical change is demanded in the effort to be faithful to God's calling in the world.

For evangelicals, Paulston's work has particular significance in addressing the widely discussed issue of schooling. Should Christian parents educate their children in public, private Christian, or home schools? For various reasons, many Christian parents have judged that the public schools in their communities do not provide the best possible education for their children. They conclude that a stance against the common culture of the public school is

35. Ibid.

TABLE 6
Theories of Social and Educational Change/"Reform"

Social Change	Illustrative Linked Assumptions Concerning Education-Change Potentials and Processes			
Paradigms / Theories	Preconditions for Educational Change	Rationales for Educational Change	Scope and Process of Educational Change	Major Outcomes Sought
Equilibrium — Evolutionary	State of evolutionary readiness	Pressure to move to a higher evolutionary stage	Incremental and adaptive; "natural history" approach	New stage of institutional evolutionary adaptation
Neo-evolutionary	Satisfactory completion of earlier stages	Required to support "national modernization" efforts	"Institution building" using Western models and technical assistance	New "higher" state of education and social differentiation/ specialization
Structural-Functional	Altered functional and structural requisites	Social system need provoking an educational response; exogenous threats	Incremental adjustment of existing institutions, occasionally major	Continued "homeostasis" or "moving" equilibrium, "human capital," and national "development"
Systems	Technical expertise in "systems management"; "rational decision making" and "needs assessment"	Need for greater efficiency in system's operation and goal achievement, i.e., response to a system "malfunction"	Innovative "problem solving" in existing systems, i.e., "research and development" approach	Improved "efficiency" re: costs/ benefits; adoption of innovations
Conflict — Marxian	Elite's awareness of need for change, or shift of power to socialist rulers and educational reformers	Adjustment of correspondence between relations of production and social relations of schooling	Incremental adjustment following social mutations or radical restructuring with Marxist predominance	Formation of integrated workers, i.e., the new "socialist man"
New Marxian	Increased political power and political awareness of working class	Demands for social justice and social equality	Large-scale national reforms through "democratic" institutions and processes	Eliminate "educational privilege" and "elitism"; create a more equalitarian society
Cultural Revitalization	Rise of a collective effort to revive or create "a new culture"; social tolerance for "deviant" normative movements and their educational programs	Rejection of conventional schooling as forced acculturation; education needed to support advance toward movement goals	Creation of alternative schools or educational settings; if movement captures polity, radical change in national educational ideology and structure	Inculcate new normative system; meet movement's recruitment, training, and solidarity needs
Anarchistic Utopian	Creation of supportive settings; growth of critical consciousness; social pluralism	Free man from institutional and social constraints; enhance creativity need for "life-long learning"	Isolated "freeing up" of existing programs and institutions, or creation of new learning modes and settings, i.e., a "learning society"	Self-renewal and participation, local control of resources and community; elimination of exploitation and alienation

warranted and that cultural revitalization necessitates the schooling of their children in distinctly Christian private schools or in a home school where the parents are the primary educators. For these parents the purpose of education is to transmit Christian culture to the next generation.

Other Christian parents decide to send their children to public schools for various reasons. Their choice represents an explicit or implicit support of the public school system. This support may not in fact be total, but may represent some desire to work within the existing system rather than opting for an alternative that may not in fact be viable. Christians also choose to work in various capacities within public schools and seek to represent their Christian commitments at least in deed, if not through direct words. Such choices by Christian parents and workers do not exclude the possibilities of working for change or renewal within the existing public school system, but accept this setting as the locus for life and ministry.

For many, the dilemma of these options can only be resolved by considering various dimensions, including one's perspective on social and educational life and change in light of the Christian faith. It is the task of evangelical educators and other leaders to raise the matter of schooling choices as they relate to the larger question of faith commitments and the Christian's call to be in but not of the world. Christians can respond in a variety of ways while recognizing the issues that Paulston's work suggests and the compromises that can be involved in school choice.

One Model for Sociological Inquiry

Building on the preceding discussions, we can propose a model for sociological inquiry that will enable Christian educators to consider the impact of society and culture on education. This model emerges from the work of Clifford Geertz, whose definition of culture is discussed earlier in this chapter.[36]

The expressions and embodiments of corporate life are experienced most directly in the groups, organizations, and institutions with which persons interact each day. These include various economic, social, educational, cultural, and political organizations and institutions—from a department store chain to the local police force, from the local community church to the regional Internal Revenue Service office. Persons relate to a host of groups in an increasingly institutionalized world.

36. Geertz, *Interpretation of Cultures*. Figure 10 was suggested by Douglas Sloan, Teachers College, Columbus University, New York, March 25, 1980, using Geertz's insights.

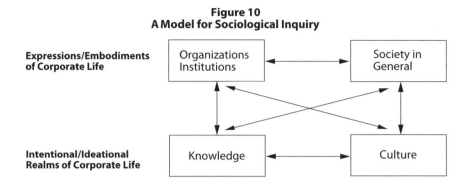

Figure 10
A Model for Sociological Inquiry

On a larger scale, persons interact with the society in general and interface with economic, political, and social structures or networks. Economically, capitalist and socialist systems set different parameters for the theory and practice of education. Politically, democratic and totalitarian structures impact education in distinct ways. Differences in social-class affiliation and commitment interact with educational philosophies and practices, resulting in distinct agendas and experiences for students.

Evangelical Christians have not traditionally been critically aware of these factors in terms of the expressions and embodiments of corporate life. Nevertheless, their impact can be seen as liberating and/or oppressive, as redemptive and/or fallen. Most organizations, institutions, and societal structures cannot be classified as exclusively liberating or exclusively oppressive, but are a combination of both.

For example, both my wife and I were taught at the elementary level in the public school system of New York City. My experience was primarily positive given the fact that my local community in Brooklyn was predominantly Jewish and the quality of the schooling was excellent. My wife's experience was primarily negative and oppressive given the fact that her local community of East Harlem in Manhattan was predominantly Hispanic and the quality of the schooling was inferior. Other examples could also be cited where students at the public school in Brooklyn had oppressive and limiting experiences as compared to students at the public school in Manhattan who may have had liberating and expansive experiences. While recognizing this contrary and exceptional evidence, one could say that the impact of local public schooling in Flatbush, Brooklyn, was generally more liberating than in East Harlem, Manhattan.

During the 1960s in New York City, general consciousness had been raised regarding the effects of racism and selective economic support on the schooling experiences in local communities. The life expectations for students attending school in East Harlem were vastly different than for those in Flatbush, and subtle messages were communicated to students regarding academic demands and the value of their cultural heritage in relation to the larger society. Following the civil rights movement, awareness had increased, but the realization of a more equitable educational experience for all children in New York or any other major city is a continual challenge. Regretfully, the evangelical church as a whole has not been responsive to this challenge.

In returning to the model of Geertz's insights, a second level of corporate life centers on the intentional and ideational realms of knowledge and culture. Knowledge is shared meanings, and education has primarily centered on the discovery, accumulation, and distribution of these shared meanings. But education has also involved in a more implicit or perhaps hidden manner the transmission of culture. Culture can be defined as shared values, attitudes, and beliefs. From the broader perspective, which includes the place of culture, education can be conceived as "the entire process by which a culture transmits itself across the generations."[37]

Such a broader perspective necessitates that evangelical Christians be less parochial and narrow in their concerns in order to explore the major impact of the wider culture on faith communities and the extent to which aspects of the wider culture can be affirmed and/or criticized.[38] Evangelical Christians, as all other Christians with distinct theological commitments, must discern what aspects of culture can be preserved, redeemed, or transformed. Such identification and analysis, with the subsequent development of strategies for action, must be included in Christian education if persons are to adequately represent Christ in the various cultures and subcultures in which they have been called to live, work, and minister. Indeed, the call is to make Christ's presence and transforming power known at all levels of corporate life. Christ is to be evident in organizational and institutional life and within larger societal structures. Christ is to be evident in the realms of shared meaning, values, attitudes, and beliefs. Such is the high calling of Christians in every society.

Why is this so? Why is this a necessary call to the Christian vocation? God is concerned for righteousness, justice, and reconciliation throughout human society in its various expressions and realms, and for the liberation of persons from every kind of oppression. This oppression includes spiritual oppression but much more. Humankind is created in God's image, and every person has

---

37. Bailyn, *Education in the Forming*, 14.

38. It is important to note the contributions of such works as Eldin Villafañe, *The Liberating Spirit: Toward an Hispanic American Pentecostal Social Ethic* (Grand Rapids: Eerdmans, 1993); and Jim Wallis, *God's Politics: Why the Right Gets It Wrong and the Left Doesn't Get It* (San Francisco: Harper, 2005).

intrinsic dignity and should be respected and served in the name of Christ. Christians, bearing the name of Christ, are called to be salt and light in the world as well as in the church. Our spiritual warfare involves confronting principalities and powers at all levels of society, of corporate life, which contribute to oppression, alienation, and discrimination. Evangelicals must address the interrelated complex of social problems suggested by Geertz's analysis with the mind and presence of Christ. Although Christians recognize that their hope is in God and not in effective service, social action, or change, they nonetheless strive to take captive every thought and expression of corporate life to make it obedient to Christ (2 Cor. 10:5).

The exploration of sociological foundations raises issues calling for attention to the wider relationships of communal and societal life. Investigation of these relationships cannot exclude consideration of the actual persons who are being taught. A concern for the wider social context cannot ignore the immediate local setting of teaching and those who are taught. Therefore, Christian educators are also drawn to consider the psychological foundations of Christian education, which are discussed in chapter 6.

Points to Ponder

- Identify the cultural factors that influence your social location in relation to educational practices.
- Bernard Bailyn defines education as the "entire process by which a culture transmits itself across the generations." How would you describe that process in the particular educational setting with which you are most familiar?
- Bailyn named the educational axles of family, church, community, and the economy. What additional axles do you identify, and how do they influence the process of transmitting your culture today?
- Which of the sociologists of education discussed in this chapter most help you understand educational processes in society and why? Pose questions you might ask them to deepen your understanding.
- With reference to Paulston's analysis in table 6, which theory of educational change would you advocate to address a current challenge in Christian education practice and why? Share the rationale for your choice using biblical, theological, and philosophical insights.

6

Psychological Foundations

The integration of a Christian educational view with psychology is particularly challenging for several reasons. First, education as it was generally conceived and practiced in the twenty-first century has been primarily dependent on psychology, with its varied theories, research findings, and practices. This follows from the fact that psychology as a discipline has included the study of human consciousness and behavior along with the processes of learning. Education is concerned with persons and the teaching-learning process, and educators can gain much through considering the insights of psychological inquiry.

Second, there are distinct psychologies or schools of psychology, including behavioral, psychoanalytic, cognitive, developmental, gestalt, humanistic, social, and transformational psychologies. Given such diverse perspectives, the issue often becomes, as was the case with educational philosophies, which psychologies, combined or integrated, provide the best mix for understanding and working with persons across the life span.[1]

Third, Christians are confronted with the need to think faithfully about psychology in general and/or develop a Christian psychology on which to build their educational thought and practice. Christianity embodies a perspective on

1. Two works that explore psychological foundations are Les L. Steele, *On The Way: A Practical Theology of Christian Formation* (Grand Rapids: Baker, 1990); and James C. Wilhoit and John M. Dettoni, eds., *Nurture That Is Christian: Developmental Perspectives on Christian Education* (Wheaton: Victor Books, 1995). See also the earlier work of Gabriel Moran, *Religious Education Development: Images for the Future* (Minneapolis: Winston Press, 1983).

human beings that has definite implications for their education. For example, if persons are viewed as basically good as created by God, then perhaps greater emphasis should be placed on freedom, discovery, and creativity in the learning process. In contrast, if persons are viewed as basically evil, as fallen in sin, then perhaps greater emphasis should be placed on structure, discipline, and responsibility in the learning process. An additional possibility is to view persons as being both good and evil in varying degrees, which necessitates some rhythm or combination of emphases on freedom and form, on discovery and discipline, on ardor and order, or on creativity and responsibility. These examples, of course, are generalizations, but they serve to underscore the importance of attempting to integrate Christian understandings with one's psychology and view of education. In this integrating it is important to recognize that every psychological perspective has an implicit theological anthropology, an implicit understanding of the origin and destiny of persons that can be discerned and evaluated. Every psychology has an understanding of what to emphasize in working with persons as they progress from birth to death to life after death. Christians may draw upon the insights from various psychological schools, but they must do so with discernment and an awareness of larger educational purposes. These larger purposes help to guide the integration of psychological understandings with faith commitments and theological perspectives on persons.

Four Approaches to Integration

To address the question of integration, it is helpful to consider the insights shared by Lawrence Crabb, a Christian psychologist, who has suggested four possible approaches. The first approach can be described as differentiated or fragmented. It maintains two "separate but equal" tracks for viewing and relating to persons. In this approach the lives of persons would be directed by psychological perspectives in all "secular" areas of life with an insistence that religious or Christian faith and development are basically unrelated to psychological processes and unaffected by them. This approach, while emphasizing a clear division of labor, can lead to religious schizophrenia and irrelevant religion. A second approach rejects psychological insights and places people in a determined religious context where their lives are totally shaped by religious insights and perspectives untainted by psychological or developmental insights. This "nothing buttery" approach maintains that nothing but the Bible or religious insights determines life and leads to a stance of heteronomy in life. In a heteronomous stance, an external law is imposed on persons without consideration of various insights and the personal appropriation of a worldview. This approach results in a provincialism or ghettoization in life that requires constant nurture and insulation to maintain the control of a religious perspective. The third approach can be described as integrated but potentially misdirected. This is a total psychological approach to Christian education and faith development that reshapes the radical demands of faith and reduces the distinctive characteristics of Christian theology (grace, salvation, sin and guilt, and a personal response of faith). This approach can be described as a "tossed salad" approach, which mixes psychological and religious concepts while giving definite priority to psychology. A fourth and final approach is one that is integrated and directed in relation to religious values. This approach requires openness and a candid evaluation by Christian educators about the assumptions and goals of both their theological and their psychological views. In this approach Christian educators must search for possible interrelationships with psychology using theological perspectives and a Christian worldview as a final authority. This approach assumes that there is discovered truth as well as revealed truth, which Christians must discern, with the proviso that discovered truth correlates with revealed truth.[2] In this approach Christians have the responsibility of careful and critical discernment in drawing upon psychology. This discernment demands that Christians carefully evaluate descriptive psychological insights before suggesting prescriptions for educational practice. Such evaluation allows for the critique and affirmation of psychological findings.

This fourth approach was described by Augustine of Hippo many centuries ago as "spoiling the Egyptians." It involves the search for truth in all areas of inquiry, including psychology, affirming that all truth is God's truth.[3] As the Israelites used the vessels and ornaments of gold and silver offered by the Egyptians to adorn the tabernacle in the wilderness (see Exod. 12:33–36; 35:30–36:38), so Christian educators must use the wisdom gained from psychology to enrich and embellish their thought and practice to the end that God might be glorified. The potential difficulty in this "spoiling" is represented by the construction of the golden calf—an idolatry with reverence for psychology finally holding sway over reverence for theism (Exod. 32). Using the integrated and directed approach demands an overriding dependence on spiritual discernment and an unwavering commitment to God's truth as revealed in Scripture and Jesus Christ. Anything less deteriorates

2. For a complete description of these four approaches, see Lawrence J. Crabb, *Effective Biblical Counseling: A Model for Helping Caring Christians Become Capable Counselors* (Grand Rapids: Zondervan, 1977), 31–56.

3. Augustine, *On Christian Doctrine*, 2.40.

into worship of the creature instead of the worship due the Creator of all creation (Rom. 1:25).

As suggested above, the task of spoiling the Egyptians requires an initial identification of one's assumptions. In relation to this task, the author proposes the following theological and psychological assumptions for consideration. Certainly others may be proposed, but these serve to introduce possibilities for the task of spoiling, which is the responsibility of every thinking Christian.[4]

1. Persons are created in God's image and have significant worth and value. The complexity and variety of their psychological nature reflect this marvelous creation and the patterns God has created.
2. Persons are affected by sin on both the personal and corporate levels of their lives. This reality does not discount the fact that persons have also been sinned against by other persons, communities, societies, and corporate structures that perpetuate oppressive patterns of life. Thus human culpability or accountability relates to both personal and corporate dimensions of life. In psychology, sins and sinful patterns are discussed in terms of dysfunctionalities.
3. Persons can be re-created in Christ, be transformed in being, and become increasingly that which God intended them to be. Conversion or conversions are a potential in human life and can be supported through caring responses to persons in various stages of their development.
4. Persons can be activated by the Holy Spirit, who is present in human life to realize this potential of transformation in Christ personally and corporately. The Holy Spirit encounters the human spirit and makes transformation possible across the life span.
5. Persons have spirits/souls as well as bodies, but are whole as body-souls. Death represents a separation of this reality, and resurrection represents a healing of this separation.
6. Persons as created are historical, cultural, economic, political, and social beings. We must see persons in relation to these wider networks of relationships. We must minister with persons recognizing the significance of these wider networks of corporate life.
7. Persons are moral, aesthetic, and creative individuals. We must nurture the potentials for freedom and expression as well as be concerned for form and responsibility in human life.

4. Readers are directed to Steele, *On the Way*, for further consideration.

In addition to these theological emphases, educators have assumptions about the psychology of persons. The proposed psychological assumptions with which I strive to operate are the following:

1. Persons have bodies, and we must attend to their physical nature, sexuality, gender, and their activity or behavior in the natural world.
2. Persons have minds, and we must consider their thinking and reasoning. Both the structure and content of cognitive processes must be considered.
3. Persons have feelings, and the affective dimension of their lives is important. We must recognize and be sensitive to feelings, motivations, and attitudes in teaching.
4. Persons have wills and make decisions in various areas of their lives. We must recognize the intentions, judgments, and decisions on which persons act. Such intentions and decisions become the basis for our inquiry into matters of responsibility, accountability, and integrity.
5. Persons are in community and we consider their relationships with other persons, groups, institutions, and social structures. Networks of care and responsibility must be discerned in ministry with persons along with concerns for righteousness, justice, and peace in corporate life.
6. Persons have intuition and aspects of character, personality, imagination, and values that transcend our analytical categories. We are called to recognize the individuality or uniqueness of persons.

Being explicit about their assumptions and the corresponding implications can assist Christians in exploring the world of psychological development while maintaining their faith identity. Bringing these assumptions to bear expands our insights beyond what is possible when we rely on any one psychological perspective.

Questions of Developmental Psychology

Given the concern in education for the changes in persons over time resulting from educational experiences, questions of development in the field of psychology have been of particular concern to educators. Human development can be defined as "an emergent reality whereby the potential structures of the personality are given particular and varied shapes over the course of a lifetime."[5] In relation to development, Gerald R. Levin, a child psychologist, has identified seven central issues that psychologists have addressed in their understanding of persons, and, in particular, of children. Each issue can be regarded as representing a continuum with contending viewpoints at each pole (see fig. 11). Each of these poles can also be envisioned as the two fixed points of an ellipse that are complementary. Truth can be found in each position on these issues, and emphasis may vary with the particular persons and context for teaching.

The first issue for Levin concerns developmental and nondevelopmental perspectives. The developmental point of view sees a person's psychological functioning as changing so radically during the course of life that one must regard developmental changes in behavior as fundamental, as basic and profound as developmental changes in physical structure that begin at conception and end when the human body is physically mature. A developmental perspective identifies various stages or cycles across the life span. The nondevelopmental point of view, at the other end of the continuum, assumes that a person's psychological characteristics remain essentially constant and regards the obvious changes in behavior that take place over time as superficial reflections of the continuing operation of stable, underlying processes.[6] The developmental perspective tends to emphasize discontinuities, whereas the nondevelopmental perspective tends to emphasize continuities in psychological functioning across the life span.

A second issue from Levin's analysis involves continuity and discontinuity positions. The continuity position asserts that developmental changes in behavior can be seen as a continuous series of minute changes. Although the cumulative effect of these changes is dramatic, the process can be thought of as analogous to the height changes between birth and maturity. Persons gain more of the same, rather than something different in development. The discontinuity position asserts that the most important changes in behavior are qualitative and discontinuous in nature. "Like the physical difference between a fertilized ovum and a newborn baby, some psychological differences involve a dramatic transformation from one stage of development to another."[7]

Levin's third issue centers on differences between the biological position and the sociological viewpoint. For those advocating the biological, development

5. James E. Loder, "Developmental Foundations for Christian Education," in *Foundations for Christian Education in an Era of Change*, ed. Marvin J. Taylor (Nashville: Abingdon, 1976), 54.

6. Gerald R. Levin, "Child Psychology: An Orientation" (unpublished paper, Lewisburg, PA: Bucknell University, 1969), 35.

7. Ibid., 35–36.

Figure 11
Various Theoretical Choices

Developmental								Nondevelopmental
	1	2	3	4	5	6	7	
Continuity								Discontinuity
	1	2	3	4	5	6	7	
Biological								Sociological
	1	2	3	4	5	6	7	
Passivity								Activity
	1	2	3	4	5	6	7	
Affective								Cognitive
	1	2	3	4	5	6	7	
Macroscopic								Microscopic
	1	2	3	4	5	6	7	
General								Differential
	1	2	3	4	5	6	7	

involves tremendous biological changes and the realization of potentials present in the genes. The helplessness of infancy, language, and sexual behavior, for example, are all products of heredity. Thus to understand normal development and its deviations, one must put the persons in biological perspective and affirm the unfolding of their nature gifted to them at birth. The sociological viewpoint counters this emphasis on biological factors by observing that development involves a great deal of learning, the acquisition of forms of behavior that are passed on from generation to generation through various cultures. The helplessness of infancy provides humans with unique opportunities for learning. Language, like other aspects of culture, must be learned through interaction with the human environment. Even seemingly biological matters such as sex take on a human character only as a result of the social context in which they are developed. Thus to understand normal development and its deviations or variations, one views persons from a sociological perspective with attention given to their nurture in distinct settings.[8]

A fourth issue Levin proposes considers persons as either passive, active, or some combination of both. The view of persons as passive or receptive sees them as being molded by powerful influences beyond their control. Driven by forces such as hunger from within and initially helpless in solving the problems of survival, children, for example, are almost completely dependent on the adults around them. As adults take care of children, they shape their behavior

8. Ibid., 36.

in numerous ways, obvious and subtle, deliberately and accidentally creating a figure in their own image. This shaping and imaging continues beyond childhood with the adult largely a passive respondent to various influences. In contrast to this view is one that emphasizes persons as active. Human children are constantly active in teaching themselves and in seeking out more challenging problems. Even a baby will frustrate his or her parents' mealtimes by playing with food, deliberately spilling milk, and seeking out endless diversions. Most of the significant achievements of life come from a person's constant curiosity and desire to master the world rather than from any interest in pleasing others. Persons expend great amounts of energy in actively exploring the world.[9] John Locke saw a child as a tabula rasa, a blank slate acted upon by various influences and forces. In contrast to Locke, Jean-Jacques Rousseau saw the child as a noble savage with an innate moral sense and intuitive knowledge requiring avenues for expression and activity. Locke's perspective supports the emphasis on passivity or receptivity, whereas Rousseau's view supports viewing persons as active and dynamic.

A fifth issue for Levin centers on the relative stress placed on the affective or the cognitive dimensions of human beings. The affective view seeks to understand persons by examining what motivates them and what determines why they select one reaction rather than another. Priority is given to feeling and the emotional-motivational side of development. The cognitive view seeks to understand how persons know the world around them. The environment is only what persons make of it, how they perceive it. Thus one must consider how persons think and what can be remembered to gain understanding of motives and emotions. Because cognitive functioning changes so radically in persons, priority must be given to this dimension.[10] The affective viewpoint has been stressed by those interested in the psychodynamics of persons; adherents of this view include Freud, Jung, and Erikson and other neo-Freudians. The cognitive viewpoint has been advocated primarily by Piaget, Kohlberg, and more recently James Fowler. Cognitive theorists stress the structures of persons' thoughts and consciousness as essential to understanding persons.

The sixth issue Levin highlights places in opposition macroscopic and microscopic viewpoints of persons. A macroscopic viewpoint considers as essential the broad patterns and features of human behavior that take years to develop. Confusing and secondary details are ignored in order to discern major trends and what influences them. An effort is made to gain the "big

9. Ibid., 36–37.
10. Ibid., 37–38.

picture" and how major shifts in society affect persons, and how various social structures influence individual development. A microscopic viewpoint stresses the minute details of behavior and the individual responses of persons. By examining details, one can discern the forces that affect persons.[11] The distinctive elements in this issue might best be compared with the differences between wide-angle and close-up photographs, with one emphasizing the broad panoramic sweeps and trends and the other concerned with the fine details of a subject.

The seventh and final issue is the debate between a general psychology position and a differential psychology position. The general position views persons as essentially similar, despite apparent differences among them. Similarity thus becomes the central focus, and the search is for basic principles that apply to everyone. By contrast, the differential position views all persons as different, despite superficial resemblances among them. This amazing variety and unique individuality provide the starting point for considering persons. Only after exploring this diversity and determining how and when differences appear should one consider the similarities among persons.[12]

This debate can be exemplified in a discussion a schoolteacher might have with a clinical psychologist who stresses the needs of the individual patient. The teacher is concerned with basic principles that will work with a large group of children and emphasizes the need for individual students to cooperate with group expectations and norms. The clinical psychologist is concerned with the best possible individualized approach that will meet the needs of a particular child within the larger classroom setting. Each practitioner will appeal to those psychological perspectives and insights that address their particular situations and needs in working with and helping persons.

Responses to these seven issues and others will greatly affect how the Christian educator formulates an educational psychology and how one acts explicitly or implicitly in teaching or interacting with others. But it must be asked which choices within each of these issues best reflect a Christian worldview and commitment. No simple choices can be made, and responses may vary with the particular social, cultural, and historical context. Nevertheless, given the high dependence on psychology in all areas of human interaction, careful thought must be given to these questions.

Some may advocate a mediating position on each of these issues, on the grounds that truth is present in each of the opposing viewpoints or perspectives on persons. But the greater challenge is to rethink one's position in light

11. Ibid., 38.
12. Ibid.

of biblical revelation and theological reflection. How does a Christian view of persons interface with modern psychology in its various expressions? A consideration of cognitive, psychosocial, moral, and faith development can provide insights for addressing this question in greater detail.

Cognitive Development: Jean Piaget

The person most closely associated with cognitive development theory is Jean Piaget, a Swiss genetic epistemologist who studied how the structures of human thought and knowledge originated and changed with maturation, particularly from birth through adolescence. His work provided a helpful bridge between the study of biology and epistemology in that he regarded knowledge as bodily activity in relation to the environment. His key concepts are assimilation and accommodation, which refer to how persons deal with varied environmental experiences in relation to their cognitive structures that change across the stages he describes. Piaget's primary concern is with reasoning and knowing, which are viewed as operations or patterns of the mind. The active body is the ground of knowledge, and interaction with one's environment is crucial for development. In relation to Levin's seven issues, Piaget opts for a perspective that is developmental, biological, cognitive, microscopic, and differential; it also emphasizes discontinuity and activity. For Piaget, the ultimate goal of education is not to fill the child's mind with an assortment of knowledge, but to advance the child from one stage of reasoning within a given hierarchy to a more mature stage. The educator's main concern, then, should be *how* the child reasons and not *about what* the child reasons. Educationally this is accomplished by producing dissonance between the child's environment and his or her particular stage of development.

While recognizing the place of cognitive dimensions, the Christian educator can criticize an exclusive emphasis on reasoning without a corresponding concern for motivation, feeling, behavior, and tendencies revealed over time. Piaget does not ignore these dimensions, but he sees them as operating consistently with intellectual functioning. Some Christians may also criticize Piaget's underlying assumption of the fundamental goodness of humanity. Piaget assumes that if human reasoning is improved to the next higher stage, growth, development, and maturation have occurred. Christians, in contrast, may recognize the fallenness of humanity that affects reasoning as well as other faculties.[13]

13. Nicholas Wolterstorff, *Educating for Responsible Action* (Grand Rapids: Eerdmans, 1980), 27–29.

Many of the insights regarding cognitive development in Piaget's theory are valid and can be affirmed. Children do learn through activity as they organize and interpret new experiences in terms of previous knowledge. In other words, they are active and constructive in relating to the world. Children's interest and ability to learn new cognitive skills do depend on existing cognitive structures. Social interaction with peers does promote cognitive development.[14] Yet while Piaget has restored a necessary appreciation of the connectedness of persons' minds and bodies, he has opted for a psychology that focuses on the structures or patterns of reasoning to the relative exclusion of other vital dimensions of human life. Theorists, like educators, make choices as to what they emphasize.

Piaget's presuppositions as a scientific naturalist and humanist contrast with a Christian worldview. Piaget would not assert that the theological and moral absolutes of the Christian view exist and affect persons. Christians recognize an objective interpersonal reality that exists apart from culture, namely, God, who stands above and judges every person's and society's cognitive constructs of reality.[15] God's revelation in Jesus Christ and Scripture provides a corrective standard for cognitive reasoning. Given this standard, true content has priority for Christian educators, whereas Piaget gives priority to internal development or cognitive structures for human development. Therefore, Piaget sees growth in terms of the restructuring of one's perceptions as new cognitive structures emerge, creating one's own reality. In contrast, a Christian understanding of growth involves integrating truth as reality into one's personality by the conjoint efforts of persons and God through the agency of the Holy Spirit. This integration for Christian educators relies on the use of Scripture along with other sources to provide a framework within which persons can build their lives. In this building process, people do make use of their reason, experience, and insights from tradition and other cultural inputs. For Piaget, God's revelation in Scripture and Jesus Christ does not provide this normative function for development.[16] In fact, exposure to Scripture may be harmful, as suggested by Ronald Goldman, who from the author's perspective uncritically applies Piaget's insights to the tasks of religious education in his study of religious reasoning.[17] Therefore, while Piaget's work is helpful, the Christian educator

14. See Harry L. Hom Jr. and Paul A. Robinson, eds., *Psychological Processes in Early Education* (New York: Academic, 1977), 17–31, for a discussion of the limitations and strengths of Piaget's theory.

15. Lawrence O. Richards, *A Theology of Children's Ministry* (Grand Rapids: Zondervan, 1983), 170.

16. See Ronald Goldman, *Readiness for Religion* (New York: Seabury, 1968).

17. Ibid.

must press beyond it to address additional factors and distinctive elements that characterize a Christian view of persons. The work of Howard Gardner, described below in the discussion of brain research, helps to expand Piaget's understanding of cognitive development and intelligence.

Psychosocial Development: Erik Erikson

Erik Erikson was a psychoanalyst and professor of developmental psychology at Harvard University. Over against Freud's emphasis on abnormal and psychosexual development, Erikson's work focuses on normal development. Erikson's main interest is social roles and self-images as these change over time. He identifies eight stages of an epigenetic cycle in which persons make choices in response to a culture's established tasks and prescribed social forms.[18]

Erikson's theory combines insights from biology, ego psychology, and anthropology in analyzing how a person's sense of body, self, and role in society interface at different points in life. In other words, he maintains that the formation of the ego is a biologically based, psychologically located, socially shaped, and culturally controlled and articulated process. Development through the life span, described as epigenesis, follows a conflict/resolution process throughout life.[19] Table 7 charts Erikson's eight stages with their corresponding personal, social, and cultural contexts.[20]

In relation to Levin's scheme, Erikson's theory can be described as developmental, equally biological and social, affective, primarily microscopic, and differential; it also emphasizes discontinuity and a combination of activity and passivity or receptivity. Like Piaget, Erikson can be criticized by those who place greater emphasis on opposing or distinct stances in any of the seven issues in Levin's scheme. But beyond these criticisms, Erikson's theory must be questioned in relation to its basic assumptions.

First, Erikson assumes that the human personality develops according to steps predetermined in the growing person's readiness to be driven toward, to be aware of, and to interact with a widening social radius. Thus for Erikson, society becomes a partner in one's development, challenging and supporting the growing individual. Vitality comes as the developing person realizes a new sense with each successive stage.[21]

18. Moran, *Religious Education Development*, 25.
19. Loder, "Developmental Foundations for Christian Education," 56–58.
20. Ibid., 59.
21. G. Temp Sparkman, *The Salvation and Nurture of the Child of God: The Story of Emma* (Valley Forge, PA: Judson, 1983), 255.

TABLE 7
Erikson's Epigenetic Cycle Model

Stage	Psychological Crises	Radius of Significant Relations	Related Elements of the Social Order	Rudiments of Ego Strength
1	Basic trust vs. basic mistrust	Maternal person	Religion and the cosmic order	Hope
2	Autonomy vs. shame, doubt	Paternal person	Law and social order	Will
3	Initiative vs. guilt	Basic family	Theater and ideal prototypes	Purpose
4	Industry vs. inferiority	Neighborhood and school	Technological elements	Competence
5	Identity vs. role confusion	Peer groups, models of leadership	Ideological perspectives	Fidelity
6	Intimacy vs. isolation	Partners in friendship, sex, competition, cooperation	Patterns of cooperation and competition	Love
7	Generativity vs. stagnation	Divided labor and shared household	Currents of education and tradition	Care
8	Ego integrity vs. despair	Humankind, "my kind"	Collective wisdom	Wisdom

Second, Erikson assumes that society, in principle, tends to be so constituted as to meet and invite this succession of potentialities for interaction and attempts to safeguard and encourage the proper rate and sequence of their enfolding. Thus Erikson views the relationship between individuals and society as primarily cooperative and mutually supportive provided there is a positive resolution of each of the successive crises. Yet he does not dismiss the possibility of negative resolutions at each stage, which reappear at later stages. Resolution of each of the developmental stages requires a balance that can be compared with the blending of major and minor notes in a musical score or major and minor roles in a theatrical performance.

Third, Erikson does not regard each stage as an achievement. The negatives always remain as dynamic counterparts. Because persons are engaged continuously with the crises and pressures of life, no one stage is resolved once and for all. Issues resurface later in life and require attention. The positive resolution of each stage results in various virtues or elements of ego strength that foster development of persons in their wider community.

In response to Erikson's first assumption, it can be pointed out that a Christian worldview can accommodate the place of development, but perhaps not in such predetermined ways. God's Spirit can intrude on the developmental process in unanticipated ways to bring about transformation in the lives of persons. The Holy Spirit encounters human spirits in gracious ways that may not always be anticipated by stages.

Erikson's second assumption must be seriously questioned if one believes that individuals can influence their society. Societies vary in fostering the development of all persons, and Erikson's assumption, while recognizing the place of personal choice, may lead to a perspective that diminishes the role of persons as agents of transformation and reform.

Erikson's third assumption indicates the open-ended character of development, which is subject to changing conditions. A Christian worldview affirms the continual processes of sanctification and/or deformation in human life. In this respect, Erikson is more sensitive to the exigencies of historical and cultural developments as compared with other developmentalists, such as Piaget and Kohlberg, who claim cross-cultural application of their understanding that may not be warranted. Whereas Erikson does not explicitly address supernatural forces as a possible source of changing conditions in human life, he recognizes the place of religion as an institution concerned with engendering hope for the human condition. The Christian educator recognizes the continual operation of God in the lives of persons. The Holy Spirit is God's agent for continual renewal not only in the lives of persons but also in the structures of society.

Erikson's conceptions of psychosocial development provide the Christian educator with working hypotheses for assessing the affective dimensions of persons' lives at various stages. The virtues of Erikson's psychosocial crises must be critiqued for a lack of sensitivity to the unique features of female development and Christian virtues that may transcend his categories.[22] Nevertheless, Erikson's sensitivity to the larger society and distinctive cultural features is noteworthy. I find much of value in Erikson's insights because of the breadth of his work, with the noteworthy exception that they do not adequately address the distinctive experiences of women.

Moral Development: Lawrence Kohlberg

Lawrence Kohlberg is most typically associated with the moral development theory. His perspective is quite similar to Piaget's in stressing the structures of cognitive reasoning in relation to moral judgment. He is concerned not so much with the content of moral development as with the structures or forms of the reasoning process that lead a person to decide on a certain solution to a moral

22. See Moran, *Religious Education Development*, 29–40, for an elaboration of these criticisms.

dilemma. Moral reasoning is the primary and determinative factor in moral education for Kohlberg. He identifies three major moral levels: the preconventional, the conventional, and the postconventional or principled level (see table 8).

TABLE 8
Kohlberg's Moral Development Model

Preconventional Level	*Stage 1* (ages 6–8)	Punishment and obedience orientation (Will I get caught? Will I get punished?)
	Stage 2 (ages 8–10)	Instrumental, relativist orientation (What is in it for me?)
Conventional Level	*Stage 3* (ages 10–12)	Interpersonal, concordance orientation (What do others expect of me? How can I please adults as the nice girl/good boy?)
	Stage 4 (ages 12–15)	Law-and-order orientation (What does the law say? What is my duty?)
Postconventional Level	*Stage 5* (ages 15+)	Social contract and consensus orientation (What is the group's agreement and my personal obligation in this matter?)
	Stage 6	Universal ethical principles orientation (What is my principle that has universal significance?)

Movement through these three levels takes a person from the pursuit of self-interest, to adherence to external standards, to the affirmation of internal autonomous principles. This developmental sequence raises serious questions from the perspective of the Christian faith. Nicholas Wolterstorff points out that Kohlberg is concerned with form to the relative exclusion of content or substance.[23] Moral development includes more than moral reasoning. Moral behavior can be seen to encompass moral judgment, the situation and its pressures, individual motives and emotions, and a sense of will. Moral judgment entails both moral reasoning (Kohlberg's primary emphasis) and moral content. Thus moral development is more complex than Kohlberg believes it to be.

In addition to Kohlberg's limited focus on form or moral reasoning, he must be criticized for his emphasis on autonomy as the highest level of moral development. This suggests that morality is based on universal principles derived solely from autonomous individual reasoning. Such a stance diminishes the place of a normative community and relationships within that community, which are fundamental to the Christian faith.[24] Rather than a stance of autonomy, the

23. Wolterstorff, *Educating for Responsible Action*, 79–100.
24. Kirk E. Farnsworth, "Furthering the Kingdom in Psychology," in *The Making of a Christian Mind: A Christian World View and the Academic Enterprise*, ed. Arthur F. Holmes (Downers Grove, IL: InterVarsity, 1985), 90–93.

Christian faith involves a theonomy in which persons are dependent on God and interdependent with others within the Christian and human community. It is in this context that moral development becomes a possibility for Christians. God introduces new possibilities into the process of moral development and addresses persons beyond the categories of Kohlberg's stages. Yet, while a theistic worldview emphasizes relationships in a community, it does not do so to the exclusion of individuality and autonomy within proper bounds. Such bounds include the faith premise that persons are creatures of God and must live in relation to God and all creation.

In relation to Levin's scheme, Kohlberg's viewpoint can be described as developmental, social, cognitive, microscopic, and differential, emphasizing discontinuity and activity. He is distinct from Piaget in his emphasis on the social dimension of life. But this social dimension is viewed only in terms of individuals having a reference point for their individual reasoning and not in terms of the basic human orientation of relationship and community, which undergirds a Christian worldview.

Several theorists have explored Judeo-Christian alternatives to Kohlberg in light of his limitations.[25] Donald Joy is an educator who has made significant contributions in this area. Joy recognizes some common ground between a Christian worldview and Kohlberg's theory in the following areas: (1) justice is complex and comprehensive; (2) justice is the core of morality; (3) justice, hence morality, is a function of perception; (4) human beings are held in positive regard; and (5) human beings are morally accountable.

But moving beyond Kohlberg to distinctive Christian elements, Joy suggests four hypotheses: (1) morality originates outside humanity; (2) justice is the core of that outside morality and also is the core attribute of the character of God; (3) human morality is bestowed on persons as the image bearers of God; and (4) since human beings are both moral and free, substantial research and theory are needed to consider moral failure, that is, sin and rebellion, in relation to the transcendent divine grace from which meaning and purpose are derived.[26]

Joy's emphasis on justice is certainly crucial in a world plagued by injustice. But an exclusive focus on justice truncates what Doug Sholl has helpfully identified as the possible sevenfold pattern of Christian relational content. Sholl

25. A good introductory work for exploring these alternatives is Donald Joy, ed., *Moral Development Foundations: Judeo-Christian Alternatives to Piaget/Kohlberg* (Nashville: Abingdon, 1983); see also Craig Dykstra, *Vision and Character: A Christian Educator's Alternative to Kohlberg* (New York: Paulist Press, 1981); and Wolterstorff, *Educating for Responsible Action*.

26. Donald Joy, "Kohlberg Revisited: A Supra-Naturalist Speaks His Mind," in *Moral Development Foundations*, 188.

suggests the following pattern: love and justice, truth and faithfulness, forbearance and patience, forgiveness and repentance, edification and encouragement, humility and submission, and prayer and praise.[27] Sholl's pattern indicates that moral development theory must consider the multifaceted network of human relationships, which, from a Christian perspective, embodies a plurality of virtues. This is also the insight of Craig Dykstra in his identification of Plato, who considered a variety of virtues, including wisdom, temperance, courage, justice, and piety, as worthy of equal concern in moral education.[28] The emphasis on justice, while important, requires expansion in relation to a Christian understanding of persons.

Having elaborated on the positive side of moral development, we must now consider amoral development. This consideration is critical given the Christian understanding that human beings are more than both moral and free; they are also fallen and responsible. But beyond the consideration of personal or individual amoral development, Christian educators can consider the effects of amoral or immoral development on the various institutions and structures of society, including the church, the family, the school, and the community in general.

The work of Richard H. DeLone for the Carnegie Council on Children in the late 1970s is particularly helpful in understanding the general insensitivity to corporate amoral development on the part of those concerned for the education of children and others in the United States. DeLone points out that the understanding of child development has traditionally included the following beliefs: individual adult characteristics determine social status; those adult characteristics are substantially determined by characteristics developed in childhood; and the microenvironment of the family, without reference to the society or macroenvironment in which it is embedded, is what substantially determines the way children develop. These beliefs have been maintained in a context characterized by cultural blindness to the significance of social structure and the dynamics of structure in the lives of persons. As an alternative to this belief system (which Christians have for the most part implicitly affirmed), DeLone suggests a theory of human development that takes account of social structures as influences in shaping individual growth, in shaping moral development. To do this, Christian educators must consider the significance of diverse social structures, the role of individuals as active participants in their

27. Doug Sholl, "Unity and Uniqueness: A Theology of Christian Relationships," in *Moral Development Foundations,* 188. See also Dykstra, *Vision and Character,* 10, for a discussion of virtues other than justice.

28. Dykstra, *Vision and Character,* 10.

own development, and the importance of history, both personal and social, as the medium within which development occurs.[29] Without such considerations, the Christian educator has a truncated view of development and does not move beyond a concern for moral psychology to consider a moral sociology, a moral philosophy, and a moral theology that views all of life as under the lordship and sovereignty of Christ.

In considering amoral development on the corporate and societal level, Christians must not only assess how the local church is a positive, inclusive, intergenerational community that fosters the development of an extended family of faith, they must also assess how the local church excludes certain individuals and is unresponsive to their needs, resulting in individual alienation and the loss of community. Christians must consider not only how the family can be a center for nurture and support but also how it has been subject to societal pressures, resulting in increased neglect and abuse with various degrees of dysfunctionality.

Christians must consider not only how various schooling choices can foster intellectual, social, and moral development but also how they may operate to limit persons and be agents of continued oppression in the lives of certain persons. Christians must not only consider the negative impact of the media—in particular, commercial television—they must also explore and support the positive uses of various media for the extension of God's kingdom. Christians must not only affirm the positive results of a world capitalist system, which has increased the possibilities of choice for persons living in certain societies; they must also assess the impact of this system on persons in "developing" or "undeveloped" nations and the increased poverty unaddressed by various development programs. Similar concerns must be raised in relation to socialist economies and their impact on basic human freedoms.

Moral and amoral development must be seen in these broader terms if persons are to be and become all that God has intended for those created to reflect God's image in their lives. The perspective suggested in this analysis is overwhelming, but to opt for a less comprehensive focus is to deny the complexity of life as created by God and the resources present in the Christian community made available by divine grace.

Christian educators must also evaluate Kohlberg in terms of his analysis of various approaches to moral education: indoctrinative moral education,

29. Richard DeLone, *Small Futures: Children, Inequality and the Limits of Liberal Reform* (New York: Harcourt Brace Jovanovich, 1979), 113–70.

values clarification, and cognitive-developmental moral education. The indoctrinative approach includes the preaching and inculcation of cultural rules and values. Kohlberg considers this approach an imposition. Values clarification involves eliciting a person's own judgment or opinion about moral issues or situations in which values conflict, rather than imposing the teacher's opinion on the students. The goal of this effort is to enable students to become more aware of personal values. This approach assumes a value relativity or neutrality in contrast to the identification of absolutes by the indoctrinative approach. Kohlberg prefers the cognitive-developmental approach, intended to foster movement to progressive stages of moral reasoning through the teacher's suggestion of reasoning at the next higher level to that level manifested by participants in the discussion.[30] For Kohlberg, the teacher is to explore with students the "why" of moral judgments more than the "what" or content of such judgments.

A Christian response to Kohlberg's cognitive-developmental approach could affirm his emphasis on discussion while recognizing his misplaced hope that discussion will affect moral reasoning sufficiently to influence moral development and behavior as well. Evangelical theology maintains the need for radical transformation in order to bring about change in moral life. Without such transformation and the continuing operation of God's grace, moral development cannot be adequately addressed.

Wolterstorff offers an alternative to Kohlberg's approach in suggesting that the best way to have children internalize Christian values and a tendency to act responsibly in light of those values is for a person (parent, teacher, friend) "who acts lovingly toward the child to combine discipline and modeling with the enunciation of a moral standard which the child perceives to fit the situations and on which he or she is willing to act."[31] Wolterstorff's suggestion can be explored as a viable alternative to exclusive reliance on Kohlberg's understanding of moral development.

Faith Development: James Fowler

James Fowler has developed a stage theory of faith development, building on the work of Piaget in cognitive development and that of Kohlberg in moral development. Fowler views faith as active, as a verb. Faith is a process of becoming rather than something a person possesses. This process involves

---

30. Lawrence Kohlberg, "The Cognitive-Developmental Approach to Moral Education," *Phi Delta Kappan* (June 1975): 673–75.
31. Wolterstorff, *Educating for Responsible Action*, 109.

continual growth through stages that are hierarchical (increasingly complex and qualitative), sequential (appearing one after the other in the life span), invariant (following the same order for all persons), and universal (applying to all cultural and societal settings).

Fowler identifies seven categories that distinguish the various stages of persons' development: form of logic, role-taking, form of moral judgment, bounds of social awareness, focus of authority, form of world coherence, and role of symbols. Fowler is concerned to distinguish the forms or structures of faith and attempts to address both cognitive and affective dimensions of faith, or the rational and the passional dimensions. Fowler's six stages of faith development are the following:

1. *Intuitive-projective faith.* Young children up to about age seven reflect the visible faith of their parents.
2. *Mythic-literal faith.* In later childhood the person takes on beliefs of persons other than parents. Some adults remain in stage 2.
3. *Synthetic-conventional faith.* Early teens conform to their "gang." Faith begins to synthesize life's increasing complexity. Many adults who are strongly influenced by peers are in stage 3.
4. *Individual-reflective faith.* In the late teens and early adulthood, the focus is on adult responsibility for one's own commitments and beliefs—doubting, questioning, and rejecting traditional assumptions. This is the period in which individual values are developed.
5. *Conjunctive faith.* A mature faith stage, seldom found before age thirty (and often never reached), which incorporates the integrity of positions other than one's own, and responds to an identification beyond race, class, or ideological boundaries. Stage 5 adults integrate traditional positions, their own doubts, and the views of others into a meaningful whole.
6. *Universalizing faith.* Persons in this stage are rare, with a few "spiritual giants" achieving it. Faith is a universal in which the individual identifies beyond self with God as a felt reality.[32]

In relation to Levin's categories, Fowler's work can be described as developmental, social, primarily cognitive (though inclusive of affective dimensions), microscopic, and differential; it also emphasizes discontinuity and activity rather than passivity. Criticisms can be raised from opposing stances on each of these issues, but the dominant Christian critique of the research and basic

---

32. This description was developed by Kenneth Stokes from James W. Fowler, *Stages of Faith: The Psychology of Human Development and the Quest for Meaning* (San Francisco: Harper & Row, 1981), 117–213.

assumptions of faith development theory as advocated by Fowler is the exclusion of God as a key factor in the faith development process.

Fowler basically seeks to generalize his concept of faith so that it has significance for all persons—whether or not they espouse a theistic world and life view. Fowler's "faith" stands in contrast to the response of the Reformation's concept of faith as solely the gift of God's grace, given uniquely in Jesus Christ. Fowler himself recognizes that critics protest his use of the term *faith*, which is an indigenously Christian category.[33] Fowler's methods of individual interviews, though providing some helpful insights for ways in which persons describe their faith commitments, restrict the relational and communal complexity of faith, which must include consideration of the mysterious workings and relationships of God with persons. Fowler essentially opts for the use of the science of developmental psychology to discern the dimensions of faith. This poses a particular problem if one distinguishes faith from science.

The discussion in the previous chapter on the place of science in relation to epistemology serves as a background to Huston Smith's pertinent observations. Smith points out that science values control, prediction, objectivity, numbers, and signs. In contrast to science, faith values surrender, surprise, subjectivity and objectivity, words, and symbols. In other words, science primarily deals with the instrumental values of utility, usefulness, service, and control, whereas faith deals with intrinsic values.[34] If one accepts these distinctions, then the limitations of Fowler's efforts must be recognized in addressing the realm of Christian faith.

Although developmental psychology can provide some intellectual concepts or working hypotheses for dealing with persons' faith, additional dimensions of faith must be considered beyond Fowler's seven categories. These additional dimensions must recognize the person and works of God and the response of human beings to God, which includes surrender, surprise, reverence, awe, and subjectivity. These dimensions are not readily available to scientific inquiry and require that the Christian educator recognize the mystery and majesty of faith. Fowler has opted for an understanding of faith that can be isolated from the content and beliefs of the Christian faith and that centers on mental structures instead of the relationships of persons with a living and active God in the context of a Christian community.[35] Some of Fowler's later works

33. Fowler, *Stages of Faith*, 91.
34. Huston Smith, "Excluded Knowledge: A Critique of the Modern Western Mind Set," *Teachers College Record* (February 1979): 419–45.
35. See Moran, *Religious Education Development*, 107–26, for an expanded critique of Fowler's perspective.

have sought to make explicit the relationships between faith development and Christian theology.[36]

A radical alternative to Fowler's work is that suggested by Ruth Beechick, who has adopted the work of Robert Havighurst in outlining the spiritual development of Christians. Havighurst identifies different roles that persons assume in life, such as child, friend, organization member, worker, spouse, parent, church member, and user of leisure time. In relation to each of these roles, Beechick defines key developmental tasks that persons are to fulfill at various ages.[37] Beechick's work can be summarized in the following outline of spiritual developmental tasks.[38]

Spiritual Developmental Tasks

I. Preschool Years
   A. Experiencing love, security, discipline, joy, and worship
   B. Beginning to develop awareness and concepts of God, Jesus, and other basic Christian realities
   C. Developing attitudes toward God, Jesus, church, self, and the Bible
   D. Beginning to develop concepts of right and wrong
II. Elementary School Years
   A. Receiving and acknowledging Jesus Christ as Savior and Lord
   B. Growing awareness of Christian love and responsibility in relationships with others
   C. Continuing to build concepts of basic Christian realities
   D. Learning basic Bible teachings adequate for personal faith and everyday Christian living
      1. prayer in daily life
      2. the Bible in daily life
      3. Christian friendships
      4. group worship
      5. responsibility for serving God

36. In particular, see James W. Fowler, *Becoming Adult, Becoming Christian: Adult Development and Christian Faith* (San Francisco: Harper & Row, 1984).

37. See Robert J. Havighurst, *Developmental Tasks and Education* (New York: David McCay, 1961), 72–98. Havighurst defines a developmental task as one that arises at or around a certain period in the life of the individual, successful achievement of which leads to happiness and to success with later tasks, while failure leads to individual unhappiness, social disapproval, and difficulty with later tasks.

38. Ruth Beechick, *Teaching Juniors: Both Heart and Head* (Denver: Accent Books, 1981), 24–25.

      6. basic knowledge of God, Jesus, Holy Spirit, creation, angelic beings, heaven, hell, sin, salvation, Bible history, and Christian literature

   E. Developing healthy attitudes toward self

III. Adolescence

   A. Learning to show Christian love in everyday life

   B. Continuing to develop healthy attitudes toward self

   C. Developing Bible knowledge and intellectual skills adequate for meeting intellectual assaults on faith

   D. Achieving strength of Christian character adequate for meeting anti-Christian social pressures

   E. Accepting responsibility for Christian service in accordance with growing abilities

   F. Learning to make life decisions on the basis of eternal Christian values

   G. Increasing self-discipline to "seek those things which are above"

IV. Maturity

   A. Accepting responsibility for one's own continued growth and learning

   B. Accepting biblical responsibilities toward God and toward others

   C. Living a unified, purposeful life centered on God

Beechick's work represents an effort to provide practical guidelines for the direction of spiritual development in a general ground plan for a Christian education program. This ground plan must be adapted in relation to individual needs and the specific beliefs of a Christian community, but it does recognize the role of content and the dimension of relationships. Some may interpret this focus as imposition because it appears to program the work of God in persons' lives (e.g., persons may not come to a personal faith in Jesus Christ until after elementary school). Also, Beechick emphasizes behavior and cognitive concepts to the relative exclusion of essential values, intentions, virtues, affections, and attitudes, which characterize the Christian faith.

While both Fowler's and Beechick's work can be criticized, their insights can be helpful in evaluating the effectiveness of existing programs in addressing the unique needs of persons in the development of their faith or their spiritual growth. Their insights can provide descriptive categories for gaining understanding, rather than exacting prescriptive guidelines for present and future programs. Randall Furushima suggests three implications from this work:

(1) programs must be intentionally developed and maintained; (2) curriculum and teaching resources must be critiqued in light of the dominant characteristics that persons in various stages generally manifest; and (3) Christian educators must be aware of and trained to anticipate the multiple dimensions of life through which faith can be expressed. Stages and developmental tasks cannot serve as restrictive labels and categories to be applied to persons, for they must be subject to the greater freedom and creativity of the Holy Spirit, who works in the lives of persons.[39] The freedom and creativity of the Holy Spirit are not readily discerned through the methodologies of developmental psychology but must be valued from a Christian perspective that affirms the place of mystery.

Other attempts to understand faith development across the life span are noteworthy. John Westerhoff provides a practical description of four faith styles that compares faith to the growth rings of a tree. As new styles are added, the old rings are retained. The first faith style is experienced faith, in which children experience the faith of significant caregivers. Children learn to trust and have confidence in others, themselves, and God as a result of assimilating faith from faithful or trustworthy persons in their lives. The second style of faith is affiliative faith, which typifies middle to later childhood. Children with this style have a sense of belonging to a self-conscious and caring community. Persons with this style have a faith that seeks to belong and to be nurtured by a community of faithing people. Identity in a community that provides for a sense of continuity and nurtures positive affections is crucial for persons with this second style. Searching or struggling faith is the third style. Persons with this style are most typically youth and young adults who encounter a time of critical reflection and questioning of their faith and that of their family and community of origin. Doubt, experimentation, testing, and the exploration of commitment typify this style. Westerhoff's fourth style is owned faith, in which people freely choose to covenant with God. This faith style attempts to bring together professed faith with one's lifestyle and actions. Owned faith involves embracing one's commitment and affiliation with a religious faith and a willingness to witness through words and deeds.[40]

39. Randall Y. Furushima, "The Developmental Faith of Youth," *New Conversations* 5 (Winter 1980–81): 41–42. Also see Randall Y. Furushima, "Faith Development in a Cross Cultural Perspective," *Religious Education* 80 (Summer 1985): 414–20, for an additional evaluation of Fowler's work. A volume that evaluates Fowler's contributions is Craig Dykstra and Sharon Parks, eds., *Faith Development and Fowler* (Birmingham, AL: Religious Education Press, 1986).

40. For a description of these styles, see John H. Westerhoff III, *Will Our Children Have Faith?* (New York, Seabury, 1976), 89–91; and John H. Westerhoff III, *Bringing Up Children in the Christian Faith* (Minneapolis: Winston, 1980), 25–27.

From a pastoral perspective, Neill Q. Hamilton makes distinctions between psychological maturing and Christian maturing that are important in considering faith development and the applicability to ministry settings. Psychological maturing is the increasing capacity of persons to love deeply and work productively, whereas Christian maturing is an increasing capacity to love God and neighbor and to work in the particular calling to spread the reign of God.[41] The ministries of the therapist and the pastor are complementary for Hamilton, with the therapist engaging in the exorcism of oppressing spirits and the pastor offering experiences of the Holy Spirit to fill the void left by a departing spirit, lest that spirit take "seven other spirits more wicked than itself, and they go in and live there. And the final condition of that man is worse than the first" (Luke 11:26).[42] It is essential that we recognize the work of the Holy Spirit with the unfolding of the human spirit through human development. The encounter of human spirits with the Holy Spirit is the concern of Christian pastors and Christian educators who have a distinct pastoral calling to nurture the faith of those within their care. Hamilton proposes three general phases of Christian maturing that include discipleship, transition in the Spirit, and maturing in church and mission. The phase of transition in the Spirit includes consciousness of worldly illusion, the experience of forgiveness, and resurrection and intimacy with the Spirit that results in being led by the Spirit in mission. Maturing in church and mission entails embracing the corporate dimensions of the Christian life.[43] One theorist who has explored in depth the relation of the Holy Spirit to the human spirit along with the possibility of transformation in this encounter is James Loder, whose works center on the dynamics of transition from one stage or phase to another more than on the particulars of each phase or stage.[44] The exploration of the distinctive elements of Christian understandings in relation to the process of maturing calls for a reconsideration of the presumptions of developmental psychology as a way to understand persons. This reconsideration is necessary in order to formulate a faithful Christian approach to teaching and ministering with persons across the life span.

41. Neill Q. Hamilton, *Maturing in the Christian Life: A Pastor's Guide* (Philadelphia: Geneva Press, 1984), 148. See also the work of Edward Robinson, *The Original Vision: A Study of the Religious Experience of Childhood* (New York: Seabury Press, 1977).

42. Ibid., 152.

43. Ibid.

44. See James E. Loder, *The Transforming Moment*, 2nd ed. (Colorado Springs: Helmers & Howard, 1989); and James E. Loder and W. Jim Neidhardt, *The Knight's Move: The Relational Logic of the Spirit in Theology and Science* (Colorado Springs: Helmers & Howard, 1992).

Neurological and Educational Research

New work on understanding the functioning of the brain and its impact on learning and religious development has contributed to an appreciation of a holistic view. Brain function has been analyzed in relation to the three areas of the brain: the brain stem, or lower brain, which oversees arousal and attention; the limbic system, or midbrain, which includes the amygdala, hippocampus, and hypothalamus, which oversee emotion, pleasure, and pain; and the cerebral cortex with its left and right hemispheres, which oversee distinct forms of thinking. The left hemisphere of the cortex is associated with logical, intellectual, rational, abstract, sequential, verbal, and scientific styles of thinking. The right hemisphere is associated with intuitive, sensual, mythical, concrete, holistic, visual/spatial, and poetic styles of thinking.[45] Research has indicated the complex interaction of all these areas of the brain as persons interact with the natural and supernatural world. Honoring the place of attention, perception, experience, emotion, and memory in learning has expanded a narrow focus on cognitive categories and dependence solely on words to communicate a living faith. Scottie May and Donald Ratcliff recommend honoring the three modalities—touch or the inward sense of the presence of God or the numinous, the visible or Shekinah presence of God, and the word of God written or spoken—in teaching and learning faith that foster spiritual experiences for children and persons of all ages.[46]

In addition to brain research, expanded understandings of intelligence itself have fostered honoring the diversity of gifts with which God has blessed humanity (Rom. 12:3–8; 1 Cor. 12:1–11; Eph. 4:1–16). Besides spiritual gifts there are also gifts of intelligence, which find expression in various ways. The work of Howard Gardner and his understanding of multiple intelligences have expanded categories for describing thinking or intelligence itself. His seven ways of thinking include linguistic, logical-mathematical, musical, kinesthetic, spatial, interpersonal, and intrapersonal intelligences or gifts.[47] Teaching and learning can honor this variety with a diversity of methods and forms of

45. For discussion of insights from brain research, see Jerry Larsen, *Religious Education and the Brain: A Practical Resource for Understanding How We Learn about God* (New York: Paulist Press, 2000); Scottie May and Donald Ratcliff, "Children's Spiritual Experiences and the Brain," in *Children's Spirituality: Christian Perspectives, Research and Applications*, ed. Donald Ratcliff (Eugene, OR: Cascade Books, 2004), 149–65; and John M. Bracke and Karen B. Tye, *Teaching the Bible in the Church* (St. Louis: Chalice, 2003), 11–42.

46. May and Ratcliff, "Children's Spiritual Experiences," 160–62.

47. See Howard Gardner, *Frames of Mind: The Theory of Multiple Intelligences*, 10th ed. (New York: Basic Books, 1993); and Howard Gardner, *Multiple Intelligences: The Theory in Practice, A Reader* (New York: Basic Books, 1993).

expression in assessment. Therefore, development must attend to individuals with their distinct array of gifts and ways of functioning in the world that can give glory to God and serve humanity and all creation. Creation itself celebrates this diversity of gifts.

Developmental Presumptions

In reviewing the developmental foundations analyzed above, we can identify five presumptions undergirding developmental perspectives. Donald E. Miller has identified these presumptions in his analysis of a developmental approach to Christian education. First, development presumes a ground plan, a preexistent structure through which persons move. For Kohlberg the ground plan is the six stages of moral development, and for Erikson it is the eight stages of epigenesis or psychosocial development. Second, development presumes an invariable sequence. Any stage presumes the previous stage and leads to the next stage. Furthermore, no stage can be skipped, and difficulties in one stage may cause difficulties in a later stage. A person cannot move from stage 1 to stage 4 in Kohlberg's scheme; and if a child does not develop sufficient basic trust in others at Erikson's stage 1, later development is hindered. Third, development presumes the integration of increasingly complex elements. This integration or synthesis remains stable until challenged by elements that will not fit, at which time the individual is driven through a period of crises toward a new integration. From Erikson's perspective, the growing capacities of the child and the increasing independence from the parent lead to a crisis of the basic trust established and a testing of the parental relationship through a new independence. The toddler is posed with the crisis: Should I obey, or should I venture out on my own? A fourth presumption of development is that individuals interact with their environment. Active interaction with the physical environment provides a sense of reality; active interaction with the social, cultural, and religious environment provides a sense of selfhood, identity, and responsibility. The fifth and final presumption is that development has a goal or end. Development does not just terminate, but rather moves toward a final level of integration that is usually referred to as maturity.[48] For Erikson, stage 8 holds the potential of integrity, whereas for Kohlberg, stage 6 represents morally principled maturity as evidenced in the lives of such persons as Gandhi and Martin Luther King Jr.

48. Donald E. Miller, "The Developmental Approach to Christian Education," in *Contemporary Approaches to Christian Education*, ed. Jack L. Seymour and Donald E. Miller (Nashville: Abingdon, 1982), 76–77.

In relation to these five presumptions, it is possible to suggest responses from a Christian worldview. Christians may or may not specify a detailed ground plan. Those who opt out of such a plan may cite their reverence for the complexity of persons created in God's image and their recognition of the place of both history and culture, which intrude on any proposed structure with a host of exceptions. Nevertheless, Christians have also affirmed the reality of structure and form in God's creation and the place of development in created life. In fact, Christians generally operate with an implicit understanding of how persons develop across the life span, as Hamilton has suggested, with distinct phases of Christian maturity.

In relation to an invariable sequence, a Christian view of persons might be more prone to affirm the place of radical transformation and conversion along with development in understanding changes over time. The work of Loder in his study of human transformation is noteworthy in this respect.[49] An emphasis on development provides key insights for Christian commitments to the processes of nurture and sanctification, but such an emphasis appears to contradict Christian commitments to personal and social transformation. Miller suggests such a judgment: "Faith development is contradicted if conversion is so defined that it includes only a one-time dramatic reorientation."[50]

Evangelical or conversionist theology assumes a onetime conversion or justification but does not exclude the operation of God's prevenient (before coming to saving faith) grace, which operates in persons' lives to draw them to Christ. Although it is an event, conversion can also imply a process. It also does not exclude God's grace as operating subsequent to justification and the possibility of subsequent turnings in persons' lives.[51] For some Christians, sanctification is an ongoing process along with edification, which is a process of growing in Christ in relation to others. Glorification is the ultimate end or goal of these processes, but, nevertheless, these processes assume development. Thus a Christian can be described as "saved" in being justified, as "being saved" in the processes of sanctification and edification, and as in a future time "to be saved" in terms of ultimate glorification at the appearance of Jesus Christ. Miller's judgment is correct if conversion as justification is only in view, but a fully orbed conversionist theology allows for development in sanctification and

49. Loder, *Transforming Moment*; and James E. Loder, *The Logic of the Spirit: Human Development in Theological Perspective* (San Francisco: Jossey-Bass, 1998). For an assessment of Loder's contributions, see Dana R. Wright and John D. Kuentzel, eds., *Redemptive Transformation in Practical Theology* (Grand Rapids: Eerdmans, 2004).

50. Miller, "Developmental Approach to Christian Education," 100.

51. For further discussion of the place of conversion, see Robert W. Pazmiño, *Principles and Practices of Christian Education: An Evangelical Perspective* (1992; Eugene, OR: Wipf & Stock, 2002), 37–57.

edification.[52] Christians are being saved on a moment-to-moment basis as God's grace continues to operate in their lives at different stages of development.

In response to the third and fourth presumptions of development, a Christian educator can affirm both the integration of increasingly complex elements and the interaction of persons with their environment. One proviso is the recognition of God as active and intrusive. In other words, interaction with the environment must include the supernatural environment, where God's presence and/or work may intrude on development to elicit a result not directly attributable to what has gone before. This understanding recognizes the place of transformation and conversion through the sovereign operation of the Holy Spirit. The work of the Holy Spirit may build on and/or negate existing elements of development in ways that bring a creative and dynamic integration that otherwise was not possible. Loder describes this possibility as a "knight's move," the creative act of Christ's Spirit to bring about transformation in unpredictable and discontinuous ways within the human game of life.[53]

The fifth presumption of development can also be critiqued in light of Christian commitments. Christian educators emphasize the ultimate goal or end of glorifying and enjoying God. In relation to Jesus Christ, the goal of Christians is that they will be like him at his appearing and that all creation will be renewed (Rom. 8:18–25; 1 John 3:1–3). This complex integration of all of life transcends the categories of developmental schemes yet also includes them to the extent to which they embody God's will. Is it God's will that all persons be at stage 6 of Kohlberg's and Fowler's schemes? This question is indeed problematic when the vision of life shared by Christian sources is compared with these attempts at providing a description of maturity, wholeness, and integrity. The Christian vision focuses on the person and work of Jesus Christ, who is the author and perfecter or finisher of faith. Descriptions of the goal or end of development pale in the light of his face.

One final question to be raised in relation to the developmental perspectives surveyed in this chapter is one raised earlier in relation to Kohlberg's work. A focus on individual or personal development must not exclude consideration of corporate and social structures and relationships that impinge on development. These too are realities of the created world and must be scrutinized in relation to the demands of the gospel and the development of persons. To neglect the corporate dimension is to truncate a Christian worldview. The

---

52. For a discussion of conversion in relation to Christian education, see also Pazmiño, *Principles and Practices,* 37–57.

53. Loder and Neidhardt, *The Knight's Move,* 2.

work of Lev Vygotsky can help Christians understand the wider cultural and sociohistorical context for psychological development.[54]

An Interactive Christian Model

In the effort to provide some form and structure in what may appear to be a web of psychological chaos, I propose the following model, which seeks to integrate developmental concepts with a Christian anthropology, a Christian understanding of persons (see fig. 12). This model is but one and must be supplemented by other models in the attempt to provide some understanding regarding persons. The terms designating different points in this network are taken from the field of human development. Human development theorists place different emphasis on the terms suggested; nevertheless, the attempt here is not to advocate one or another emphasis. Rather, this model serves to identify the various dimensions of human beings suggested by biblical sources, which must be considered in ministering with and teaching persons.[55]

God's sovereignty and grace serve as both the umbrella and the foundation of this model. God's providential care and grace is a faith understanding that follows from the doctrine of creation and providence. Questions have been raised regarding God's sovereignty in the midst of human exigencies and suffering, but a Christian worldview has affirmed this perspective on human life.

Heredity is the genetic and structural nature and makeup of persons, which they receive from parents and ancestors. There are biological, cognitive, and emotional aspects of heredity. At the beginning of life, the social fabric is evident; a biblical perspective also suggests the presence of a spiritual heritage or inheritance operating in the human family. This spiritual heritage centers on the faith affirmations that persons, male and female, are created in God's image; that persons are fallen in sin; and that persons can be re-created or transformed by Christ. By virtue of their created nature, persons have intrinsic dignity and are worthy of respect, love, and service in all areas of their lives. By virtue of their fallen nature, persons are in need of instruction, correction, and discipline that recognizes the operation of God's grace at every point of human inadequacy. Sin is manifest in both personal and social interactions, and amoral as well as moral development is a concern. By virtue of Christ's life, death, and resurrection, persons can potentially experience

54. See Cynthia Jones Neal, "The Power of Vygotsky," in *Nurture That Is Christian: Developmental Perspectives on Christian Education*, ed. James C. Wilhoit and John M. Dettoni (Wheaton: Victor Books, 1995), 123–37.

55. I am indebted to the work of Gerald R. Levin in this model, taken from his lectures at Bucknell University, Lewisburg, PA, September–December 1969.

Figure 12
Integration of Developmental Concepts with Biblical Anthropology

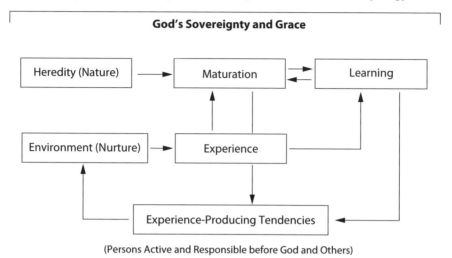

renewal and transformation in their lives at various points and in various dimensions that include both personal and corporate realities.

Maturation refers to biological growth processes that unfold the hereditary nature of persons and is distinct from learning. If a behavior matures through regular stages irrespective of intervening practice, the behavior is said to develop through maturation and not through learning. One example of maturation is the reflexes that newborns manifest at birth irrespective of practice and intervening experience. Having made this distinction, we must note that many activities develop through a complex interplay of maturation and learning. The Old Testament uses various words to describe children at different ages, suggestive of a maturation process:

yeled—a newborn babe (Exod. 1:17)

yônēq—a nursing child (1 Sam. 15:3)

ʿôlēl—a young child beginning to ask for food (Lam. 4:4)

gāmûl—a weaned child (Isa. 28:9)

ṭap—little children clinging to their mothers (Jer. 40:7)

naʿar—a growing child who "shakes free" (Isa. 11:6)

bāḥûr—a young adolescent, twelve to fourteen years of age (a ripened one) (Isa. 31:8)

In 1 Corinthians 13:11, Paul states, "When I was a child, I talked like a child, I thought like a child, I reasoned like a child. . . ." Children's ways of knowing are distinct from those of adults and change as a result of maturation. The observation of infants and children at various ages confirms the biblical descriptions.

As a psychological term, *learning* has been defined as the process by which behavior or the potentiality for behavior is modified as a result of experience.[56] Learning can also be defined as the process of change in knowledge, beliefs, values, attitudes, feelings, skills, or behaviors as a result of experience with the natural or supernatural environment. In relation to their created nature, persons are called to learn to love, live in, and obey God within the grasp of their understanding and ability. God's grace enables persons to learn in ways that fulfill divine expectations for and gifts to humanity. The greatest challenge is for Christians to be involved in lifelong learning in communities that provide such access to them at points of readiness. Learning most often involves a transmission of a cultural heritage in one form or another.

Environment denotes the total context in which a person grows or develops. Physical, psychological, familial, communal, economic, political, social, cultural, educational, aesthetic, and religious dimensions of the environment affect persons. Those theorists and practitioners in the field of human services who emphasize the impact of the environment on persons are said to maintain a "nurture" stance as compared with those who emphasize the impact of heredity on persons (a "nature" stance). Locke stressed the role of the environment on persons, whom he viewed as blank slates, whereas Rousseau emphasized the unfolding of each person's nature, which was given at birth. Key biblical passages emphasize the need for adults to consider the environment for the nurture of children. Both Deuteronomy 6:4–9 and Psalm 78:1–8 emphasize parental responsibilities for passing on to the next generation God's commandments and accounts of God's historical activities. Ephesians 6:4 admonishes parents not to exasperate their children, but to bring them up in the training and instruction of the Lord.

The environment in its variety of expressions, then, influences persons via their experiences. Personal experiences are the only direct experience persons have. In particular, the world of children is an experiential world, and persons who raise or teach children must be aware of this. The book of Proverbs is a guidebook of practical wisdom for supervising the experiences of others. A frequently quoted verse addressing the experiences of children is Proverbs 22:6:

56. For a study on learning, see Klaus Issler and Ronald Habermas, *How We Learn: A Christian Teacher's Guide to Educational Psychology* (Grand Rapids: Baker, 1994).

"Train a child in the way he should go, and when he is old he will not turn from it." "Way" can refer to the child's natural endowments and disposition or the intention of the child's mentors.[57] The first interpretation is preferable, as it emphasizes the need to be sensitive to each child, respecting her or his unique, God-given individuality. This perspective stresses the need to allow for creative self-fulfillment and a careful reading of each person's character. In raising children, we should stress choosing what God wants them to be and do and not forcing them to conform to the parents' way.[58] These insights regarding children also apply to the experiences of youth and adults.

Although people are influenced by their inborn nature and the nurture they receive, they are active as well as receptive. In Isaiah 29:22–23, the very presence of children is said to be a reminder of God's faithfulness. Scripture affirms the place of children in ministering to God and others (1 Sam. 1–3). The psalmist declares that from the lips of children and infants God has ordained praise (Ps. 8:2). From the very beginnings of life, persons are viewed as active and responsible before God at the level of their understanding and competence. They have experience-producing tendencies.

God created persons with minds and wills and a disposition to gain competence and abilities in a vast variety of endeavors. Often, despite limitations, people express their curiosity, creativity, and uniqueness. Where diversity is affirmed in human responses, educators in the home, church, school, and community witness persons' capabilities to initiate activity and gain experience, which influences the environment and potentials for learning. As indicated in the model, one person's experience-producing tendencies are influenced by previous learning and maturation, and the impact of nature and nurture in each person's case cannot be precisely predicted, given the reality of a person's own active engagement with such influences. Therefore, it is impossible to guarantee that certain outcomes will occur in any educational setting. This means, for instance, that identical twins may have similar home and educational influences and yet gain different perspectives and learn different things.

A complex web of elements must be accounted for in considering a biblical view of persons. Various theorists have stressed one element or another, but careful consideration must be made of each of the suggested elements in the model. In scholarship and research, serious questions have been raised regarding dominant developmental understandings that have excluded and devalued the unique characteristics of women in their development. In particular, the

57. J. Coert Rylaarsdam, "The Proverbs," in *Peake's Commentary on the Bible*, ed. Matthew Black and H. H. Rowley (London: Nelson & Sons, 1962), 454.

58. Marvin J. Wilson, "The Hebrew Model of Education" (lecture presented at Gordon-Conwell Theological Seminary, South Hamilton, MA, September 17, 1977).

work of Carol Gilligan in *In a Different Voice: Psychological Theory and Women's Development* and the work of Mary Field Belenky and others in *Women's Ways of Knowing* have posed fundamental challenges to traditional ways of understanding persons.[59] Gilligan points out the need to consider attachments along with separations in development, and the need to affirm affiliation and interconnection as well as achievement. She focuses on responsibility and care in addition to justice and personal rights in considering moral development. *Women's Ways of Knowing* explores the distinctive experiences of women that also have significance for men, and cultural settings outside dominant Western traditions. These conceptions, along with others, promote the formulation of a holistic understanding of persons more in harmony with a Christian worldview. As God's creatures, persons are multifaceted in their makeup and relationships, and this must be reflected in both theoretical and practical conceptualizations.

The interactive model proposed above does not claim to be the final word in considering the psychological foundations of education, but it does suggest a framework for considering the unique complexities of persons as created by God. Beyond the insights of such an analysis are the affirmations that persons are whole and that each individual is unique and worthy of our consideration, concern, and care. To do otherwise is to distort the image of the Creator in each one of us. A Christian understanding of persons affirms both the individuality of each person and the mutual relationships in the human community.

As Christian educators function in their faith community, they are called upon to propose, implement, and evaluate various curricula. To accomplish their responsibilities, educators must consider the curricular foundations of their ministries, which is the topic of chapter 7.

Points to Ponder

- Why might the approach of "spoiling the Egyptians" following the insights of Augustine be the best option for integrating psychology and Christian faith today? Suggest other approaches to consider.

59. Carol Gilligan, *In a Different Voice: Psychological Theory and Women's Development* (Cambridge, MA: Harvard University Press, 1982); and Mary Field Belenky et al., *Women's Ways of Knowing: The Development of Self, Voice, and Mind* (New York: Basic Books, 1986). See also Catherine M. Stonehouse, "Learning from Gender Differences," in *The Christian Educator's Handbook on Adult Education*, ed. Kenneth O. Gangel and James C. Wilhoit (Wheaton: Victor Books, 1993), 104–20.

- Revise the theological and psychological assumptions proposed to better reflect your understanding of persons.
- Map out your positions on the various theoretical issues from Levin in developmental psychology and suggest the biblical and theological warrants for your particular view.
- To whom among the developmental theorists discussed (Piaget, Erikson, Kohlberg, Fowler, Beechick, Gilligan, Belenky, and Loder) are you most attracted in terms of their view of persons? Explain why.
- Where do you agree and disagree with the "Integrative Christian Model" proposed in figure 12? Propose your own model or changes to make to the model presented here.

7

Curricular Foundations

The Christian educator must make decisions that directly affect the actual practice of education. These decisions are particularly necessary in the planning, implementation, and evaluation of a curriculum. Christian educators can explore curricular foundations with a focus on concrete realities and a concern to develop practical guidelines for teaching. The content and methods of that teaching are drawn from the various educational foundations explored in the first six chapters of this text and additional sources that are identified in the introduction. The fashioning of a curriculum provides the occasion to integrate insights drawn from various foundations in a connective way.

An issue of immediate concern in considering curriculum is that of definition. What is meant by curriculum if its foundations are to be considered? Various definitions and conceptions of curriculum have been suggested reflecting distinct value orientations and commitments in the field. Among suggested definitions are the following:

1. Curriculum is the content that is made available to students.[1]
2. Curriculum is the planned and guided learning experiences of students.[2]

1. Dwayne F. Huebner, "From Theory to Practice: Curriculum," *Religious Education* 77 (July–August 1982): 363.
2. John Dewey, *Experience and Education* (New York: Macmillan, 1944), 16, 86.

3. Curriculum is the actual experiences of a student or participant.[3]
4. Generally, curriculum includes both the materials and the experiences for learning. Specifically, curriculum is the written courses for study used for Christian education.[4]
5. Curriculum is the organization of learning activities guided by a teacher with the intent of changing behavior.[5]

Each of these definitions suggests a distinct emphasis in planning for and implementing teaching. Some theorists define curriculum as that which is planned or intended by educators, whereas instruction is that which is actually experienced by students. In this case, that which is experienced may be quite similar or quite distinct from that which is planned or intended. Some of the best laid teaching plans may not come to fruition as every experienced teacher knows. In contrast to this distinction, the definition of curriculum I propose includes aspects of instruction. Curriculum can be defined as that content made available to students and their actual learning experiences guided by a teacher. This definition implies that the teacher must assume responsibility in terms of content and experience in the planning, implementation, and evaluation of teaching. This responsibility results not in the determination or imposition of students' experiences but in the guidance of these experiences as students are invited to participate. Students' experiences are guided in ways that contribute to their information, formation, and transformation. The teacher's responsibility in relation to students' experiences is to foster a process in which experiences become informed and are examined with reflection. These possible experiences are shared and reflected upon with others to gain wisdom for living.

In justifying this perspective, the comments of Lois LeBar are helpful as she draws on the educational wisdom of John Amos Comenius (1592–1670) and the progressive education movement in the United States, which included the work of John Dewey (1859–1952). She observes that Christian content without experience is empty and that experience without content is blind.[6] The challenge in curriculum construction is to merge or blend both Christian content and experience so that the minds and lives of students are influenced and

3. Alice Miel, *Changing the Curriculum: A Social Process* (New York: Appleton-Century-Crofts, 1946), 9.

4. Iris Cully, *Planning and Selecting Curriculum for Christian Education* (Valley Forge, PA: Judson, 1983), 11–12.

5. Lois E. LeBar, *Education That Is Christian*, rev. ed. (Old Tappan, NJ: Fleming H. Revell, 1981), 211.

6. Lois E. LeBar, "Curriculum," in *An Introduction to Evangelical Christian Education*, ed. J. Edward Hakes (Chicago: Moody, 1964), 89.

transformed by God's truth. An exclusive emphasis on content in orthodoxy (true or right belief) can ignore the essential dimension of Christian experience, without which Christian education is empty. Likewise, an exclusive emphasis on experience in orthopraxis (true or right practice) can ignore the essential dimension of Christian content, without which Christian education is blind. An effective curriculum weds Christian content and experience and thereby is potentially life transforming. This potential requires the active and receptive participation of persons who seek to learn and are open to God's instruction as mediated through human teachers.

No simple formula to accomplish an adequate blending of content and experience exists, but certain guidelines can be shared. Teachers are called to be knowledgeable and sensitive to the dimensions of the content and to the various experiences of the students within their particular context. Through this knowledge and sensitivity, teachers can tailor the presentation of material to their students. This blending implies complementary concerns for truth and love in a Christian worldview along with sensitivity to a host of Christian virtues that teachers seek to model.

Truth is the essential content of Christian teaching—truth as revealed in Christ and in Scripture through the ministry of the Holy Spirit, and truth as discerned in all creation. As observed through history, all truth is God's truth. Love is the medium through which this truth is effectively communicated. Christians are commanded to love and witness about their faith through this love (John 13:34–35). The Scriptures blend these two virtues in the exercise of Christian ministry; they have particular import in teaching ministries. In Ephesians 4:15, Paul describes the need to "speak the truth in love." In 2 John 1–2, John describes his relationship with the chosen lady and her children, most likely referring to a church and its members. He states that he loves these persons in the truth because of the truth that lives within them. Therefore, to blend both content and experience, Christian teachers must faithfully live out a concern for both truth and love in their teaching and the experience of students. Teachers are called to care for the persons they are teaching with their diverse backgrounds and experiences. Teachers also are called to care for the content they are sharing, given its transformative potential in the lives of their students. Third, teachers are called upon to care for the context in which their students live, including their communities, their societies, and eventually their world reflecting God's love for all of creation.

A concern for truth not tempered by an equal concern for love can lead to harshness. A concern for love not tempered by an equal concern for truth can lead to license. Truth without love becomes hard, whereas love without truth becomes soft. Too often evangelical Christians have so proclaimed the truth to a world in need of love, that the gospel message has gone unheeded because it is inappropriately hard and unresponsive to the areas in which persons are living and hurting. Likewise, liberal or progressive Christians have so often emphasized love to a world in need of hearing God's truth that the gospel message has been viewed as insignificant because it is inappropriately soft. This limited comparison of evangelicals and liberals points out the desperate need for a balanced curriculum in dealing with just these two essential Christian virtues with implications for other virtues that may be identified.

Basic Questions

Decisions regarding curricula are crucial because it is through the curriculum that educational values and commitments actually become embedded in practice or take form. Curriculum is the vehicle or medium through which educational vision takes root. In relation to decisions regarding curriculum, several basic questions are either explicitly or implicitly answered by those involved in the process.[7]

What specifically should be taught?

In answering this question, areas of knowledge, understanding, values, attitudes, and skills can be identified by the Christian educator. It is essential to establish biblical and theological basics at this point along with areas of Christian life to be addressed. Even at the youngest ages, children can be exposed to theological concepts.

Why should these areas be taught?

In answering this question, the educator outlines the general purposes and specific goals of the particular ministry as discerned through Bible study, prayer, conscious dependence on the Holy Spirit, and a careful assessment of student needs. Needs must always be compared with God's demands and our responsibilities before God. There are genuine needs, but a culture may define needs that must be questioned in relation to biblical values.

7. Thomas Groome poses the first six basic questions in *Christian Religious Education: Sharing Our Story and Vision* (San Francisco: Harper & Row, 1980), xiv. These questions parallel those identified by D. Campbell Wyckoff in *Theory and Design of Christian Education Curriculum* (Philadelphia: Westminster, 1961).

Where is the teaching being done?

One's situation or setting affects what can be reasonably accomplished with the given resources and limitations. Unique cultural, social, and economic factors must be considered by the educator. The context of teaching may set clear limits that affect curricular decisions.

How is the teaching to be done?

One must consider the methods that are most appropriate for teaching. A variety of methods that are consistent with the truths being taught can be used in teaching. Also, in a media-oriented Western society more visual materials must be used to maintain students' interest. This "how" question also involves decisions regarding the organization of the content to be taught and the interrelationship of various components of the curriculum that may facilitate the integration and transfer of learning to other situations.

When should various areas be taught?

Christian educators determine the readiness of students and teachers to deal with the various areas of the Christian faith selected for teaching. Chronological age and spiritual maturity are factors to consider. A sense of timing is important in relation to previous and anticipated learnings and to unanticipated events.

Who is being taught, and who is teaching?

Understanding the lives and needs of students provides an important basis for the choice and development of any curriculum. Christian educators must also understand their own unique gifts, strengths, and weaknesses. Everyone involved in educational ministries is in need of the personal support and encouragement that characterizes Christian fellowship. Relationships become a vehicle for communicating God's living truth.

What organizing principle holds it all together?

What serves to provide unity, integration, and culmination to the educational experience in terms of planning, implementation, and evaluation?[8] In Christian education the appeal to distinctive biblical, theological, and philosophical elements can provide the means by which to identify principles that can have

8. Wyckoff identifies this question in *Theory and Design*.

universal significance and reveal what may be true for everyone in relation to faithful Christian education.

Cam Wyckoff posed yet an additional question to consider in curricular practice: *In what atmosphere does Christian education best take place?* He proposed a response to this question: "In an atmosphere of prayer, coupled with justice and love."[9] This additional question deals with the ethos—tone, character, or quality—of life fostered in education. It honors the affective area of experience that is related to Jonathan Edwards's concern for religious affections.[10]

Answering these essential educational questions enables the Christian educator to approach specific decisions about the curriculum from an informed and examined perspective. Various other criteria must be explored in dealing with specific ministries. In using teaching materials distributed by denominational and independent publishing houses, educators should be in basic agreement with how curriculum writers and editors have answered these seven questions or supplement the published curriculum in areas of disagreement. In developing one's own curriculum, agreement may be assured, but the writing of curriculum can be demanding in terms of material and time resources. Sometimes, however, developing one's own curriculum is the best solution to address a particular group of persons in their setting.

If one chooses to use a published curriculum, several key areas must be explored. First, does the theology of the publisher and curriculum writers agree with the theology of the particular church or ministry? Are theological concepts presented that are appropriate for various age levels and comprehensive in exposure?

Second, does the curriculum affirm the Scriptures as authoritative in the sense embraced by the particular church or community served? Is the whole counsel of the Scripture addressed in the sequence of the curriculum across the age groups? Besides the Scriptures, what other authorities functionally operate in curricular decisions?

Third, are the activities for learners varied and relevant to their life situations? Are students actively involved in the learning and challenged to deal with appropriate questions of the Christian faith?

Fourth, do the lesson plans allow for adapting materials to deal with time constraints, available resources, class size, and differing student ability? Can inexperienced teachers effectively use the materials? Can experienced teachers creatively use or adapt the curriculum?

9. D. Campbell Wyckoff, letter to the author, September 20, 1997.

10. For Edwards's thoughts on the aesthetic transformation possible in Christian education, see Ola Elizabeth Winslow, *Jonathan Edwards: Basic Writings* (New York: New American Library, 1966), 84–85.

Fifth, does the material deal with the needs, interests, and concerns of the students? Are students provided with appropriate ways in which to apply Christian truth and encouraged to respond to the lordship of Christ in all areas of their lives?

Finally, are the layout, colors, and quality of the materials attractive and attention-getting? Are racial and sexual representations appropriate? Can the curriculum be used more than once?

The relative importance of positive responses to each of these questions must be determined by those evaluating a variety of published curricula. Evaluators must be aware of the strengths and weaknesses of published materials and the unique needs of their particular education setting. It may be helpful to develop scales for comparing curricula in the areas mentioned. Additional questions beyond those suggested may need to be asked. Once a curriculum is chosen, the greater task is equipping teachers to effectively use and adapt that choice to their individual classes. Teacher training sessions can be planned to assist teachers in this area.

If the choice is made to develop a curriculum, the Christian educator must consider questions of continuity, sequence, and integration. Continuity is a measure of the extent to which biblical, theological, or life-related themes are adequately repeated for any one age group throughout the course of study. Sequence is a measure of how current teaching and learning builds on previous learning and contributes to future learning. Integration assesses the extent to which efforts in one aspect of the educational program, such as church school, relate to other aspects, such as Sunday worship and youth-group activities. These questions are generally addressed by publishers in their planning but are frequently ignored in personalized curricula.

Any decision concerning curriculum must be eclipsed by a greater concern for the life and ministry of the teachers themselves. Teachers need to consciously rely on the guidance of the Holy Spirit and demonstrate a genuine love for their students. God's curriculum transcends published or developed materials, and teachers must be flexible in the use and adaptation of the curriculum. The teachers themselves are a key element of the curriculum in teaching ministries. Paul's instructions to Timothy illustrate this perspective in 1 Timothy 4:11–12, 16: "Command and teach these things. Don't let anyone look down on you because you are young, but set an example for the believers in speech, in life, in love, in faith and in purity. . . . Watch your life and doctrine closely. Persevere in them, because if you do, you will save both yourself and your hearers." Timothy was encouraged to consider not only his teaching or doctrine but also his life, as it teaches by way of example. The modeling of teachers can set the terms of what content is embraced and what is dismissed over time.

Proposed Metaphors for Curriculum

Herbert M. Kliebard has provided an insightful analysis of the metaphorical roots of curriculum design. He identifies three metaphors that have influenced the thought and practice of curriculum creation in both general and Christian education: production, growth, and travel.[11] Figure 13 places these metaphors along a continuum. One pole emphasizes teacher direction and the other pole, student direction.

Figure 13
Curriculum Metaphors

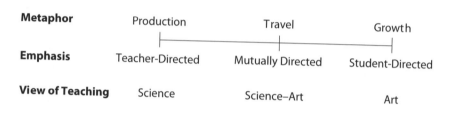

It is helpful to explore each of these metaphors as they relate to curricular decisions. Each will be discussed in terms of its general description, view of the teacher and teaching, advocates, and potential strengths and weaknesses. Other metaphors can be proposed, but these capture the dominant orientations in curricular foundations

The Metaphor of Production

In this metaphor, the curriculum is the means of production in education, while students are the raw material that will be transformed into a finished and useful product under the control of highly skilled technicians, namely, the teachers. The outcome of the production is carefully plotted in advance according to rigid design specifications with a concern to eliminate waste and maximize efficiency. Other descriptors of this approach have been "teacher-directed education," or "pedagogy," referring to the art and science of teaching children. Student learning goals in this metaphor are often structured competitively or comparatively by teachers with a concern to shape students in relation to predetermined objectives.

11. Herbert M. Kliebard, "The Metaphorical Roots of Curriculum Design," in *Curriculum Theorizing: The Reconceptualists*, ed. William Pinar (Berkeley: McCutchan, 1975), 84–85. Kliebard's descriptions are drawn from and elaborated upon in what follows.

The teacher is viewed as a sculptor or the social engineer, actively shaping and chipping away at the raw material of the students. Wherever possible, teaching is viewed as a science that specifies, measures, and combines various factors to maximize its impact on the lives of students.

The strongest advocate of this concept in general education is B. F. Skinner, who has stressed the need to shape the behavior of persons through careful and systematic conditioning, or behavior modification. There have also been various advocates in the area of instructional design, such as Robert Mager, Robert Gagne, and William E. Hug, who have emphasized efficient management of various educational elements. In the area of curriculum formation, Ralph Tyler developed a rationale that is the dominant framework for curricular planning and writing. The four basic steps of this rationale are identifying education objectives, selecting appropriate learning experiences, organizing learning experiences, and evaluating the learning.[12]

An extensive analysis of Tyler's metaphor is warranted, given its dominance in the curriculum field of Christian education. First, its potential strengths:

1. This framework has generally been successful and popular, given its basic rationality. A logical and sequential order is provided.
2. Tyler's framework does not stress minute details in the writing of objectives as compared with Mager and others working in the area of instructional design and technology.
3. It is a powerful model for the technical aspects of curriculum, those aspects that can be measured, quantified, and readily evaluated.
4. Tyler emphasizes a neutral or value-free position in dealing with competing conceptions for objectives.
5. Tyler defines education as the "process of changing the behavior patterns of people." In so doing, he uses behavior in a broad sense to include thinking, feeling, and action.
6. Tyler views the learner as active in the sense of responding to appropriate input. Learning experiences should balance discipline and freedom. Thus Tyler's emphasis is distinct from Skinner's commitment to discount the place of human freedom and dignity in education.

12. Ralph W. Tyler, *Basic Principles of Curriculum and Instruction* (Chicago: University of Chicago Press, 1949). Also see Robert F. Mager, *Preparing Instructional Objectives* (Palo Alto, CA: Fearson, 1962); Robert M. Gagne, *The Conditions of Learning* (New York: Holt, Rinehart & Winston, 1970); and William E. Hug, *Instructional Design and the Media Program* (Chicago: American Library Association, 1975).

7. Tyler's rationale diverts the focus in curricular planning from testing and places it on the objectives of the educational program.[13]

Next, the potential weaknesses of this metaphor for curriculum construction:

1. Philip Jackson, in *Life in the Classrooms*, suggests that Tyler's understanding is oversimplified in relation to what actually goes on in classroom teaching. The ordinary teacher is too busy to focus on preplanned objectives exclusively. Teaching, and therefore curriculum planning, must consider the opportunistic nature of classroom interactions. Because teachers must work with a high degree of uncertainty and ambiguity, albeit creative ambiguity, Tyler's rationale is inadequate.[14]

2. Curriculum planning and implementation are more an art or craft than a science. The imposition of a scientific and systematic approach is therefore not appropriate for the best results.

3. Tyler's rationale can exclude other considerations, such as differing styles of teaching and learning that would limit the effectiveness of identifying common objectives for any group. A teacher must be aware of responsiveness, variety, and flexibility in teaching, which this framework does not adequately encourage.

4. The statement or formulation of objectives, which is the crucial step in Tyler's rationale, may not adequately encourage the consideration of one's values and philosophy. Nor may it allow for adequate collaboration with others, including students when appropriate.

5. It is questionable whether stating objectives, when they represent external goals allegedly reached through the manipulation of learning experiences, is a fruitful way to conceive of the process of curricular planning. A broader and more comprehensive approach is called for.

6. Tyler's concept of a learning experience—the interaction between the learner and external conditions in the environment—fails to address interpersonal relationships, which are fundamental to teaching and learning.

7. Evaluation may ignore latent outcomes in concentrating on manifest and anticipated ones. Latent outcomes, those unanticipated insights or

13. Herbert M. Kliebard, "The Tyler Rationale," *School Review* 78 (February 1970): 259–72.

14. Philip W. Jackson, *Life in the Classrooms* (New York: Holt, Rinehart & Winston, 1968), 165–66.

results of teaching often described as incidental learning, may be just as important as stated objectives.[15]

The metaphor of production supports precision in emphasizing the learning of content. The metaphor of growth as compared with production focuses on persons.

The Metaphor of Growth

In this metaphor, the curriculum is like routine care provided in a greenhouse situation where students will grow and develop to their full potential under the wise and patient attention of the teacher. The plants that grow in the greenhouse are of every variety, but the gardener cares for each plant in unique ways so that each comes to flower. Each person is taught in accordance with personal needs; individualized instruction is the norm.

The teacher is viewed as the gardener caring for the individual needs of each growing plant or life. The teacher needs a great deal of sensitivity and insight in order to maximize appropriate growth at various points in development. Every effort is made to accurately discern the unique characteristics of students and the best-tailored plan to foster growth. Teaching from this perspective is perceived as an art, similar to the patient art of nursery care or gardening.

Given the impact of psychology on education, Carl Rogers has been most closely associated with this perspective.[16] In the field of education, those emphasizing progressive education in the tradition of John Dewey have placed a similar emphasis on the growth and nurture of persons.

The potential strengths of this metaphor include its focus on individual needs, a concern for persons beyond their responses, and a freedom to emphasize differences and distinctive elements. The growth metaphor stresses the individuality of each student and attempts to tap into intrinsic motivations to learn. A potential weakness of this metaphor is its assumption that students are to a certain extent self-directed and capable of pursuing tasks on the basis of increased intrinsic motivation. This metaphor can potentially deemphasize the place of structure and discipline as necessary prerequisites for growth and creativity. Growth in itself may be an inadequate goal if it is misguided and random. While stressing the importance of the individual, this metaphor may ignore the importance of the community and the larger social context.

15. Kliebard, "Tyler Rationale," 259–72.
16. For an introduction to Rogers's work, see Carl R. Rogers, *Freedom to Learn* (Columbus, OH: Charles E. Merrill, 1969); and Carl R. Rogers, *On Becoming a Person: A Therapist's View of Psychotherapy* (Boston: Houghton Mifflin, 1961).

The Metaphor of Pilgrimage

This metaphor represents a balance between teacher- and student-directed approaches. Students are relatively interdependent with teachers, as compared with being primarily dependent in the teacher-directed metaphor of production and being primarily independent in the student-directed metaphor of growth. Student learning goals are structured in a cooperative or collaborative way that assumes a degree of responsibility on the part of students. Teaching is related to a pilgrimage or route over which students will travel under the leadership of an experienced guide or companion. Each traveler or student will be affected differently by the journey since its effect is at least as much a function of the expectations, intelligence, interests, and intentions of the travelers as it is of the contours of the route and the skills of the guide. No effort is made to anticipate the exact nature of the effect on the traveler. But great effort is made to plot the route so that the journey will be as rich, as fascinating, and as memorable as possible.

The teacher is the experienced guide and companion who cares for and stimulates those with whom she or he is traveling. Teaching is viewed as a cooperative endeavor that employs both artistic and scientific elements in such a way that creativity from the realm of art and validity from the realm of science are both preserved.[17]

Theorists who have emphasized the place of pilgrimage as communicated through story support this metaphor. Both James Fowler and Richard Peace have emphasized the place of pilgrimage as related to development or growth.[18]

This metaphor is appealing, given the story nature or narrative quality of human experience. Teachers have served as guides and companions with students in exploring various areas of study. Possible weaknesses of this metaphor include the time required to develop personal relationships between teachers and students. It also assumes a measure of creativity and flexibility on the part of the teacher in responding to distinctive characteristics of the route and of the students at the same time.

Which metaphor is best and should therefore guide curriculum conceptions and decisions? No simple answer can be given. Sensitivity is required in relation to purposes, content, student/teacher needs, and styles. In teaching a highly technical skill, the metaphor of production would be warranted. In teaching a creative sensitivity that entails individual learning, the metaphor of

17. James Michael Lee describes teaching in these terms in *The Flow of Religious Instruction* (Dayton, OH: Pflaum/Standard, 1973), 215–21.

18. See James W. Fowler, *Stages of Faith: The Psychology of Human Development and the Quest for Meaning* (San Francisco: Harper & Row, 1981); and Richard Peace, *Pilgrimage: A Workbook on Christian Growth* (Los Angeles: Acton House, 1970).

growth would be best. In teaching a survey course of a richly diverse subject, the metaphor of pilgrimage would be the choice. A larger question at stake in the choice of a metaphor or metaphors in curriculum planning is the question of values that must be explicit in curricular planning.

The Place of Values in the Explicit Curriculum

A curriculum embodies values in relation to those understandings, attitudes, skills, and behaviors chosen to be shared with students. Values are generally defined as conceptions to which worth, interest, and goodness have been attributed. Once Christians identify values in education that are consistent with a Christian world and life view, they are under certain obligations to consider those values in curricular planning and teaching. These obligations are fourfold and call for theological accountability in the practice of educating.[19]

First, Christians must own and live out the values they profess. This is a call to integrity in curricular decision making and planning. Three examples can be cited. If Christians affirm the value of individuals as created in the image of God, they must adapt or adjust teaching styles to enable various persons to learn and apply God's truth in ways that are consistent both with God's demands and with their own learning styles. If this is not the case, curricular planning and teaching are subject to the inappropriate imposition of content and method on students.

If Christians affirm the view of a heavenly parent who disciplines children for their benefit, they must uphold appropriate discipline and order in curricular planning and teaching that benefits students and glorifies God. This obligation is an especially difficult task in a generally undisciplined and unrestrained societal context that ironically also struggles with abuse of various kinds in epidemic proportions. If Christians affirm the creative potential of each person who has been created, they must allow for creative expression in curricular planning. A slavish adherence to behavioral objectives in curricular planning may in fact stifle the freedom and open-ended responses necessary for creative expression in the classroom. Such adherence may not enable students to think for themselves.

A second obligation in curricular planning can be noted. To live out Christian values, Christians must translate their values into the purposes and goals of the curriculum. Christian educators often state purposes and goals without questioning their relation to underlying values endemic to a Christian worldview. The result is a truncated educational experience that can claim to be

19. See the discussion of values in chap. 3, pp. 101–7; and John W. Gardner, "Engagement of Values in Public Life," *Harvard Divinity Bulletin* (October–November 1984): 5–6.

Christian only in name but not in substance. For example, Christians have affirmed that all truth is God's truth. This implies the necessity of enabling students to think "Christianly" about any area of study. It also implies the need to integrate truth in various areas to God's truth as revealed in the Bible wherever possible. Furthermore, love and truth must be balanced. In the curriculum, this implies the need to teach the truth and encourage students to love the truth. It also implies the necessity of encouraging love between teacher and students and among students. Whereas these purposes may be viewed as simple and assumed in curricular planning, they are in actuality profound and pervasive in their impact on teaching.

A third obligation involves the need to pursue values in the institutional orders of everyday life. These institutional orders include the home, the church, the school, the community, the society, and other groups.[20] Values can become so privatized that they become less rooted in life. Life is inherently social and corporate. Institutions, groups, and communities embody various values, which unfortunately are often unexamined. The consideration of the sociological foundations of education, especially the questions posed by John Eggleston, serves to address this third obligation.

A fourth obligation is related to the constant need for renewal in curricular formation, the need to reaffirm basic values and goals. The real danger of "morphological fundamentalism" exists in curriculum.[21] This term refers to the fact that certain forms or structures may take on the character of being sacred and therefore exempt from question or examination. They become fundamental and essential. With curriculum, this danger implies the need for constant evaluation and adaptation. Change and transformation are realities to consider and plan for in developing any curriculum. Those who use a curriculum must be encouraged to adapt the material to their particular group and setting. Without a certain degree of flexibility and adaptability, a curriculum can become outdated and inappropriate.

The Hidden Curriculum

According to Elizabeth Vallance, the "hidden curriculum" identifies those nonacademic and systematic side effects of education that are sensed, but which

20. For a discussion of educational agencies or structures, see Robert W. Pazmiño, *Principles and Practices of Christian Education: An Evangelical Perspective* (1992; Eugene, OR: Wipf & Stock, 2002), 59–90.

21. See J. C. Hoekendijk and Hans Schmidt, "Morphological Fundamentalism," in *Planning for Mission: Working Papers on the Quest for Missionary Communities,* ed. Thomas Weiser (New York: U.S. Conference for the World Council of Churches, 1966), 134–37.

cannot be adequately accounted for by reference to the explicit curriculum. The explicit curriculum is the stated or public purposes and particulars of an educational program or event. Vallance suggests three dimensions along which aspects of the hidden curriculum can be considered:

1. Hidden curriculum can refer to any of the contexts of education, including the student-teacher interaction, the classroom structure, or the whole organizational pattern of the education establishment as a microcosm of the social value system.
2. Hidden curriculum can bear on a number of processes operating in or through schools, churches, or homes, including values acquisition, socialization, and maintenance of a social structure.
3. Hidden curriculum can embrace differing degrees of intentionality and depth of "hiddenness" ranging from incidental and quite unintended by-products of curricular arrangements to outcomes more deeply embedded in the historical social function of education in different communities.[22]

How do Vallance's insights relate to Christian education? Examples from one educational context may help. An evangelical college or theological seminary may maintain the following elements within its hidden curriculum:

1. Each person in the community should have had a personal experience with Jesus as Lord and Savior.
2. Scholarship, service, discipline, or piety is the highest ideal in Christian ministry.
3. Liberals are to be viewed as enemies of the evangelical faith.
4. Graduates of specific evangelical colleges or institutions are to be revered.
5. A faithful evangelical is a member of the Republican Party; or a thinking evangelical is a member of the Democratic Party.
6. Evangelicals are not communists, social activists, or successful capitalists. Evangelicals are suspect if they are inappropriately aligned politically or economically.
7. Evangelicals are the backbone of middle-class society in the United States.

22. Elizabeth Vallance, "Hiding the Hidden Curriculum: An Interpretation of the Language of Justification in Nineteenth-Century Educational Reform," *Curriculum Theory Network* 4 (1973–74): 5–21.

8. Evangelical faith is the faithful embodiment of historic orthodox Christianity in the modern world.

9. If Jesus were alive today, he would be an evangelical.

These aspects of the hidden curriculum are held in varying degrees and with varied effects on students.

Lawrence Richards, in his analysis of seminary training, maintains that the hidden curriculum of most programs also includes the conceptual structuring of content. As a result, students are often trained to study and master Scripture in an intellectual rather than a personal or relational way. The hidden curriculum also includes a largely impersonal learning setting that transfers to an impersonal style of ministry following seminary. The emphasis is on Bible information over against modeling the Christian life. Finally, in Richards's analysis, seminary training emphasizes that learning is primarily individual and competitive to the relative exclusion of corporate and cooperative patterns.[23] Richards's insights are generally accurate, but developments since 1975 indicate some movement away from this pattern of seminary training.

Richards contends that the hidden curriculum is the most powerful educational force with which Christian education deals. This is the case not only at the seminary level but at all levels of education. This contention naturally follows from his emphasis on socialization and nurture through modeling. Richards, in fact, defines the hidden curriculum as those elements of every setting in which believers interact that support or inhibit the transformation process.[24] For Richards this transformation process is the essence of Christian education that communicates the Christian faith as life.

In relation to Richards's contention, I believe that both explicit and hidden curriculum require equal attention. Both are powerful forces and must complement each other. An emphasis on the hidden curriculum should not diminish a concern for the explicit, academic dimensions of the curriculum. Likewise, an emphasis on the explicit curriculum should not diminish a concern for the hidden curriculum. The Christian educator is called upon to assume responsibilities in both areas and to complement academic and nonacademic emphases wherever possible. Both content and experience must be addressed. Both formal and nonformal educational components are matters for curricular planning. Both explicit and hidden curricula are matters

23. Lawrence O. Richards, *A Theology of Christian Education* (Grand Rapids: Zondervan, 1975), 251–52.

24. Ibid., 321.

for curricular planning. Both explicit and hidden curricula are concerns for the Christian educator in planning for and implementing an effective educational program.

The Null Curriculum

In addition to both the explicit and the hidden curricula, which operate in any educational setting, be it the church, the home, or the school, there is also the "null curriculum." Elliot Eisner defines the null curriculum as that which is not taught by choice or oversight. He posits that what is not taught may be as important as what is taught because ignorance affects the kinds of options one can consider.[25] Any educational program or event cannot address everything that is possible or even desirable. In light of this reality, educators must acknowledge the choices that have been made and suggest additional opportunities for students to explore options that were not selected. The identification of the null curriculum enables teachers to be honest about both their limitations and the assumptions that undergird their efforts. These assumptions about the content, persons, and contexts of their teaching serve to indicate the parameters of curricular foundations.

Therefore, beyond the explicit and the hidden curricula, Christian educators must consider the null curriculum in curricular planning, implementation, and evaluation. The null curriculum as first described by Eisner is that which is not taught, with the explicit curriculum referring to what is taught.[26] The hidden or implicit curriculum refers more to what is caught by persons than to what is directly taught in the course of instruction. In other words, the explicit curriculum focuses on content, the hidden curriculum addresses the implicit formation of persons, and the null curriculum is disclosed by considering the wider context of what is possible but not selected for sharing or just forgotten. Maria Harris helpfully explores the implications for noting the null curriculum:

> The null curriculum is a paradox. This is the curriculum that exists because it does not exist; it is what is left out. But the point of including it is that ignorance or the absence of something is not neutral. It skews the balance of options we might consider, alternatives from which we might choose, or

25. Elliot W. Eisner, *The Educational Imagination: On the Design and Evaluation of School Programs*, 2nd ed. (New York: Macmillan, 1985), 97. See also Ronald T. Habermas, "Even What You Don't Say Counts," *Christian Education Journal* 5 (Autumn 1984): 24–27.
26. Eisner, *Educational Imagination*; 87–107. See also Pazmiño, *Principles and Practices*, 91–115.

perspectives that help us see. The null curriculum includes areas left out (content, themes, points of view) and procedures left unused (the arts, play, critical analysis).[27]

The identification of the null curriculum provides a basis for critique of existing curricula and the invitation for future changes for a more inclusive curriculum. But with inclusion educators always struggle with the reality of limits and questions of feasibility that call for a larger vision. A larger vision calls for surveying one's educational landscape and considering new invitations such as those explored in this work's appendices while affirming points of continuity with the past.

A Larger Vision

A survey of most printed curricula reveals that the vast majority specify what students are to know, feel, or do as a result of a particular class or course. This derives from emphasizing behavioral objectives in teaching and learning. Clarity and specificity in relation to purposes, goals, and objectives are to be affirmed, but a larger vision is suggested by exploring biblical models. In curricular matters, how does the dominant model, emphasizing the identification, realization, and evaluation of behavioral objectives, compare with a model implied in the context of a New Testament ministry? In relation to this question, the book of Titus provides helpful insights:[28]

> You must teach what is in accord with sound doctrine. Teach the older men to be temperate, worthy of respect, self-controlled, and sound in faith, in love and in endurance.
>
> Likewise, teach the older women to be reverent in the way they live, not to be slanderers or addicted to much wine, but to teach what is good. Then they can train the younger women to love their husbands and children, to be self-controlled and pure, to be busy at home, to be kind, and to be subject to their husbands, so that no one will malign the word of God.

27. Maria Harris, *Fashion Me a People: Curriculum in the Church* (Louisville: Westminster John Knox, 1989), 69, 122, 174.

28. The use of the New Testament book of Titus as a pastoral epistle may be problematic for Christian feminists who appropriately object to the perceived limited role of women advocated in this section of Scripture as compared with Jesus's affirmation of their ministry as described in the Gospel accounts. My use of the letter to Titus recognizes the cultural context in which women did not have extensive access to education and patriarchal patterns persisted. The contemporary cultural context is distinct, and I affirm the full participation of women in teaching ministries at all levels of the Christian church and wider society.

Similarly, encourage the young men to be self-controlled. In everything set them an example by doing what is good. In your teaching show integrity, seriousness and soundness of speech that cannot be condemned, so that those who oppose you may be ashamed because they have nothing bad to say about us.

Teach slaves to be subject to their masters in everything, to try to please them, not to talk back to them, and not to steal from them, but to show that they can be fully trusted, so that in every way they will make the teaching about God our Savior attractive.

For the grace of God that brings salvation has appeared to all men. It teaches us to say "No" to ungodliness and worldly passions, and to live self-controlled, upright and godly lives in this present age, while we wait for the blessed hope—the glorious appearing of our great God and Savior, Jesus Christ, who gave himself for us to redeem us from all wickedness and to purify for himself a people that are his very own, eager to do what is good.

These, then, are the things you should teach. Encourage and rebuke with all authority. Do not let anyone despise you. (Titus 2:1–15)

Titus was a Gentile convert to Christianity who became a fellow worker and assistant to Paul. Paul's letter to Titus finds him in Crete, where he has the responsibility of supervising the work of the church. Part of this supervision involved Titus in teaching various groups with their distinct needs and responsibilities. Paul addresses the content and methods of teaching these various groups (older men, older women, younger women, younger men, and slaves). Titus is advised both what to teach and how to teach. Paul outlines age-graded specifics along with general guidelines for the curriculum. Paul's insights are suggestive for current efforts, provided one recognizes the historical setting of this letter and the social context it addressed. Critical understanding is also necessary in interpreting the place of women and slaves in this setting.

In general terms, Titus is encouraged to teach various groups *to be* something or other. No doubt knowing, feeling, and doing are implied in the call to be, but a concern for being implies a larger purpose, a larger vision. Titus is to be concerned with character formation, the values persons are embracing and living out. Good works and conduct flow from sound doctrine and from a person's being in a right relationship with God and others. Christian educators must be concerned for Christian values and virtues, which persons are called upon to embody in their very lives.

Titus is to teach the older men *to be* temperate, worthy of respect, self-controlled, and sound in faith, in life, and in endurance. Titus is to teach the older women *to be* reverent in the way they live, not to be slanderers or addicted to much wine, but to be teachers of what is good. Younger women are *to be* taught by older women to love their husbands and children, to be self-controlled and pure, to be busy at home, to be kind, and to be subject to their husbands. The young men are *to be* taught to be self-controlled. Titus, himself a young man, is to be an example by doing what is good and showing integrity, seriousness, and soundness of speech. By implication, other young men are to be encouraged to be like Titus. Slaves are taught *to be* subject to their masters in everything, to try to please them, not to talk back to them, and not to steal from them, but to show they can be fully trusted. This curriculum, even in terms of each age and social group, is quite extensive. How is Titus ever to accomplish this task? How can teachers teach others *to be*?

Several answers can be suggested. In commenting on Titus 2, Wilbur Wallis has stated that God's grace not only saves persons but also teaches and trains them in sober and godly living.[29] This is one possible answer. Every Christian teacher can confess the need for God's grace to accomplish any results in the lives of students. God's grace is realized not only through the abilities and sensitivities of teachers and students alike in the classroom but also through the medium of prayer as all participants rely on God's wisdom and work. Thus prayer and the expectation of the work of the Holy Spirit are essential elements.

A second possible answer is also suggested in the text of Titus itself. Titus is encouraged to set an example by doing what is good and by showing integrity, seriousness, and soundness. Titus is to teach others "to be" by "being" himself. Likewise, teachers can hopefully encourage students to be of a certain character by embodying that very character themselves. This ministry does not eliminate the possibility of students exceeding their teachers and manifesting abilities and aspects of character beyond their examples. But teachers must be aware that they are examples or models that are being examined by their students. Teachers mentor others through the hidden and null curricula as well as through the explicit curriculum.[30]

A third answer involves the two Christian virtues of love and truth. Titus is instructed by Paul to teach what is in accord with sound doctrine (2:1) and rebuke with all authority (2:15). Titus is to affirm the standard of God's truth. This standard requires that persons say "no" to ungodliness and worldly passions and live self-controlled, upright, and godly lives. A concern for truth implies a serious grappling with God's standards for

---

29. Wilbur B. Wallis, "The Epistle to Titus," in *The Wycliffe Bible Commentary*, ed. Charles F. Pfeiffer and Everett F. Harrison (Chicago: Moody, 1962), 1395.

30. For a discussion of these three dimensions of curricula, see Pazmiño, *Principles and Practices*, 93–114.

holiness and purity in one's personal and corporate life. Holiness includes the call to confront injustice and to advocate for Christian values in the wider society.

In addition to this concern for truth, Titus is instructed to encourage various persons in their need to be taught. For him to effectively accomplish this, he must love them, a theme not addressed here but in other portions of Scripture. Some Christians in the past have used this text to support slavery, whereas others have raised serious questions about the presence of Christian love in relation to slavery. This indicates the need for critical awareness of what one is in fact teaching using the biblical sources and how one is appropriating a text or context.

In conclusion, Titus is to teach others by relying on the grace of God, by being himself an example, and by teaching in accord with truth and in love. These are simple yet profound answers to questions of how to encourage others to be in Christ. To live out these answers requires the diligent efforts of a teacher in a working relationship with God.

This chapter completes the survey of the various foundations that Christian educators should consider in their thought and practice. No final answers have been provided, but the hope is that grappling with such matters will make a difference in the advance of God's work in our time. The important work of formulating principles and guidelines for practice remains for the Christian who seeks to be faithful in the various dimensions of Christian education.[31] This work has sought to provocatively identify key foundational issues that Christians are called to consider in the faithful practice of Christian education. The postscript provides a summary of insights the author has sought to share in this third and earlier editions.

Points to Ponder

- Consider a particular Christian education lesson or class and attempt to answer the basic questions for a curriculum from what is planned for it.
- Advocate for one of the proposed metaphors for curriculum (production, growth, or pilgrimage) and outline how it can assist teachers in planning to teach a particular topic or theme. Suggest additional metaphors such as midwifery, cooking, or quilt making to guide curricular foundations.

31. For the author's description of these principles and guidelines for practice, see Pazmiño, *Principles and Practices*, which is a companion volume to this work.

- Describe the lessons of both the hidden and the null curricula in your current course or class from the perspective of the students or participants. Compare the descriptions with what the teacher or teachers intend.
- Besides the Titus 2 passage, suggest other key biblical passages from chapter 1 that can serve to expand our curricular visions in Christian education. A favorite passage for the author is Nehemiah 8. How might Nehemiah 8 provide an alternative to Titus 2? Elaborate.[32]

---

32. See Robert W. Pazmiño, *Latin American Journey: Insights for Christian Education in North America* (Eugene, OR: Wipf & Stock, 2002), 123–44, for my thoughts on this passage.

Appendix **A**

Singing the Lord's Song in a Foreign Land

Proclaiming Truth in a Postmodern Setting

The Hebrew psalmist raises a question for Christians grappling with the possibility of truth in a postmodern era: "How can we sing the songs of the LORD while in a foreign land?" (Ps. 137:4). Christians affirm the existence of truth. Christians celebrate in word and song the reality of truth in the person of Jesus Christ. But as Christians we struggle with the reception of truth in a postmodern world that often denies the very possibility of truth, particularly on the universal scale claimed by Christians. Truth for all is too often viewed as foreign to postmodern sensitivities. As a result, Christians feel and think that they are residing in a foreign land, residing in a land foreign to what Christians hold as foundational to their faith.

The dilemma in our contemporary context is compounded by the calling that Christians have to witness to their faith and its truth claims. Christians have an obligation, a mission to sing the Lord's song wherever they are called to be. The Lord's song is one of truth. Indeed, truth is one of the notes of the melody begun at creation and continuing through all the ages. Certainly other notes make up the melody and harmony of the Lord's song. They include love, faith, hope, joy, righteousness, justice, peace, holiness, reverence, and wonder along with a host of other Christian virtues. But the note of truth is sounded clearly from the beginnings of the gospel message. John's Gospel claims that "the law was given through Moses; grace and truth came through Jesus Christ" (John 1:17). The coming of grace and truth in Jesus Christ challenges persons in every age to consider God's revelation and its implications for all of life. The singing of the Lord's song and the disclosure of its truth require the discernment of Christians in both a modern and a postmodern age.

The process of discernment calls upon Christians to consider whether they are living in a foreign land. Is it a foreign land that does not embrace the possibility or even the desirability of truth? What did Jesus confront in disclosing the truth in his land of birth and in his age of the first century? What can Christians today discern from the response of others to Jesus in his time and context? How receptive were people to what Jesus shared with them about God's truth embodied in his very person? One example comes from Jesus's encounter with Pilate in the last days of his earthly ministry described in John 18:28–38. Of particular interest is the account of verses 37 and 38:

> Pilate asked him, "So you are a king?" Jesus answered, "You say that I am a king. For this I was born, and for this I came into the world, to testify to the truth. Everyone who belongs to the truth listens to my voice." Pilate asked him, "What is truth?" (NRSV)

In this and other accounts Jesus claimed to be testifying to the truth. He also claimed that every person who belongs to the truth will listen to him. In effect, Jesus is claiming to embody in his life and person the truth for humankind. Pilate's response is noteworthy. His response historically has been viewed as evidence of his moral bankruptcy. Nevertheless, Pilate's question is what is hailed as a new question for Christians in a postmodern age. What is truth if no truths can be claimed that have universal significance? The reception of Jesus in his world of the first century may provide insights for Christians in the current age.

The Reception of Jesus in His World

It is instructive to explore how Jesus was received at different points in his earthly journey. These responses to Jesus by his contemporaries have implications for understanding the receptivity to truth in postmodernity. With Jesus as a model or exemplar, Christians can gain perspective as suggested by Matthew 10:24–25a:

A disciple is not above the teacher, nor a slave above the master; it is enough for the disciple to be like the teacher, and the slave like the master. (NRSV)

Four examples of the reception of Jesus in the world will be considered. They include the reception on earth, the reception at Bethlehem, the reception in Nazareth, and the reception at Jerusalem. Related respectively to each of these settings for receiving Jesus I have identified a theme for reflection: incarnation, intimidation, rejection, and crucifixion. Each of these themes relates to how Christians might respond to the challenges of postmodernity.

Earth: Incarnation

Jesus's entry into the world itself marks the distinctive claim of the Christian faith. God has chosen to assume human form in the person of a first-century Jewish child, conceived by an unmarried woman. How is it possible that God, the Second Person of the Trinity, could be revealed in such a way? The utter impossibility, the scandal to human consciousness of such an event as the incarnation can lead to either disbelief or wonder. The truth of such a revelation about the person and character of God confronts humanity with a choice. Ultimately, this choice is between life as offered in the Son of God or a refusal of God's gift of eternal life described graphically in the following passage of Scripture:

> This is the one who came by water and blood, Jesus Christ, not with the water only but with the water and the blood. And the Spirit is the one that testifies, for the Spirit is the truth. There are three that testify: the Spirit and the water and the blood, and these three agree. If we receive human testimony, the testimony of God is greater; for this is the testimony of God that he has testified to his Son. Those who believe in the Son of God have the testimony in their hearts. Those who do not believe in God have made him a liar by not believing in the testimony that God has given concerning his Son. And this is the testimony: God gave us eternal life, and this life is in his Son. Whoever has the Son has life; whoever does not have the Son of God does not have life. (1 John 5:6–12 NRSV)

Such a choice is not received well in an age of inclusivity, and the scandal of God's revelation in Jesus Christ is an offense to many persons and communities. But this response does not refute the truth of God's revelation and what God has offered humanity in Jesus Christ.

What might this suggest for Christians and their sharing testimony, their bearing witness in a postmodern world? Paul in writing to the Corinthian church described the challenge in his setting that has direct parallels for Christians today:

> For Jews demand signs and Greeks desire wisdom, but we proclaim Christ crucified, a stumbling block to Jews, and foolishness to Gentiles, but to those who are the called, both Jews and Greeks, Christ the power of God and the wisdom of God. (1 Cor. 1:22–24 NRSV)

Christians are called to proclaim the truth of Christ being God's revelation and the incarnation of God's power and wisdom for all creation. In a postmodern setting, many will reject this proclamation and will refute its truth, but this should not deter Christians from the mission of preaching and teaching the wonders of the gospel. These wonders are shared as a gift with humanity and not imposed as a judgment. This is the case because Christians must always allow for the gracious working of God's Spirit on the hearts and minds of persons who reject the gospel. In their very lives Christians are called to incarnate the grace and truth of the gospel. The truth is to be revealed continually in the lives and words of those who claim to be Christians and followers of the Son of God. In this way the miracle of the incarnation extends into the contours of a postmodern world in the faithful witness of the Christian community. This is how the apostle Paul describes the ministry of the Christians at Corinth:

> You yourselves are our letter, written on our hearts, to be known and read by all; and you show that you are a letter of Christ, prepared by us, written not with ink but with the Spirit of the living God, not on tablets of stone but on tablets of human hearts. (2 Cor. 3:2–3 NRSV)

In a postmodern world it may well be that some persons must first read the truth of the gospel in the lives of Christians before they can hear our words witnessing to the truth. But the mysterious workings of the Spirit of the living God cannot be programmed by human minds and hearts. For this we can be grateful in the midst of various threats and intimidation.

Bethlehem: Intimidation

From his birth in Bethlehem Jesus posed a threat to others and was in turn threatened. King Herod sought the life of Jesus upon hearing of the wise men's inquiry about one who was to be born the king of the Jews, a position he cherished for himself. The birth of Jesus, while a source of great joy for his parents, the shepherds, and all of humanity who has sought a savior, was also a source of great suffering. The Gospel of Matthew records the massacre of the infants, the slaughter of the innocents who died at the hands of Herod (Matt. 2:16–18). All the children in and around Bethlehem who were two years old or under were killed. The political implications of Jesus's birth were apparent to those in power.

In response to Herod's threat, Jesus and his parents fled to Egypt, but in their wake weeping and mourning was the experience of many families. The saving of Jesus's life occurred in the context of a greater loss of life for those whose only crime was that of being born at the wrong time and place. This was the case because of the tyranny and evil perpetuated by those in political power who felt threatened by a child and what he represented for humanity. Today the loss of life at Bethlehem is relived as children are born into what is called the "permanent underclass" in the United States.

The terms of life have not radically changed in too many places around the globe. The coming of one who embodies truth and an alternative can be just as intimidating today as in the first century. Jesus's forced exile to Egypt along with his family is repeated in the experience of a vast host of exiles whose numbers increase annually. The massacre of children continues in the steady rise of child abuse and random violence against children even in what are regarded as advanced societies like the United States. The disclosure of truth poses a threat to patterns of living and governing that promote oppression. All this calls for a response of advocacy that can be costly. The threat of truth to political, social, and economic powers continues in the postmodern world just as it did in the first century.

One additional thought in relation to the threat in Bethlehem is the significance of the flight of Jesus and his family to Egypt. Augustine of Hippo in reflecting on the discernment of truth wrote about the spoiling of Egyptians in the earlier flight of the Israelites from their oppression. The spoiling of the Egyptians refers to the various gifts that were bestowed on the departing slaves by the Egyptians themselves, who offered gold, silver, and precious jewels (Exod. 3:21–22). The Israelites used the vessels and ornaments of gold and silver to adorn the tabernacle in the wilderness (Exod. 25 and 26). The negative potential or threat in this "spoiling" is represented by the idol of the golden calf (Exod. 32). Augustine suggested that Christians could selectively incorporate truths from various sources, the spoils, and integrate them into a life of worship and adoration of God.[1] Jesus's own flight to Egypt can symbolically represent the affirmation of truth wherever it is discovered. Jesus, like Joseph, Moses, and Israel, escaped to and returned from Egypt thus fulfilling what God had spoken through the prophet Hosea, "Out of Egypt I have called my son" (Hos. 11:1;

---

1. Augustine, *On Christian Doctrine*, 2.40.

Matt. 2:15 NRSV). Egypt represents a place of both safety and danger that requires careful discernment. For Christians the trends of postmodernity can offer both promise and threat, thus requiring discernment. In a postmodern world Christians can themselves be threatened and intimidated by other truths that do not directly emerge from Christian sources. In recognizing that Jesus was a Jew and that he imbibed the truths that were current in Palestine of the first century, Christians can be open to the gifts God intends to share with the spoiling of the Egyptians. This spoiling fulfilled God's plan but required careful discernment as it also does today.

Nazareth: Rejection

The rejection of Jesus at Nazareth held a double jeopardy for him both in his hometown and in the wider circle of Jewish society. When he disclosed the truth about his ministry in his hometown synagogue, the reception he received was not all that cordial. The account in Luke 4:16–30 points out that "no prophet is accepted in his hometown," but Jesus's public ministry results in the rage of his neighbors, who drove him out of town and attempted to hurl him off a cliff. This is a direct rejection of the truth Jesus shared regarding God's favor being shed on outsiders, even Gentiles, to the exclusion of those in Israel who were perceived as favored.

The additional rejection that Jesus experienced is described in the words attributed to Nathanael in John 1:46: "Nazareth! Can anything good come from there?" Not only was Jesus rejected in his hometown of Nazareth, but he was rejected initially for being associated with Nazareth in the wider society. Galilee, the region in which Nazareth was located, had a bad reputation for being a culturally mixed wasteland or a backwater setting from which nothing of worth could emerge. Yet, remarkably, the Son of God took on the form of a man who dwelt the majority of his life in such a place. The upwardly mobile would have long deserted such a region. How is it that any sayings from an inhabitant of Nazareth or Galilee can be identified as truth? The unorthodox character of any declarations that issue from Nazareth or Galilee could be easily assumed.[2]

Christians in a postmodern society confront a similar pattern of rejection where the disestablishment of the church is the norm within a "culture of disbelief."[3]

2. For a discussion of Galilee, see Virgil Elizondo, *Galilean Journey: The Mexican-American Promise* (Maryknoll, NY: Orbis, 1983); and Robert W. Pazmiño, *Latin American Journey: Insights for Christian Education in North America* (Cleveland: United Church Press, 1994), 108–11.

3. See Stephen L. Carter, *The Culture of Disbelief: How American Law and Politics Trivialize Religious Devotion* (New York: Anchor Books, Doubleday, 1994).

As law professor Stephen L. Carter suggests, we in the wider pluralistic society have no settled rules to determine truth claims concerning moral knowledge.[4] The voices of Christians and other religiously devoted persons are discounted if they claim to be speaking from within their faith traditions. Whereas the Declaration of Independence of the United States declares that certain truths are self-evident, the questions today are: Are any truths self-evident? Does God's truth endure or abide forever? Does any truth endure? Can truths be passed on from one generation to the next?

To some it appears that postmodern society has drastically moved from a position in modernity that affirms a freedom *for* and a freedom *of* religion. The culture of disbelief has perpetuated a freedom *from* religion and religious truth. Regarding the extent to which religious truth discloses God, the words of the psalmist can be shared today as in ancient Israel: "The fool says in his heart, 'There is no God'" (Ps. 14:1).[5]

There is no limit to the foolishness of humanity in whatever century one lives. Postmodernity is subject to the same forms of idolatry and paganism that have plagued humanity from the beginnings of time. The terms may vary, but the shadows of the human mind and spirit persist as they deny access to the light of God's truth. The rejection of truth may take on distinct nuances, but the fruits of such a rebellion are passed across the generations.

Jerusalem: Crucifixion

It is ironic that Jerusalem, the city of peace, should receive the Prince of Peace with death on a cross. The ultimate rebellion against God and God's truth revealed in Jesus Christ is the taking of his life. As noted above, Pilate's question to Jesus about the nature of truth revealed his bankruptcy before the one who embodied truth. Jesus's entry into Jerusalem on Palm Sunday revealed the hunger of human hearts for a king and savior, one who would bring deliverance to the whole society suffering under Roman occupation. But the deliverance Jesus brought served to reveal the true motives and desires of the people and the leadership of the Holy City. Except for a small group of faithful followers who were primarily women, Jesus was ultimately not well received in the urban center of his land. He was betrayed for thirty pieces of silver, abandoned, and even denied by a member of his most intimate circle of disciples. The truth he had hoped to share was not widely accepted in the halls of power and privilege, and his life was taken

4. Ibid., 215.
5. See also Ps. 53:1.

as a result of the offense he posed. His truth claims were not acceptable to those entrusted with guarding the traditions. The penalty for this was death on a cross.

What implications can be suggested for Christians today? Christian truth can be contextualized but never accommodated to the world that rejects its ultimate significance. The initial welcome of Palm Sunday readily transforms itself into the shouts for crucifixion as voiced by the crowds. Christians are posed with the questions: If we can't proclaim the truth, what can we proclaim? What is a viable alternative to the truth? What response is possible if there is no place for truth?

I venture some thoughts. As Christians we cannot allow the strangeness of our intellectual landscape to silence the proclamation of Christian truth, including the scandal of the cross. If we refrain from such a proclamation, we like Esau will have sold our birthright for a bowl of porridge. In his entry into Jerusalem, Jesus suggested such in his response to the Pharisees in the crowd of his time who sought to silence his disciples:

> Some of the Pharisees in the crowd said to Jesus, "Teacher, rebuke your disciples." "I tell you," he replied, "if they keep quiet, the stones will cry out." (Luke 19:39–40)

It is a sin not to be a faithful witness to the truths God has revealed. Christians cannot remain silent when it is time to speak. Christians are called to proclaim in their teaching and preaching the wonders of the gospel whatever the costs. The ultimate cost may be death conceived in a variety of ways, but the promise of resurrection awaits all who remain faithful.

The reality of crucifixion may also require of Christians a death to patterns and forms of proclaiming the truth that are not contextualized in a postmodern landscape. A concern for relevance can be distorted but must not be ignored in any contemporary context. The need is to contextualize the gospel without succumbing to contextualism. In relation to postmodernity, if we embrace the impossibility of universal truth, we have compromised the claims of the gospel. In this case we are messengers who forget the message and embrace contextualism.[6] Likewise, if we fail to present gospel claims in ways that are intelligible to postmodern hearers, we have limited the outreach of the gospel in our context. In this second case we are messengers without an audience who fail to appropriately contextualize the Christian faith.

6. Samuel H. Dresner, *I Asked for Wonder: A Spiritual Anthology, Abraham Joshua Heschel* (New York: Crossword, 1995), 43.

Yet the questions can be asked: Why a concern for relevance in a post-modern setting? What factors warrant this concern? Three can be suggested. First, relevance is implied by the incarnation. God was made real to persons in first-century Palestine in the person of Jesus, a Jew from Nazareth. Second, the very occasional nature of Jesus's teaching is also noteworthy throughout the various Gospel accounts. Jesus addressed the immediate needs of the folk he encountered, but with a concern for universal significance. Third, the example of Paul, the apostle to the Gentiles, is suggestive. Paul was a task theologian who spoke to the specific needs of various Christian communities as they sought to live out the Christian faith. In this he was fulfilling the commission of the resurrected Christ as recorded in Matthew 28:18–20 and Acts 1:8. For Christians this requires bearing a daily cross in the service of their Lord (Luke 9:23).

Educational Implications

Those who teach and learn are committed to discern and in various ways to proclaim the truth. But educators must be aware of the seduction of our particular version of the truth or the seduction of the version in current vogue. This includes the version of postmodernity, but also our own current version, which may not recognize the place of mystery and new truth that God seeks to reveal in this age.

The quest for truth is to be open ended lest we usurp the place reserved for God alone as the source of all truth. The danger of idolatry is real and calls for our openness to the possibility of transformation or conversion throughout the educational process. Sharing truth in teaching is like carefully holding sand in our hands so that others can observe it. Postmodernity would have us not cup our hands or connect our fingers to retain the sand at all. With any movement or wind, the sand is lost. Modernity would have us close our hands so tightly that nothing remains as the grains fall to the ground. Both approaches disperse the grains of sand that others desperately need to see. Avoiding both approaches is necessary for Christians to sing the Lord's song of truth in the foreign land of postmodernity. But Christians are reminded of what James Russell Lowell observed in an earlier age. Lowell was an avid abolitionist, and his poem quoted here was concerned with the choice facing the country, whether to choose the way of evil represented in slavery or to choose the way of truth. In poetic form Lowell captures the challenge and hope that Christians can embrace in confronting postmodernity:

Truth forever on the scaffold, Wrong forever on the throne—
Yet that scaffold sways the future, and behind the dim unknown,
Standeth God within the shadow, keeping watch above his own.[7]

Educational implications and a concern for truth lead to consideration of educational invitations. Such invitations explored in appendix B seek to incarnate a complementary concern for love affirming the biblical injunction to live and speak "the truth in love" (Eph. 4:15).

7. James Russell Lowell, "The Present Crisis," in *Poems*, vol. 7 of the Riverside Edition of the Writings of James Russell Lowell (Boston: Houghton, Mifflin, 1890), 181.

Appendix B

Crossing Over to Postmodernity

Educational Invitations

Crossing over is an experience affirmed in biblical accounts. Crossing over is central to our calling as pilgrims or sojourners in faith. The anticipation of crossing over is fraught with a sense of adventure, awe, and apprehension. Nevertheless, the experience of crossing over from one locale or realm to another invites the possibility of transformation. Transformation is central to the journey of faith with our Triune God. God is in the business of bringing new life and sustaining life beyond what humans conceive is feasible or desirable. The cultural shifts identified as postmodernity provide an occasion for the transformation that God will bring to individuals, families, communities, churches, societies, structures, and creation itself. The occasion of a cultural shift does not assume faithfulness to God's purposes or intentions. Spiritual discernment is required to affirm those changes that God intends and oppose those that distort God's will for humanity and all creation.

In May 2000, I traveled along with eighteen other delegates from Andover Newton Theological School to Mainland China. This was the first occasion I had to cross the Pacific Ocean to visit Chinese churches and seminaries. I witnessed the spiritual vitality of Christians who suffered much during the Cultural Revolution. My sense of hope was renewed in seeing how God has sustained the faith of persons, honoring their prayers and those of other Christians across the globe. The fervent commitment of Chinese Christians to mission in a rapidly changing society encouraged all members of our delegation. Crossing over to China with open hearts and minds provided fertile ground for God's Spirit to work and foster vision. This contemporary experience of crossing over parallels what the Bible describes in both the Old and the New Testaments.

Old Testament Crossings

The most dramatic accounts of crossing over describe how the nation of Israel was both formed and transformed at critical points in its history. The classic film *The Ten Commandments* portrays the dramatic crossing of the Red Sea (Exod. 14) in Hollywood fashion. In that crossing from Egypt to Sinai, the nation itself in its infancy was delivered by God's mighty hand. A diverse or mixed crowd of people departed from Egypt (Exod. 12:38), and their liberation came at great cost to their oppressors. But every stranger or alien had access to the spiritual blessings of the new covenant forged with God, provided they fulfilled its obligations (Exod. 12:48).[1] A second crossing is recorded in the crossing of the Jordan River (Josh. 1–4). The first crossing, though dramatic, led not to full liberation but to a forty-year wilderness trek. A second crossing was required to enter the promised land on the terms God intended. Even Moses, the nation's leader, was ineligible for this second crossing and had to step aside for new leadership to emerge in the person of Joshua. New crossings may well require the emergence of younger leadership in a time of significant transition in faith communities. This shift can be seen more dramatically in the case of Elijah and Elisha with their personal crossings of the Jordan.

Second Kings 2:1–14 recounts how Elisha crossed over the Jordan River and was empowered to address new challenges of prophetic ministry following the earthly crossing of Elijah to God's realm of heaven in a whirlwind. The transference of leadership from Elijah to Elisha was symbolized by Elisha's receiving Elijah's mantle. Elisha persisted in pursuing Elijah across the river and requested he receive the firstborn's inherited portion of spirit and power. It is noteworthy that in the case of both Moses and Elijah, who stand as anchors for Israel's faithful leadership, crossings loom as central to addressing new challenges nationally and personally.

1. Hywel R. Jones, "Exodus," in *The New Bible Commentary*, ed. D. Guthrie and J. A. Motyer, rev. ed. (Grand Rapids: Eerdmans, 1970), 127–28.

New Testament Crossings

In the New Testament, the person and ministry of Jesus are preeminent. Jesus crosses over from his pre-incarnate state to his humanity in a profoundly simple and dramatic fashion reversing Elijah's departure. He comes as an infant born in the humblest of settings and under difficult circumstances. Those circumstances include the Roman domination of the nation Israel. In the multicultural setting of Galilee, he crosses over many barriers in his teaching to include Gentiles, women, and children. He also crosses over from the multicultural backwater of Galilee to Judea and Jerusalem in proclaiming outrageously the kingdom of God in his person. In addition to Jesus's public crossings, in his own teaching through parables he honors the more personal crossing of the Samaritan in Luke 10:25–37. In the parable of the Good Samaritan, the Samaritan crosses over from one side of the road that went from Jerusalem to Jericho to minister to the injured Jewish merchant. The Samaritan was recognized by Jesus for all time and perhaps later by Paul as being a true Jew of the heart (Rom. 2:28–29).

Crossing Over to Postmodernity

Commentators on popular culture and philosophical trends note that we are in the process of crossing over to postmodernity. What invitations might God be making in this crossing especially to those who teach? These invitations include the crossing over of hearts, minds, spirits, and even bodies in actual teaching practices. God delights in using those who are willing to cross over. In the crossing, we must ask ourselves: Does this particular crossing bring us a wilderness or a promised land, or some combination of both? Jesus, the author and finisher of our Christian faith, was willing in his incarnation and earthly ministry to cross over. If Jesus serves as the exemplar or model for teaching, can Christian teachers do less?

A consideration of the theological foundations of Christian education in this work has celebrated the Trinity as the main taproot. The life revealed in the Trinity and offered to humanity and all creation satisfies the deep spiritual hunger of postmodern persons. How the Christian faith is shared with postmodern persons, speaking to their context with sustaining and sustainable teaching content, is the challenge facing Christian educators.

The realities of postmodernity find expression in the rising influence of Generation X (Gen X) and the call to reevaluate teaching in relation to their participation in Christian education. In my earlier writing on postmodernity in *Foundational*

Issues in Christian Education, I stressed the place of truth that is appropriately questioned within postmodernity.[2] The necessary complement to that discussion is one that considers the place of love or care in Christian education. This follows from the scriptural principle in education of "speaking the truth in love" (Eph. 4:15), which can include actions as well as words.[3] To speak the truth in love in a postmodern context requires giving attention to the deep hunger for genuine or truthful relationships and community voiced by members of Gen X.[4] Christians claim that the ultimate fulfillment of that hunger can be found in the experience of the love of God and the care of the Christian community. For that to be the case, Christians engaged in education need to consider the following seven invitations in their educational thought and practice:[5]

1. Return to relational bonds revealed in the Trinity (Ephesus, Rev. 2:1–7, be relational).
2. Revisit the communal commitments that shape our lives (Sardis, Rev. 3:1–6, be done in partnership).
3. Reaffirm the "common good" in the societal and global context and form a public theology (Smyrna, Rev. 2:8–11, be relevant).
4. Reconsider the place of conscience in the search for wisdom (Laodicea, Rev. 3:14–22, have clarity of vision and mission).
5. Reinvest in the prophetic calling in pursuing God's politics in the world (Pergamum, Rev. 2:12–17, have strong leadership).
6. Reappropriate the joy of celebration in corporate worship and public festival (Thyatira, Rev. 2:18–29, have story and celebration at its center).
7. Recognize the continual demand for renewal, reformation, and revolution that God intends until the consummation (Philadelphia, Rev. 3:7–13, be innovative).

The relevance, order, and embrace of these invitations will vary with the particular context of ministry, but the challenge remains if Christians are to minister effectively in postmodern settings.

2. Robert W. Pazmiño, *Foundational Issues in Christian Education: An Introduction in Evangelical Perspective,* 2nd ed. (Grand Rapids: Baker, 1997), 243–51.

3. See my discussion of this principle in Robert W. Pazmiño, *Basics of Teaching for Christians: Preparation, Instruction, and Evaluation* (Grand Rapids: Baker, 1998), 67–68, 75–76, 88, 98–99.

4. For a discussion of this hunger, see Tom Beaudoin, *Virtual Faith: The Irreverent Spiritual Quest of Generation X* (San Francisco: Jossey-Bass, 1998).

5. These invitations can be compared with the mandates or invitations shared with the churches in Revelation 2 and 3, noted in chap. 6 of Robert W. Pazmiño, *God Our Teacher: Theological Basics in Christian Education* (Grand Rapids: Baker Academic, 2001), 152–56.

Be Relational

The return to relational bonds revealed in the Trinity requires Christians to clarify their theological grounding. I affirm that the Trinity can serve as an organizing theological theme for Christian education. This idea is not new, but its application to postmodern realities calls for a return to this distinctive Christian element. James Smart, in his classic work *The Teaching Ministry of the Church*, has suggested that the doctrine of the Trinity is the essential starting point for understanding the theological bases of Christian education.[6] Nels Ferré, a systematic theologian, who worked with D. Campbell Wyckoff, a renowned Christian educator, proposed in his work *A Theology for Christian Education* a trinitarian model with God the Father as the educator, Jesus Christ the Son as the exemplar, and the Holy Spirit as the tutor.[7] Christian education strives to enable students to explore the mystery and wonder of the Trinity and to taste of the community life modeled for humanity in the life of the Trinity. This monumental task calls for the reflection, commitment, and hard work of Christian educators.

Trinitarian language also applies to the general tasks of education suggested by the work of Peter Hodgson in *God's Wisdom*. Hodgson, for example, proposes three basic elements for higher education, which include critical thinking, heightened imagination, and liberating practice.[8] These three relate to my educational trinity in that critical thinking relates to *content*, heightened imagination to *persons'* creativity, and liberating practice to the *context* of the community and society. I define education as the process of sharing *content* with *persons* in the *context* of their community and society. God the Father as Creator is the educator from whom all the *content* of education issues. God's wisdom is what can distinguish education that results in transformation. Jesus the Son as the exemplar or mentor is the model or master teacher who in his *person* exemplifies all that teachers should be in their relationships with students, with other *persons*. The hunger for love and care finds fulfillment in the person of Jesus and all who follow him in their teaching ministries. The Holy Spirit as the tutor is the counselor or community consultant who sustains the life of the Christian community and the wider society in ways that fulfill God's purposes for the *context*. The Holy Spirit encounters human spirits to bring new life on the

---

6. James D. Smart, *The Teaching Ministry of the Church: An Examination of the Basic Principles of Christian Education* (Philadelphia: Westminster, 1954), 10.

7. Nels F. S. Ferré, *A Theology for Christian Education* (Philadelphia: Westminster, 1967). See my discussion of this work in Robert W. Pazmiño, *By What Authority Do We Teach? Sources for Empowering Christian Educators* (Eugene, OR: Wipf & Stock, 2002), 20–29.

8. Peter C. Hodgson, *God's Wisdom: Toward a Theology of Education* (Louisville: Westminster John Knox, 1999), 8, 114–24.

personal, communal, societal, and global levels. Spiritual renewal applies to the public levels of discourse and life as well as the personal and private domains. In relation to theological education, Hodgson's basic elements can be renamed to include theological reflection, spiritual imagination, and transformative practice that fulfill the Triune God's purposes and politics in the world.

Be Done in Partnership

In light of the life revealed for humanity by the Trinity, Christians are called to revisit the communal commitments that shape our lives. Postmodernity shatters the myth of the autonomous individual totally divorced from the bonds of tradition, family, and the wider community. Postmodernity also destroys the claim for objective reason divorced from the place of human interests and existential concerns. The use of language itself represents communal practices and nuances. The viewing subjects and their history affect the terms and directions of communication. Knowledge itself is recognized as a social construction, and the veracity of various information from media such as the Internet must be questioned. Public disclosures are subject to a variety of "spin doctors" who provide a host of interpretations in making connections with the recipients or, more often in a visual culture, the viewers of the message. The variety of contacts and inputs in postmodern life require careful discernment to sort out the barrage of information packaged and disseminated. To extract the wisdom from the vast amount of information and knowledge with its claims for immediate attention, Christians must discern the nature and extent of their commitments to various human associations.

Educators have explored the variety of influences by considering the educational configurations or the educational ecology of persons. An educational configuration is a cluster or network of agencies that pass on a culture or educational content to persons. This concept was fully developed in the pioneering work of the educational historian Lawrence Cremin.[9] From the work of Bernard Bailyn, Cremin identified the four educational agencies or axles in the colonial experience (1607–1783) of the United States to include the home, the church, the community, and the economy.[10] In the national period (1783–1876), additional educational agencies or institutions emerged, including the schools and a host of voluntary associations such as libraries, museums, and child advocacy or support groups such as the YMCA and the YWCA.

9. Lawrence A. Cremin, *Traditions of American Education* (New York: Basic Books, 1976).

10. Bernard Bailyn, *Education in the Forming of American Society: Needs and Opportunities for Study* (New York: W. W. Norton, 1960), 45.

During the metropolitan period (1876–2000), the rise of the body politic and the media is noteworthy. The relationships and interactions of these various agencies or institutions represent an educational configuration. Cremin's shorthand for describing these relationships is his observation that agencies confirm, complement, and/or contradict each other and have varied impact on individuals in particular communities depending on their distinctive learning styles and histories. Communal commitments can be explored by assessing educational configurations and considering the varying contours over time. Postmodern shifts have resulted in increased contradiction across educational configurations with the resulting sense of fragmentation. In light of this situation, Christians must clarify their basic commitments as the people of God who are called to incarnate Christian values in the community and society. In relation to the church and its interface with other agencies, the educational agenda calls for a response to preserve, redeem, or transform the explicit or implicit curriculum of the corresponding agency. This task requires discernment and often the weighing of compromises.

Be Relevant

While assessing educational configurations, Christians must reaffirm the "common good" or the public good in the societal and global context. This must be done without the loss of their Christian identity. Christians affirm the bonds they share with all of God's creatures and all creation. The pursuit of the common good itself is a major task that requires sustained dialogue and a willingness to demonstrate love in the social arena through the pursuit of justice and peace (shalom). The Scriptures describe shalom in terms of the fullness of relationship and communion that God intends for all creation. The identification of the "common good" for Christians results in educational efforts that affirm both Christian identity and openness to the other.[11] The affirmation of identity preserves distinctive Christian elements, which include the recognition that God has created all persons with intrinsic dignity and worth. The affirmation of openness signals the need to respect and care for all others in educational encounters and, more generally, in life. The extent of the globe's ecological crisis demands attention be given to the common fate that Christians share with humanity and all created life.

The "common good" for humanity necessitates occasions to *mix* with others, with non-Christians, as well as occasions to *huddle* with persons of

---

11. Constance Tarasar, "The Minority Problem: Educating for Identity and Openness," in *Religious Pluralism and Religious Education*, ed. Norma Thompson (Birmingham, AL: Religious Education Press, 1988), 195–210.

like faith in wrestling with past, current, and future challenges that our world confronts.[12] Truth can be discerned in both the particulars of the Christian faith and insights from other religious and nonreligious sources.[13] In drawing from these various sources, Christians in their public discourse affirm the place of politics, which can be defined as the art of making and keeping persons truly human.[14] Christians share with all other persons the care for creation and the possibility of the fullness of life sustained for future generations. This fullness of life the Scriptures describe as shalom, which God intended from creation and will complete at the consummation.

Have Clarity of Vision and Mission

With the identification and reappropriation of the "common good" comes the need to reconsider the place of the conscience in the search for wisdom. Barry Harvey draws on the work of Paul Lehmann in proposing that Christians focus on conscience as an organizing principle for their shared life and education.

> According to Lehmann, it is only as human motivation and human judgment actually converge within conscience that God and humans "have directly and insistently to do with one another (as) the aims and the direction, the motivations and the decisions, the instruments and the structures of human interrelatedness are forged into a pattern of response—a style of life."[15]

The conscience as the seat of the will or intentions requires attention to God's demands in a Christian understanding. God's demands include responsible living in the created world. This living is as social, political, economic, intellectual, aesthetic, cultural, and spiritual beings-in-relationship. As relational beings, persons are accountable to God, to others, and to themselves. The conscience is that dimension of persons where matters of value, virtue, and character take form. The Christian community is the context for the formation of Christian conscience.

12. I discuss the strategy of "huddle and mix" in Robert W. Pazmiño, "Surviving or Thriving in the Third Millennium?" in *Forging a Better Religious Education in the Third Millennium*, ed. James M. Lee (Birmingham, AL: Religious Education Press, 2000), 82–83.

13. I discuss this perspective in *By What Authority Do We Teach?* 119–46.

14. In the tradition of Aristotle, George W. Webber proposes this definition in *The Congregation in Mission* (New York: Abingdon, 1964), 49. In this definition, Webber draws on the work of Paul L. Lehmann, *Ethics in a Christian Context* (New York: Harper & Row, 1963), 74–101.

15. Barry Harvey, *Politics of the Theological: Beyond the Piety and Power of a World Come of Age* (New York: Peter Lang, 1995), 12–13. Harvey quotes from Paul L. Lehmann, *Ethics in a Christian Context*, 288.

With the increased fragmentation in the human community and educational configurations, the appeal in public discussions of education is to attend to matters of character formation. With the increase in violence and abuse in communities viewed as safe havens from urban decline and minority intrusion, the concern in the United States intensifies. The expectation that schooling efforts at the primary, secondary, and higher levels can alone bridge the gaps in both public and private morality must be questioned. The formation of conscience and character requires strategies that influence all the agencies and institutions of any educational configuration. In light of the increased sense of societal and educational crisis, the question of Christian vocation must be posed. With the persistent interest in transformation in education, Christians can share the source of transformation they have in their faith.

Have Strong Leadership

As Christians engage their mission in the educational world, they can reinvest in their prophetic calling. The prophetic calling involves pursuing God's politics in the world. What are God's politics, and in particular how do they relate to education? In one sense, education is slow-fuse politics that seeks transformation in the human situation. The transformation or change sought is not directly through the legislative, executive, or judicial processes of political and civic bodies. Rather the audacious claim is that education can transform persons and life through study, dialogue, interaction, research, and expression with others in formal, nonformal, and informal arrangements. The sharing of educational content includes cognitive, affective, intentional, and behavioral components and their interface as the whole being of persons takes on new shape.

The prophetic calling involves the posing of questions, the creation of reflective space, and the wrestling with alternatives to current arrangements. A necessary prior task is the identification of the current condition and its precedents. The commonly identified sequence of learning in a prophetic mode is *to see*, *to judge*, and *to act*. It must be noted that to act also requires seeing the results of actions. Seeing the results of actions thereby continues the cycle and calls for judgment in evaluation. The sequence presumes certain realities. First, it presumes the prior ability to see, which itself may require learning, although seeing can imply various modalities. Second, it presumes the understanding of categories for judgment and a basis for comparison. Third, in the case of action, it presumes the empowerment of persons with the voice, choice, and means to act effectively. The hope in prophetic teaching is to equip persons to be all that God intends for them as subjects of God's love and care. God's care implies that Christians should care enough to confront realities that oppress persons and limit the fulfillment of God's shalom in all creation. From a Christian perspective, this is possible only through the person and work of the Holy Spirit working in partnership with persons. The reinvestment in the prophetic calling is often associated with struggle in the recovery of hope. The great North African teacher Augustine commented on hope: "Hope has two lovely daughters, anger and courage. Anger at the way things are, and courage to see that they need not remain as they are."[16] The complement to the anger and courage of hope is the experience of joy, which is crucial to teaching and life.

Have Story and Celebration at Its Center

Christians engaged in education are called to reappropriate the joy of celebration in public worship and festival. Gabriel Fackre helpfully distinguishes the inreach and the outreach of the church in relation to the task and spiritual gift of *leitourgia*, or celebration. The inreach of celebration finds expression through the ministries of corporate worship. The outreach of celebration finds expression in festival.[17] Outreach in public festival serves as an extension of Christian mission in the world. Both worship and festival are vehicles for the sharing of joy as the complement to the expression of anger and courage in the embodiment of hope. Joy is the emotion closest to the heart of God in my evangelical perspective. The gospel denotes good news that leads to the experience and expression of joy. This joy is experienced even in the midst of loss and suffering. Joy finds its fullest expression in the shared human experiences of worship. In a different mode, this joy is also experienced on occasions of public festival when the gift of life and human community is celebrated.

The expression of joy in worship and festival is a form of nonformal and informal education in which life is viewed from the perspective of God's heart. In worship, the conscience is engaged, but much more. Archbishop William Temple described the "more": "To worship is to quicken the conscience by the holiness of God, to feed the mind with the truth of God, to purge the imagination by the beauty of God, to open the heart to the love of God, to devote the will to the purpose of God."[18] Worship of this kind is formative and

16. As cited in Wilbert J. McKeachie, *Teaching Tips: Strategies, Research, and Theory for College and University Teachers*, 9th ed. (Lexington, MA: Heath, 1994), 384.

17. Gabriel Fackre, *The Christian Story: A Narrative Interpretation of Basic Christian Doctrine*, rev. ed. (Grand Rapids: Eerdmans, 1984), 71.

18. William Temple, *The Hope of a New World* (London: Student Christian Movement Press, 1941), 30.

transformative. In festival, the very gift of life to humanity and the beauty of creation are celebrated. Opportunities for creative expression in the arts and music can give glory to God as they are shared in public settings. Recounting the history and recognizing the cultures of various communities can glorify the Creator of all culture and history itself. The hunger in postmodernity is for the genuine experience of joy, which Christians can share through worship and festival.

Be Innovative

The seventh invitation of postmodernity is to recognize the continual demand for renewal, reformation, and revolution that God intends until the consummation. Given the nature of created life reflected in the changing seasons of nature and in the human life span, openness to transformation is required. New life springs forth in a variety of ways, and the rising generations inevitably see the world with different eyes, postmodern eyes. Christian sources describe the need for a continuous process of being reformed, transformed, and renewed by the gracious ministry of the Holy Spirit. In relation to education, this implies a reforming, transforming, and liberating approach.[19]

In any Christian education effort, evaluation is a crucial element that invites the possibility of change in future efforts.[20] Evaluation can also signal the need for openness to the work of the Holy Spirit in recognizing the limits of human efforts. The danger in all education is idolatry that baptizes the content, methods, forms, or relationships as divine equivalents. Any of these vehicles can be graciously used by God to accomplish God's purposes. Nevertheless, they all fall short of God's ideals as modeled in the life and ministry of Jesus the Christ. The inevitable gaps serve as an incentive to rely prayerfully on God's resources in the person and ministry of the Holy Spirit and the critical role of the Scriptures. Such reliance welcomes the place of renewal, reformation, and on occasion revolution in Christian education. The Spirit brings new life as Christians spiritually discern alternatives to existing patterns and rely on the Spirit's transformation. The Scriptures present new vistas and interpret us and our educational efforts from the perspective of perennial, enduring forms and principles grounded in our Triune God. Postmodernity provides an occasion for reflection and reconsideration of educational theory and practice.

19. See my discussion of liberation and transformation in Robert W. Pazmiño, *Latin American Journey: Insights for Christian Education in North America* (Cleveland: United Church Press, 1994), 28–75.

20. See my discussion of evaluation in Pazmiño, *Basics of Teaching*, 75–99.

Conclusion

This appendix has identified seven potential educational invitations of postmodernity for Christian educators. These invitations encourage theological reflection, spiritual imagination, and transformative practice in Christian education beyond current efforts. Discernment is required in responding to these along with openness to the one seated on the throne who declares, "See, I am making all things new" (Rev. 21:5 NRSV).

Points to Ponder for Appendixes

- Compare and contrast the views of postmodernity portrayed in the two appendixes in conversation with your particular view.
- Discuss the perceptions and portrayals of Jesus popular today in the global culture and how they relate to the receptivity to the Christian gospel.
- Discuss how Christians are effectively crossing borders and boundaries in sharing Christian truth and love in particular multicultural and intercultural ministry settings.
- Identify additional educational invitations presented to Christians in societal changes.

Postscript

After writing the first edition of this work, I was reviewed by a committee of my faculty colleagues for tenure consideration. One helpful insight shared by one of the committee members was that my text, *Foundational Issues in Christian Education*, had identified a number of pearls, but that the connective strand that held together the pearls was not as evident to a first-time reader. As I have thought about that helpful comment over the years, I have had two reactions. One has been to hope that the readers in surveying the various foundational issues and questions I posed would begin to develop their own connective strand linking any pearls they may have discovered in interacting with the text. My writing of a sequel to *Foundational Issues*, the work *Principles and Practices of Christian Education*, proposes my personal strand in an explicit manner. This first reaction assumes that readers are capable and challenged to think deeply and reflectively in reading this and any other book. With this first reaction, the basic intent of the work is to pose foundational questions and suggest issues of importance that require our careful attention and response. Such a response encourages critical and creative thought by those who teach the Christian faith in various settings. But a second reaction is also warranted and appropriate in a postscript to this edition. Assuming that readers have grappled with the questions and issues, I can state for myself and others more explicitly what I have attempted to say in this work and why. In teaching the foundations of Christian education and in courses on theological research, I have pressed students to identify the "what" and "why" of their own work. These questions are of first-order significance and are often ignored to the peril of any ministry venture. Thus a fitting conclusion to this edition is to explicitly state what I hope is communicated in this work and why. This second response serves as a review of the text and an effort to identify the underlying connective strand.

The "what" of this work can be summarized in five points. The first point is that Christian education is a vital ministry that deserves our best efforts and can be a source of joy and renewal in the life of the Christian church. Without effective education, the faith is not faithfully passed on to the rising generations and Christians are not obedient to their educational commission (Matt. 28:18–20).

The second point is that Christian education is an interdisciplinary and integrative field that is "preparadigmatic" in character. The interdisciplinary and integrative character calls for discerning appropriation by educators from a variety of foundations, sources, or wells. Beyond drawing on various sources comes the task of integration. The preparadigmatic character calls for use of the imagination and a commitment to contextualize a teaching ministry in real-life settings. In theological terms, this is an incarnational perspective that seeks to bring to life one's understanding of the Christian faith.

The third point is that Christian education is an active partner with theology in the teaching ministry. The dialogue with theology helps to ground teaching and learning in the church. Also, Christian education itself can be seen as one dimension of a practical theology. Without this grounding in theology, the distinctive elements of Christian education can be lost in our conforming to the latest educational fads in society and the most recent insights from the social sciences that are too often uncritically appropriated.

A fourth point is that the need for reformation and reconstruction is upon us in the field of Christian education. The watchword of the Reformation is a demand on us today. That watchword is *semper reformanda*, always being reformed by the gracious work of the Holy Spirit in our time. Openness to the Spirit's reforming and transforming work is essential to maintaining the vitality of Christian education and any ministry.

The fifth and final point is based on what I have taught and learned over the years. Christian education is a lifelong, ongoing dialogical process that seeks to discern God's truth and to foster through loving relationships the expression of God's reign. This process calls for advocacy by laity and clergy who sense God's delight in teaching that transforms persons, communities, and the wider society.[1]

1. For further discussion of the transformative aspects of education, see Robert W. Pazmiño, *Latin American Journey: Insights for Christian Education in North America* (Cleveland: United Church Press, 1994), 55–75.

The "why" of this work can be captured in three purposes that have been suggested in the introduction but are worth emphasizing again in the conclusion to this work. First, Christian education must be rethought by each generation to avoid a cultural captivity. Without raising the foundational questions anew, Christian educators may well be perpetuating conceptions and practices that are *not* faithful to the gospel of Jesus Christ.

Second, this work is an expression of nurturing that I received in three distinct academic communities among others. At Teachers College, Columbia University, in cooperation with Union Seminary, I embraced the value of critically returning to our sources of faith in both conceiving of and practicing education. At Gordon-Conwell Theological Seminary, I embraced the importance of proclaiming the good and joyful news of Jesus Christ with a sense of biblical and theological integrity. At Andover Newton Theological School, I have embraced the demands of an ecumenical ministry within the Christian church that calls for a "transpositional theology" for our time.[2] In a transpositional theology, the truths of Christian sources are interpreted to address contemporary challenges in fresh and joyful ways.

Third, my identity as a North American Hispanic person with the vocation of ecumenical evangelical Christian educator has meant that I have worked on the border of various communities of discourse. This position has provided a distinct perspective on the field that I personally have been privileged to share through this and other writings. This third edition, as was the case with earlier editions, is shared with the hope that Christians will experience the joy of teaching the Christian faith in transformative ways by grappling with foundational issues that ground, inform, and enrich our practice while glorifying God.

---

2. George Peck, former president of Andover Newton Theological School, used this term in drawing on the work of C. S. Song, *The Compassionate God* (Maryknoll, NY: Orbis, 1982), 5–12, 16–17.

Select Bibliography

Biblical Foundations

Barclay, William. *Educational Ideals in the Ancient World*. Grand Rapids: Baker, 1974.

Boys, Mary C. *Biblical Interpretation in Religious Education*. Birmingham, AL: Religious Education Press, 1980.

Bruce, A. B. *The Training of the Twelve*. Grand Rapids: Kregel, 1971.

Brueggemann, Walter. *The Creative Word: Canon as a Model for Biblical Education*. Philadelphia: Fortress, 1982.

Giles, Kevin. *Patterns of Ministry among the First Christians*. Melbourne, Australia: Collins Dove, 1989.

Grassi, Joseph A. *Teaching the Way: Jesus, the Early Church, and Today*. Washington, D.C.: University Press of America, 1982.

Heschel, Abraham J. *Between God and Man: An Interpretation of Judaism from the Writings of Abraham Heschel*. Edited by Fritz A. Rothschild. New York: Free Press, 1959.

Horne, Herman H. *The Teaching Techniques of Jesus*. Grand Rapids: Kregel, 1920.

LeBar, Lois E. *Education That Is Christian*. Old Tappan, NJ: Fleming H. Revell, 1981.

Marino, Joseph S. *Biblical Themes in Religious Education*. Birmingham, AL: Religious Education Press, 1983.

Stein, Robert H. *The Method and Message of Jesus' Teaching*. Philadelphia: Westminster, 1978.

Theological Foundations

Browning, Robert L., and Roy A. Reed. *The Sacraments in Religious Education and Liturgy*. Birmingham, AL: Religious Education Press, 1985.

Bushnell, Horace. *Christian Nurture*. Grand Rapids: Baker, 1979.

DeJong, Norman. *Education in the Truth*. Nutley, NJ: Presbyterian & Reformed, 1969.

Downs, Perry G. *Teaching for Spiritual Growth: An Introduction to Christian Education*. Grand Rapids: Zondervan, 1994.

Fackre, Gabriel. *The Christian Story*. Vol. 2, *Authority: Scripture in the Church for the World. A Pastoral Systematics*. Grand Rapids: Eerdmans, 1987.

Ferré, Nels F. S. *A Theology for Christian Education*. Philadelphia: Westminster, 1967.

Foster, Charles R. *Teaching in the Community of Faith*. Nashville: Abingdon, 1982.

Francis, Leslie J., and Adrian Thatcher, eds. *Christian Perspectives for Education: A Reader in the Theology of Education*. Leominister, UK: Fowler Wright, 1990.

Freire, Paulo. *Pedagogy of the Oppressed*. Translated by Myra Bergman Ramos. New York: Continuum, 1970.

Gaebelein, Frank E. *The Christian, the Arts, and the Truth: Regaining the Vision of Greatness*. Edited by D. Bruce Lockerbie. Portland, OR: Multnomah Press, 1985.

———. *The Pattern of God's Truth: Problems of Integration in Christian Education*. New York: Oxford University Press, 1954.

Getz, Gene A. *A Sharpening Focus of the Church*. Chicago: Moody Press, 1974.

Groome, Thomas H. *Sharing Faith: A Comprehensive Approach to Religious Education and Pastoral Ministry*. San Francisco: Harper & Row, 1991.

Habermas, Ronald, and Klaus Issler. *Teaching for Reconciliation: Foundations and Practice of Christian Education Ministry*. Grand Rapids: Baker, 1992.

Harris, Maria. *Teaching and Religious Imagination: An Essay in the Theology of Teaching*. San Francisco: Harper & Row, 1987.

Little, Sara. *To Set One's Heart: Belief and Teaching in the Church*. Atlanta: John Knox, 1983.

Marthaler, Berard. *The Creed*. Mystic, CT: Twenty-Third, 1987.

Moore, Mary Elizabeth Mullino. *Teaching from the Heart: Theology and Educational Method*. Minneapolis: Fortress, 1991.

O'Hare, Padraic, ed. *Tradition and Transformation in Religious Education*. Birmingham, AL: Religious Education Press, 1979.

Pazmiño, Robert W. *By What Authority Do We Teach? Sources for Empowering Christian Educators*. Eugene, OR: Wipf & Stock, 2002.

———. *Principles and Practices of Christian Education: An Evangelical Perspective*. 1992; Eugene, OR: Wipf & Stock, 2002.

Richards, Lawrence O. *A Theology of Christian Education*. Grand Rapids: Zondervan, 1975.

Schipani, Daniel S. *Religious Education Encounters Liberation Theology*. Birmingham, AL: Religious Education Press, 1988.

Seymour, Jack L., and Donald E. Miller, eds. *Theological Approaches to Christian Education*. Nashville: Abingdon, 1990.

Thompson, Norma H., ed. *Religious Education and Theology*. Birmingham, AL: Religious Education Press, 1982.

————, ed. *Religious Pluralism and Religious Education*. Birmingham, AL: Religious Education Press, 1988.

Van Til, Cornelius. *Essays on Christian Education*. Nutley, NJ: Presbyterian & Reformed, 1977.

Westerhoff, John H., III. *Will Our Children Have Faith?* New York: Seabury, 1976.

Wilhoit, Jim. *Christian Education and the Search for Meaning*. 2nd ed. Grand Rapids: Baker, 1991.

Philosophical Foundations

Astley, Jeff. *The Philosophy of Christian Religious Education*. Birmingham, AL: Religious Education Press, 1994.

Boys, Mary C. *Educating in Faith: Maps and Visions*. Kansas City, MO: Sheed & Ward, 1989.

Burgess, Harold W. *Models of Religious Education: Theory and Practice in Historical and Contemporary Perspective*. Wheaton: Victor, 1996.

DeJong, Norman. *Philosophy of Education: A Christian Approach*. Nutley, NJ: Presbyterian & Reformed, 1977.

Frankena, William K. *Philosophy of Education*. New York: Macmillan, 1965.

Knight, George R. *Philosophy and Education: An Introduction in Christian Perspective*. 2nd ed. Berrien Springs, MI: Andrews University Press, 1989.

Moran, Gabriel. *Interplay: A Theory of Religion and Education*. Winona, MN: St. Mary's Press, 1981.

Petersen, Michael L. *Philosophy of Education: Issues and Options*. Downers Grove, IL: InterVarsity, 1986.

Historical Foundations

Bailyn, Bernard. *Education in the Forming of American Society*. New York: University of North Carolina and W. W. Norton, 1960.

Cremin, Lawrence A. *Traditions of American Education*. New York: Basic Books, 1977.

Cully, Kendig B. *Basic Writings in Christian Education*. Philadelphia: Westminster, 1960.

Dworkin, Martin S. *Dewey on Education: Selections*. New York: Teachers College Press, 1959.

Gangel, Kenneth O., and Warren S. Benson. *Christian Education: Its History and Philosophy*. Chicago: Moody Press, 1983.

Hauerwas, Stanley, and John H. Westerhoff III, eds. *Schooling Christians: "Holy Experiments" in American Education.* Grand Rapids: Eerdmans, 1992.

Kennedy, William B. *The Shaping of Protestant Education.* New York: Association Press, 1966.

Knoff, Gerald E. *The World Sunday School Movement: The Story of a Broadening Mission.* New York: Seabury, 1979.

Lynn, Robert W., and Elliott Wright. *The Big Little School: Two Hundred Years of Sunday School.* Rev. ed. Birmingham, AL: Religious Education Press, 1980.

Osmer, Richard R. *A Teachable Spirit: Recovering the Teaching Office in the Church.* Louisville: Westminster John Knox, 1990.

Sawicki, Marianne. *The Gospel in History: Portrait of a Teaching Church: The Origins of Christian Education.* New York: Paulist Press, 1988.

Seymour, Jack L. *From Sunday School to Church School: Continuities in Protestant Church Education in the United States, 1860–1929.* Washington, D.C.: University Press of America, 1982.

Sherrill, Lewis J. *The Rise of Christian Education.* New York: Macmillan, 1944.

Towns, Elmer L., ed. *A History of Religious Educators.* Grand Rapids: Baker, 1975.

Westerhoff, John H., III, and O. C. Edwards Jr. *A Faithful Church: Issues in the History of Catechesis.* Wilton, CT: Morehouse-Barlow, 1981.

Wyckoff, D. Campbell, and George Brown Jr. *Religious Education, 1960–1993: An Annotated Bibliography.* Westport, CT: Greenwood, 1995.

Sociological Foundations

Berger, Peter L., and Thomas Luckmann. *The Social Construction of Reality: A Treatise in the Sociology of Knowledge.* Garden City, NY: Doubleday, 1966.

Durkheim, Émile. *Education and Sociology.* New York: Free Press, 1956.

Eggleston, John. *The Sociology of the School Curriculum.* London: Routledge & Kegan Paul, 1977.

Geertz, Clifford. *The Interpretation of Cultures.* New York: Basic Books, 1973.

Habermas, Jürgen. *Knowledge and Human Interests.* Boston: Beacon, 1971.

Hesselgrave, David J. *Communicating Christ Cross-Culturally.* Grand Rapids: Zondervan, 1978.

Kraft, Charles. *Christianity in Culture.* Maryknoll: Orbis, 1979.

Lawton, Denis. *Class, Culture and the Curriculum.* London: Routledge & Kegan Paul, 1975.

Lines, Timothy A. *Systemic Religious Education.* Birmingham, AL: Religious Education Press, 1987.

Niebuhr, H. Richard. *Christ and Culture.* New York: Harper & Brothers, 1951.

Paulston, Rolland G. *Conflicting Theories of Social and Educational Change.* Pittsburgh: University Center for International Studies, University of Pittsburgh, 1976.

Psychological Foundations

Aleshire, Daniel O. *Faithcare: Ministering to All God's People through the Ages of Life*. Philadelphia: Westminster, 1988.

Barber, Lucie. *Teaching Christian Values*. Birmingham, AL: Religious Education Press, 1984.

Belenky, Mary Field, Blythe McVicker Clinchy, Nancy Rule Goldberger, and Jill Mattuck Tarule. *Women's Ways of Knowing: The Development of Self, Voice, and Mind*. New York: Basic Books, 1986.

Bronfenbrenner, Urie. *The Ecology of Human Development*. Cambridge, MA: Harvard University Press, 1979.

Cully, Iris V. *Christian Child Development*. San Francisco: Harper & Row, 1979.

Dykstra, Craig. *Vision and Character: A Christian Educator's Alternative to Kohlberg*. New York: Paulist Press, 1981.

Dykstra, Craig, and Sharon Parks, eds. *Faith Development and Fowler*. Birmingham, AL: Religious Education Press, 1986.

Erikson, Erik. *The Life Cycle Completed: A Review*. New York: W. W. Norton, 1982.

Fowler, James W. *Becoming Adult, Becoming Christian: Adult Development and Christian Faith*. San Francisco: Harper & Row, 1984.

———. *Stages of Faith: The Psychology of Human Development and the Quest for Meaning*. San Francisco: Harper & Row, 1981.

Gilligan, Carol. *In a Different Voice: Psychological Theory and Women's Development*. Cambridge, MA: Harvard University Press, 1982.

Havighurst, Robert J. *Developmental Tasks and Education*. New York: David McKay, 1961.

Johnson, Susanne. *Christian Spiritual Formation in the Church and Classroom*. Nashville: Abingdon, 1989.

Joy, Donald M., ed. *Moral Development Foundations: Judeo-Christian Alternatives to Piaget/Kohlberg*. Nashville: Abingdon, 1983.

Kohlberg, Lawrence. *Essays in Moral Development*. Vol. 1, *The Philosophy of Moral Development*. San Francisco: Harper & Row, 1981.

Loder, James E. *The Transforming Moment: Understanding Convictional Experiences*. 2nd ed. Colorado Springs: Helmers & Howard, 1989.

Moran, Gabriel. *Religious Education Development*. Minneapolis: Winston Press, 1983.

Piaget, Jean, and Barbel Inhelder. *The Psychology of the Child*. New York: Basic Books, 1969.

Rizzuto, Ana-Maria. *The Birth of the Living God*. Chicago: University of Chicago Press, 1979.

Steele, Les L. *On the Way: A Practical Theology of Christian Formation*. Grand Rapids: Baker, 1990.

Wilcox, Mary M. *Developmental Journey*. Nashville: Abingdon, 1979.

Curricular Foundations

Cully, Iris V. *Planning and Selecting Curriculum for Christian Education.* Valley Forge, PA: Judson, 1983.

Eisner, Elliot W. *The Educational Imagination: On the Design and Evaluation of School Programs.* 2nd ed. New York: Macmillan, 1985.

Harris, Maria. *Fashion Me a People: Curriculum in the Church.* Louisville: Westminster John Knox, 1989.

Jackson, Philip W. *Life in Classrooms.* New York: Holt, Rinehart & Winston, 1968.

Lee, James M. *The Content of Religious Instruction: A Social Science Approach.* Birmingham, AL: Religious Education Press, 1985.

———. *The Flow of Religious Instruction.* Dayton: Pflaum/Standard, 1973.

Miel, Alice. *Changing the Curriculum: A Social Process.* New York: Appleton-Century-Crofts, 1946.

Richards, Lawrence O. *Creative Bible Teaching.* Chicago: Moody Press, 1970.

Stenhouse, Lawrence. *An Introduction to Curriculum Research and Development.* New York: Holmes & Meier, 1975.

Tyler, Ralph W. *Basic Principles of Curriculum and Instruction.* Chicago: University of Chicago Press, 1949.

Wyckoff, D. Campbell. *Theory and Design of Christian Education Curriculum.* Philadelphia: Westminster, 1961.

Scripture Index

General Index

acculturation, 51, 145
activism, 76–77, 78–79
advocacy, education for/of, 49–51, 53
aesthetics, 93, 101–7
African American church, 80
Against Hermogenes (Tertullian), 126–27
Amish, 155
Anselm of Canterbury, 149
anthropology, 93, 94
Apostles' Creed, 69
Aqua Church (Sweet), 123
Aristotle, 138–39
assensus, 47
Augustine, 33, 49, 149, 159, 197, 257
authority, biblical. *See* biblical authority
authority, of teachers, 111, 112
autonomy, 209–10
axiology, 93, 101–7

Bailyn, Bernard, 88–89, 135
balance, in life, 58
banking education, 79
Bantock, G. H., 168, 170
beauty. *See* aesthetics
Becker, Arthur, 50
Beechick, Ruth, 216–17
behaviorism, 119, 124
Belenky, Mary Field, 228
believing, 149, 150
believism, 62
Berger, Peter L., 167, 177
Bethlehem, 256–57
Beversluis, N. H., 170

Bible. *See* Scripture
biblical authority, 10–11, 58–59, 71, 94
Bloch, Marc, 129–30
body/soul dualism, 72
Bonhoeffer, Dietrich, 62
brain function research, 220–21
Bruderhof community, 155
Brueggemann, Walter, 21
Butts, Freeman, 138
By What Authority Do We Teach? (Pazmiño), 28n17

Calvin, John, 151
canon, 21, 55, 142
Caswell, Hollis L., 125
catechesis, 59
catechisms, 149–50
celebration, 27–28
celibacy, 145
change, social and educational, 10, 189
The Child and the Curriculum (Dewey), 124
children. *See* students
Children without Childhood (Winn), 146
Christian Education and the Search for Meaning (Wilhoit), 10n2
Christian Education in a Democracy, 159
Christianity, early, 36, 142–44
Christian Religious Education (Groome), 66, 234n7
"chronological fallacy," 164
Church
    as body of Christ, 71
    and community values, 136